NEAL GARNHAM is a lecturer in hist(
and is currently researching aspects o
partition Ireland. He is also the auth
criminal law in Ireland, 1692–1760

LARRY WILL SEE JUSTICE DONE

'We hear that our worthy friend was waited upon recently by a deputation of Association football players from Dublin, who declare that they have a real grievance, in so much that although there are seven senior clubs, in addition to six military combinations in that city, while there are only five in Belfast, yet, notwithstanding, the international players are invariably selected from the Belfast teams. Our friend who was fittingly attired for the occasion received the deputation with due respect, and promised to give his most serious attention to the matter, and also to use his utmost endeavour to see justice done.'

Ireland's Saturday Night

Association football and society in pre-partition Ireland

NEAL GARNHAM

ULSTER HISTORICAL
FOUNDATION

In memory of William Charles Garnham
born Boxing Day 1909,
died April Fool's Day 1998;
and Eva Garnham
born 7 April 1927,
died 30 June 2002

First published 2004
by the Ulster Historical Foundation
12 College Square East, Belfast BT1 6DD
www.ancestryireland.com

Except as otherwise permitted under the Copyright, Designs and Patents Act 1988, this publication may only be reproduced, stored or transmitted in any form or by any means with the prior permission in writing of the publisher or, in the case of reprographic reproduction, in accordance with the terms of a licence issued by The Copyright Licensing Agency. Enquiries concerning reproduction outside those terms should be sent to the publisher.

© Neal Garnham
ISBN 1-903688-34-5

Printed by Biddles
Design by Dunbar Design

Contents

	ACKNOWLEDGEMENTS	viii
	PREFACE	ix
1	The game 1878–1914 *development and dissemination*	1
2	Clubs	42
3	Players	65
4	Crowds	101
5	Football and politics	132
6	The game 1914–1924 *decline and division*	159
7	Conclusions	197
	APPENDIX Winners of major association football competitions in Ireland 1881–1922	201
	NOTES	203
	BIBLIOGRAPHY	235
	INDEX	252

Acknowledgements

While all the errors it contains remain my sole responsibility, during the planning and writing of this book I have incurred a number of debts. In the first place I must thank the Leverhulme Trust for co-funding my former post at the Queen's University of Belfast. My former colleagues in Belfast, especially Sean Connolly, David Hayton and Alvin Jackson, deserve many thanks for their comments on earlier drafts of parts of this work. For very generously granting me access to their records, I am extremely grateful to the Irish Football Association and the Irish Football League. I also wish to thank the staffs of the Public Record Office of Northern Ireland, the National Library of Ireland, and Belfast Central Library. Many individuals who are interested or involved in football in Ireland have offered useful advice and encouragement, and I wish to thank all these. In particular, however, I am grateful to Stephen Byrne, William Campbell, Herbert Johnstone, Michael McGuigan and Dawson Simpson for their help. Finally I wish to thank Brian Graham, Director of the Academy for Irish Cultural Heritages, and the Ulster Historical Foundation for allowing this work to finally appear.

Preface

Much has been written about the history of football,
although the game in Ireland remains somewhat aloof.
No great chronicler, or even studious amateur, has
given the game its deserved memorial.
Alas this work is not that book either,
nor yet is it written to skit or to scathe.
It tries only to consider the game in its context,
seeking to place the clubs and the players
amidst their times, their trials and their tirades.
No particular axe is ground here,
and the attempt is made to treat all fairly and well.
Reading it, please consider my objects:
solely to entertain, instruct and inform.
Ensure, if only initially, you capture its meaning.

NEAL GARNHAM

Allegations of a pro-Belfast bias in the selection of the Irish international side prompted this cartoon in 1898.
Ireland's Saturday Night

1

The game 1878–1914
development and dissemination

> Football's a game that's so jolly dashing.
> Football's a game to give your foes a thrashing.
> Then hip, hip, hurrah, for the game that beats them all,
> There's nothing half so jolly as to play Football.
>
> *Sport*, 7 November 1885

THE SELECTING COMMITTEE AT WORK

QUIET GENT (who loves to give a dig) looking at the map – "Yes there is such a place as Dublin."

BELFAST GENT – "Yes, but Belfast is the commercial capital and deserves all the spoil."

Ireland's Saturday Night

THE URGE FOR GROUPS OF YOUNG men to collect together, and then to indulge in kicking an object of some sort in play, seems to be a universal one. From China to Cheshire the practice of playing football in some form was an apparently common activity from early times.[1] Ireland was no exception. Although football in Ireland lacks the place in Gaelic mythology and antiquity accorded to the game of hurling, there is evidence to show that from at least the sixteenth century a game involving kicking a ball was being played in Ireland. Perhaps the earliest explicit mention of the game comes in 1518, when an ordinance of the Archbishop of Dublin decreed that in the diocese of Ossory 'clerks playing football' should be fined and were to pay for any damage they caused to church property.[2] A decade later, by-laws enacted for the town of Galway echoed the earlier Statute of Kilkenny in outlawing 'the playing at horlinge of the litill balle with hockie sticks or staves'. Use of 'the great foote balle', however, was actually encouraged.[3]

Through the following centuries, isolated reports continued to be made of football being played across the country. In 1706 a press gang in Waterford used the ruse of organising a football match against the local townsmen to allow them to identify the twelve fittest men in the town. John Dunton, the English publisher, had earlier noted that the Irish 'do not play often at football', though the Irish Sunday Observance Act of 1695 had explicitly sought to prohibit 'hurling, commoning, foot-ball playing' and most other popular amusements on the sabbath.[4] Exactly what form these games took is uncertain. A long poem celebrating a game in Co. Dublin was published in 1720. It suggested a game in which both handling and kicking the ball were accepted tactics.[5] Later reports were less specific about such details, but certainly implied that games were vigorous, physical and potentially dangerous. An attempt by the watch to prevent a game being played in Dublin in April 1780 resulted in the shooting dead of one player, and the conviction of a watchman for his murder.[6]

Whatever form they took, the close of the eighteenth century and the beginning of the nineteenth seem to have heralded a distinct decline in such pastimes. In the years before the rebellion of 1798 and in the ensuing period of political uncertainty, football games and other sports were suppressed by the authorities as potentially subversive. Large gatherings of young men were not to be tolerated in such troubled times.[7] If such actions perhaps led to a diminution in the frequency and popularity of football games, later events were also to play a significant part in the decline of such informal and unregulated pastimes.

Traditionally the Great Famine of the 1840s has been seen as an important watershed in the popular culture of Ireland. The massive depopulation that occurred at the time, and the subsequent alienation of the surviving inhabitants of the country from practices that were reminiscent of the old, failed order, have been seen as responsible for the near disappearance of many aspects of the existing popular culture.[8] In some areas, though, earlier economic disruption had already led to the modification of patterns of behaviour. For example, in one Co. Antrim parish it was reckoned in 1838 that among the population in general the 'taste for amusement has within the last ten or twelve years greatly declined. They have not the same means either as to circumstances or time for enjoying themselves.' In another it was noted that although various activities had once been popular in the area, parishioners now found that 'all their industrious exertions and energies are called forth to meet the pressure of the times and to cope with the decline in prices'.[9] Changing manners and perceptions of which modes of conduct were correct and becoming may also have played a part in transforming the popular culture of the day. Reformation and revival in the major churches were important factors in the establishment of new cultural values. Football may, along with more sanguinary practices such as duelling and animal baiting, have become a less socially acceptable practice.[10]

The riot, revelry and hard drinking that often accompanied football games made them a particular focus for would-be reformers of various types. In one particular case it was suggested that 'first the cholera panic, in 1833, and then teetotalism' were primarily responsible for the death of a local sports meeting.[11] In Belfast the borough police opposed football, along with other public nuisances, in the town's streets.[12] It seems therefore that social, economic and political factors conspired to create a situation in which, by 1850, football in Ireland was, if not completely extinct, something of a rarity.[13]

While visiting Scottish seamen may well have played the game along Ireland's north coast in the intervening years, it was to be almost another three decades before the first recorded game of association football took place in Ireland. This being the case, any link between the earlier 'folk game' and the association game in Ireland must be seen as a very tenuous one.[14]

It is in fact possible to date precisely the commencement of association football as a pastime in Ireland. On the 24 October 1878 the Caledonians and Queen's Park, two Scottish teams, played a demonstration game at the grounds of the Ulster Cricket Club in Belfast. The game had been arranged by J.A. Allen, the captain of the Caledonians, with the help of J.A. McAlery, the manager of a gentleman's outfitters in Belfast: the latter allegedly became interested in the game after seeing a match played while on honeymoon in Scotland.[15] Earlier attempts by members of the Scottish Football Association and those of a Dublin rugby club to introduce the game had been frustrated by both a lack of enthusiasm and the lack of a pitch.[16] Thus in a United Kingdom context the game of association football came late to Ireland. The Football Association had been formed in England fifteen years before, in 1863, and a regular cup competition introduced under its auspices in 1871. Scotland's first club, Queen's Park, had been founded in 1867. By 1877 even the principality of Wales had its own Football Association and a domestic trophy.[17]

Despite the fact that the game was already long established elsewhere, its immediate prospects in Ireland were seen as uncertain. A report in the Dublin press was rather less than complimentary. The players were described as 'butting at the ball like a pack of young goats', and as a result it was thought unlikely that 'the natives will take kindly to the innovation'. In Belfast the view differed to some extent. A letter to the *Northern Whig* suggested that if the game could 'once get a start' it would 'soon commend itself to both players and onlookers..[18] Such contradictory attitudes were to be perpetuated for some time.

The first step towards establishing the sport in Ireland on a regular footing was the formation of a number of teams and clubs between whom domestic matches could take place. Little could be done in the immediate aftermath of the 1878 demonstration, as the young men who were likely to take part in the game were committed to the large number of rugby clubs which already existed in the country. However, by the summer of 1880 at least four clubs had been playing regular matches. Two of these, Cliftonville and Knock, were situated in the rapidly growing conurbation of Belfast. The other two were Moyola, based in Castledawson, and Banbridge Academy in Co. Down.[19]

The final component in the creation of an Irish footballing infrastructure came on 18 November 1880. Following an invitation issued to other clubs in the Belfast area by the Cliftonville club, a meeting was convened at the Queen's Hotel in Belfast, and the Irish Football Association (IFA) was formed to organise, govern and promote the association game in Ireland. It immediately set about drawing up the rules for the Irish Cup competition, a trophy which would be competed for between Irish clubs. [20]

The manner in which the game then developed and spread is not easy to chart. Judging from the number and location of clubs which affiliated to the IFA, the progress of the game was initially slow and geographically confined. By 1886 there were still fewer than forty clubs in Ireland paying affiliation fees to the IFA, the majority of whom were in the province of Ulster. By 1890, however, the game was both apparently more popular and more widespread. In that year the demand of some of the Belfast-based clubs for regular fixtures led to the creation of the Irish Football League, in which seven clubs from the city, and Milford from near the town of Armagh, competed.[21] Regional associations had been formed in the counties of Antrim, Down, and Derry, and a Mid-Ulster Association had been formed from clubs in the north Armagh and adjacent areas. A total of 124 affiliated clubs were now in existence.[22] There was little rural representation outside Ulster, however, and one area in which the progress of association football had already had a chequered history was Dublin.

The Dublin Association Football Club had been formed in

November 1883, and was apparently the first in the capital. Both opposition and credibility were hard to find. The report of the club's first game noted that only twelve men turned up to take part, including a bearded, pipe-smoking goalkeeper.[23] By the following autumn there were five teams playing in Dublin, one of which was from a Scottish infantry battalion resident in the city's garrison, with the remainder representing educational establishments. The facts that the soldiers were frequently on leave, and that the students who made up the other teams were not resident in Dublin outside term time, meant that fixtures were often not completed, and the teams fielded were rarely at full strength. The result was that the interest of neither players nor spectators could be maintained.[24]

Further complications came when Dublin teams tried to take on opposition from outside the capital. Logistical difficulties were relatively easily overcome with teams travelling back and forward between Belfast and Dublin by train. However, in 1890 a dispute arose between the IFA and the Dublin Association team over a contested result in an Irish Cup semi-final tie. The outcome of the dispute was the disbanding of the Dublin side, though some of its members did go on to form the Leinster Nomads club, and continued in the game.[25] By 1890, though, prospects for the game in Dublin seemed grim, and one Belfast sports newspaper thought that the 'hope of establishing the game there, for the present at least, is very visionary'.[26]

Despite these misgivings, two years later the Leinster Football Association (LFA) was founded in Dublin, affiliated to the IFA, and began the promotion of its own competitions for affiliated clubs in the Dublin area.[27] As the administrative network for association football expanded, so the number of clubs coming under the umbrella of the IFA grew. By 1901 there were 259 such clubs, and in October of that year the Munster Football Association (MFA) was founded and linked to the IFA. Three years later the Fermanagh and South Tyrone Football Association, later to be the Fermanagh and Western Association, was admitted to the IFA.[28] The result was that the administration and control of association football across all Ireland was now effectively vested in the Belfast-based IFA and its constituent bodies.

Between 1905 and 1910 the number of affiliated association football clubs in Ireland rose from 278 to 420. Despite a major crisis in the game in 1911/12 when the majority of the senior clubs disengaged from the IFA and established the 'new Football Association', by 1914 the game in Ireland was to reach new heights of popularity and success.[29]

The last Saturday before St Patrick's Day in 1914 was seasonably cold and wet in Belfast. Even these conditions, however, could not deter a crowd that one newspaper estimated at 30,000 from attending that afternoon's football match between Ireland and Scotland in the south of the city.[30] The previous three weeks had seen the Irish national side narrowly defeat the Welsh at Wrexham, and trounce an English eleven in Middlesbrough. As a result, the game against Scotland offered the Irish their first ever chance of both taking the Triple Crown, by defeating all three of the other home nations, and being outright winners of the Home Championship. In the event the Irish team, handicapped by injuries and withdrawals of players, could only secure a draw. However, while the result was the loss of the Triple Crown, victory in the overall championship was secured for the first time in three decades of competition. The reaction was tremendous. The players were carried shoulder-high from the pitch by their supporters, and praise for the team flooded in from all sections of the press. In Belfast the Liberal Unionist *Northern Whig* declared that it was a day that would 'have a place of its own in football history'. The politically more conservative *Belfast News Letter* saw the victory as the 'happy consummation of the long-cherished hopes of Irish footballers'; while the Nationalist *Irish News* revelled in the fact that 'Ireland was asserting not merely equality with, but superiority over, her powerful neighbours'. In Dublin the similarly aligned *Freeman's Journal* boasted that 'we can now acclaim our team as champions;' and the *Sunday Independent* took pride in Ireland's victory in this 'remarkable soccer struggle'. Even the rather more staid *Irish Times* was forced to admit that the match had generated 'a scene of enthusiasm unparalleled in the history of Irish Association Football' and provided ' a remarkable struggle and a thrilling finish'.[31] For others it was 'a memorable achievement', and 'a wonderful exposition of pluck and endurance'.[32]

The path to this position, in which association football in Ireland was in an apparently robust and healthy condition, and at the zenith of its achievements, was neither as simple nor as straightforward as these bare facts might suggest, however. The progress of the game had been aided by a number of factors, while others had served to impede it. The result was the uneven growth and spread of the game, both chronologically and geographically.

Most important, perhaps, in facilitating the growth of football in Ireland were a number of fundamental changes which were taking place in Irish society in the later decades of the nineteenth century. The cumulative effects of these were to make sport in general more prominent and popular, and also incidentally described the nature of football's future development. In the first place, rising incomes and the greater availability of leisure time for some of Ireland's population meant that for them participation in sport became a possibility for the first time. For example, between 1850 and 1900 the wages paid to individual farm labourers in Ireland more than doubled, in actual if not real terms.[33] Meanwhile, various factory acts, as well as some local initiatives, gradually reduced the working hours of some industrial operatives.

In addition to these economic changes, demographic developments occurred that indirectly encouraged greater sporting activity. Although the overall level of population in Ireland continued to fall over the decades following the famine, the greater proximity of some of the population due to growing urbanisation meant that the holding of competitive sports meetings, attracting large numbers of spectators, was now more feasible. Between 1841 and 1891 the proportion of the Irish population living in towns of 2,000 or more inhabitants almost doubled, rising from less than a sixth to over a quarter of the total population.[34] Ireland did of course remain an overwhelmingly rural society, and its population in general was relatively sparsely spread, but the growth of provincial urban centres, and the expansion of the Belfast and Dublin metropolises in particular, facilitated the growth of organised mass sports of all sorts.

Rising literacy rates and the growth of the popular press, seen as crucial in the political development of Ireland, also aided a growing interest in sporting events. By 1871 two thirds of the Irish population were reckoned to be literate, a proportion which continued to rise.[35] Accompanying this growth was one in the Irish press. In addition to the vibrant Dublin press, by 1860 there were already more than a hundred newspapers being published in provincial Ireland, and the number was to grow further in the following decades.[36] Among this plethora of printing activity, there eventually emerged a specialist sporting press. The *Irish Sporting Chronicle*, arguably Ireland's first sporting newspaper, began publication in 1840. The more athletically minded and influential Dublin-based *Sport* was first published in 1880. In 1887 the *Ulster Football and Cycling News* became the country's first paper to concentrate overwhelmingly on reporting and debating association football matters. It was followed in 1894 by *Ulster's Saturday Night*, soon to become *Ireland's Saturday Night*, a more general paper, but which had the added advantage of including the day's results in its copy. During the 1890s at least a dozen newspapers that concerned themselves primarily with athletic and sporting news, most of which were admittedly short-lived, appeared in Ireland.[37] As commercial ventures these newspapers must have been launched to cater for a perceived existing demand, but at the same time they acted to familiarise their readers with the finer points of sports, to make them aware of the wider dimensions of games, and to expose them to the likenesses and exploits of men who were to emerge as sporting heroes.[38]

Simultaneously developments were taking place in transportation that made mass participation in sport a real possibility. By 1879 Ireland had 2,285 miles of railway track, and the rolling stock employed on it carried more than 16,000,000 passengers annually.[39] The availability of comparatively rapid and cheap transportation not only meant that teams and competitors could travel with economies of time and financial cost, but that spectators were able to travel considerable distances to venues. The growth of tramway networks in urban centres also ensured that individuals could travel from city centre locations to newer sporting venues in the suburbs, and that the growing number of suburbanites might journey cheaply and efficiently to established city stadia. Dublin's first trams ran in February 1872, though a more efficient service was signalled with the creation of the Dublin United Tramways Company in 1880. In Belfast, although electrification only came in 1906 through public ownership, it was the pre-existing network of tramlines that largely shaped the expansion of the growing city.[40]

The development of sporting venues, especially publicly available pitches and courses, also acted to promote sport in general. Under the provisions of an 1859 act, Irish municipal authorities were permitted to grant land for recreational grounds. Under the 1869 Public Parks Ireland Act they were then empowered to purchase land for such use. Three years later similar powers were delegated to non-municipal authorities.[41]

However, these changes were not all felt with equal measure in all areas of Ireland, and neither did they occur in Ireland at the same time as they emerged elsewhere in the United Kingdom. As a result, the development of Irish sport in general, and association football in particular, followed patterns that differed both in relation to the rest of the British Isles, and regionally within Ireland.

In the context of the United Kingdom, as already noted, the development of association football in particular was comparatively late in Ireland. This situation may to some extent be explained by differing economic circumstances. For the five decades from 1861 Ireland's gross domestic product per head of population was consistently lower than that of any of the other constituent countries of the United Kingdom.[42] Individual incomes in Ireland were rising, though, and by 1914 skilled wage rates in Ireland were almost at parity with those in Britain. However, unskilled men in urban Ireland earned only just over half of what their British counterparts received, and there was an even greater disparity in rural areas.[43] Thus it could be argued that a lack of resources prohibited the earlier development of football in Ireland, and would continue to retard its growth in rural areas. Ireland also remained more sparsely populated than most other areas of the United Kingdom, denying association football the seedbed of contiguous communities in which it prospered elsewhere.

Regional variations in the development of association football within Ireland can also, to some extent, be attributed to differing social and economic circumstances. For example, the effects of the Factory and Workshops Acts must have been felt most heavily in Ulster, and especially Belfast, where the linen industry employed such a large proportion of the workforce. Although the limitations on working hours contained in the 1874 act actually applied only to women and youths, the fact that it was uneconomic to run factories with adult male labour alone meant that from this date many working men in Belfast came to enjoy Saturday afternoons off work for the first time. Additionally, after the Belfast Chamber of Commerce sought subsequent clarification of the act from the Home Office, it became apparent that the half-dozen half-holidays required to be granted could be arranged by employers for Saturday mornings. Thus from the early 1880s a sizeable proportion of the Belfast workforce was working a five and a half day week, with on six or more occasions each year a full Saturday of leisure. A decade later most linen workers were also receiving a week's paid holiday.[44] The linen industry, through the provision of employment for females, also led to total household incomes, and thus disposable income in Belfast, being comparatively high; a situation noted by at least one contemporary in Dublin.[45] The other main Belfast staple, shipbuilding, provided the city with a disproportionately large number of well-paid skilled workers, both in the industry itself and in subsidiary enterprises such as rope making.[46] The Belfast working population, more than any other in Ireland, therefore seems to have had the necessary leisure time and financial resources to participate in some form of modern sporting pastime.

In Dublin, Ireland's other main industrial centre, less than a quarter of the city's male workforce was employed in any kind of manufacturing by 1881, making them far less likely to benefit from factory legislation.[47] Simultaneously, the working population in Dublin, half of which was reckoned to be unskilled, experienced generally higher overall levels of unemployment than their counterparts in Belfast, as well as lower wages and a higher cost of living.[48] It could therefore be argued that a very sizeable proportion of the Dublin workforce had its potential participation in sport of any kind curtailed by its economic situation.

For those for whom the want of time and money were not impediments, however, the sporting facilities available in the Irish capital, and especially those for association football, were remarkable. Complaints in 1898 and 1900, the former by the late secretary of the LFA, that association football's progress in Dublin was being seriously impeded by a lack of facilities did not, perhaps, fall on deaf ears.[49] In 1901 the Commissioners of Public Works, in an attempt to prevent accidents caused by the erection of temporary unauthorised goal posts, and to preserve the existing cricket pitches and flower beds from abuse, laid out a number of football pitches in the Phoenix Park in north Dublin. The following season there were almost a thousand applications for their use. By the 1903/4 season that number had doubled, and the following year there were more than 3,000. In 1907 dressing rooms were erected for use by players.[50] In February 1906 the fact that of the 31 football pitches by then available 29 were for the association game, and only two for Gaelic football, was raised in the House of Commons by the Nationalist member for Co. Dublin. The allegation that this betrayed a bias against 'Irish games' was answered with the observation that this in fact reflected public demand. An additional Gaelic pitch was added, however, though a further question on the same issue was again met by the suggestion that this situation was 'fully proportionate to the relative demand'.[51] The extent to which this situation did in fact truly represent the level of demand may be judged by the fact that by 1925 a survey commissioned by the Irish Free State government reckoned that the 24 association pitches by then available in the park was an 'inadequate' number.[52]

Levels of wages and working conditions in Cork, the third largest urban centre in Ireland, were even less conducive to the promotion of popular sport than those in Dublin. Building workers, for example, were expected in 1892 to work a six-day, 60 hour week. The small number of manufacturing workers in the city were still overwhelmingly employed in small-scale enterprises, effectively beyond the reach of working time regulation. Wages 'were generally lower than those of Dublin.'[53]

Over time it was also variously alleged that nearly all the other material factors, or rather the lack of them, conspired to thwart the growth of association football in the Cork area. 'The lack of a general half-holiday' in Cork was cited in one newspaper in 1909 as a primary reason that participation in the game was limited there. The paucity of pitches 'in or near the city' was raised the following year, and the lack of reliable rail services into the area's interior the year after that.[54] Although levels of literacy in Munster were not appreciably lower than in Leinster or Ulster, it was also suggested that the lack of coverage of local matches in the region's press was countering the spread of the game.[55] As funds for each divisional association were derived primarily from the subscriptions of its member clubs and the gate monies collected at cup-final ties, this lack of both players and spectators in turn created further difficulties. The 'want of money in spreading the light' was reckoned to be a crucial factor in the game's failure to attract wider support by 1912.[56]

As well as these material changes and developments in Irish society, the rise of certain beliefs among men of power and influence in Ireland was crucial in aiding the growth of sports of various kinds, not least association football. Participation in the game was widely acknowledged as leading to greater physical prowess among individuals. A speaker at the IFA AGM in 1887 suggested that 'anything which develops the stamina and power of the people must ultimately be a good thing for the land'. Four years later another commentator agreed, noting the need for more public pitches to be made available in Belfast, 'where the sons of artizans can exercise their frames and enable them to grow up strong, hardy men, with a constitution to enable them to labour, and become a credit to the city, and an ornament to the state'.[57] Thus football was welcomed as a means of physically preparing men for service in both factories and the empire. As well as its beneficial physical effects, football was reckoned to have a moral influence. It was seen as inevitable that 'during a game … the best qualities of a man are brought to the surface'; and the ability to 'play the game' in a gentlemanly manner was seen as promoting strength of character and fair-mindedness. Association football led to 'health – mental, moral and physical'.[58]

Involvement in football and its attendant activities also encouraged self-reliance among the working classes. The raising of money through benefit games and subscriptions, especially when devoted to a worthy cause such as the construction of a working men's institute, where 'the artisan might rest his weary limbs and improve his mind', provided indisputable evidence of this.[59] Another aspect of the improving nature of football was its alleged ability to refresh and rejuvenate those who watched it. 'Business men go away from a match like new men, ... the poorer classes ... have a brief period of excitement and uplifting, which makes up for the weary and sordid days of the past week.' In the words of one Irish football administrator:

> It cheers us up like friendship's cup,
> And drives care to the wall,
> For there's no sport half so jolly,
> As a good game at Football.[60]

At the heart of the ideological support for football, however, was an apparent belief that the game could, by various means, promote greater social stability. On a grand scale, international games between teams representing the four home nations were seen as promoting greater national understanding and solidarity through 'international intercourse'.[61] At a more local level, football was seen as diverting men from potentially more harmful activities. The game acted as 'a great temperance reformer by providing amusement for young men during the two hours on a Saturday when they are most assailed by the temptations of the public house'. Whether they attended them as players or spectators, football matches kept men 'away from the public-house and its baneful influences'.[62] Association football was also seen as directly promoting greater social cohesion and understanding by facilitating the mixing of men of 'all classes, creeds, and religions together, and help[ing] more than anything to provide a friendly feeling among all'. One Congregationalist minister in Belfast concurred in 1896, to the extent that he suggested football's ameliorative powers had led to 'the old spirit of prejudice ... dying a natural death' in the city[63] Many of the hopes that were attached to the game of football in

Ireland were summed up by three speakers at the North-West Football Association's President's Dinner, in Londonderry in 1898. One said simply that there was 'nothing so good for the youthful part of the community' as the exercise the game entailed, and the fact it made them fit 'for almost every class of work'. Another, a Catholic Home Ruler, commented on the fact that through the game 'people were brought together in equality, free from the friction of everyday life', and that football itself had earned 'a congenial halo of civil and religious liberty'. The Unionist mayor of the city thought 'there was something beautiful' in this gathering 'composed of men representing different religious persuasions and different lines of politics'. All the speakers were greeted with calls of acclamation.[64]

Such glowing praise for football was not, of course, universal. One commentator suggested that it generated an 'unchristian-like spirit' in players, while the fact that public houses in Belfast displayed signs saying 'Football results received here' to attract customers must have undermined the game's efficacy as an antidote to drink.[65] In the event, the extent to which such hopes and fears were to be finally realised remained debatable.

Just as the changes in Irish society which had necessarily precipitated the spread of mass sports in the country had been various, and disparate ideologies had acted to foster them, so the means by which association football was actually disseminated across Ireland were many and varied. Both their efficacy and their nature were to have both short- and long-term effects on the game's popularity and perception in Ireland.

At various periods from its founding in 1880 the IFA engaged in missionary work to promote a greater interest in the game. A match under its auspices in Londonderry in December 1883 was watched by 'a goodly number of spectators', despite the inclement weather. A few days before that match the IFA had arranged for a game in Coleraine in an attempt to introduce 'the dribbling game' into the area.[66] Exactly how successful these efforts were is debatable, however. Earlier exhibition games in Limavady, Lisburn, Dublin and

Monaghan all went unremarked upon in local newspapers, and in 1890 the Co. Antrim FA still thought it worth its while to play a demonstration game and distribute rule books in one Ulster town.[67] In fact, in later years the IFA seems to have displayed something of a lack of enthusiasm for such proselytising ventures.[68]

If the actions of the sport's controlling bodies in attempting its dissemination were probably only of a limited effectiveness, the efforts of individuals seem to have more than made up for the former's failings. Although the initial introduction of the game to Belfast is generally credited to, and was enthusiastically claimed by, J.A. McAlery, the manager of the Irish Tweed House in the city, the secretary of the Scottish Football Association had already been attempting to stage an exhibition match somewhere in Ireland.[69] Once the game was placed on a firmer footing in Belfast, the Scottish influence continued to be felt. The very first practice of the Distillery club in 1880 saw 'several Scotchmen, who have played the game in Glasgow' taking part, while the following year the 'cross channel friends' of the Cliftonville club were seen as a distinct asset to the team. In 1882 'Simms, late of Renfrew' was appearing for the Avoniel team in Belfast.[70] In later years the Queen's Island team that won the Irish Cup in 1882 was remembered as being composed solely of Scots employed in the city's shipyard, and the Avoniel club was reckoned to have been formed from Scotsmen employed in establishing the new distillery of that name. The Oldpark team who competed in the first Irish Cup competition in 1881, when they were accused by their opponents of 'unseemly conduct', were allegedly formed by Scottish printers employed in two recently established Belfast companies.[71] The Scottish link did not end there. Early games in Belfast were reported as being played under 'Scottish Association Rules'.[72] The adoption by the IFA of 'the Scotch rule book' gave a formality to the link that was further reinforced by the decision of the SFA to subscribe the sum of £5 towards the cost of the first Irish trophy.[73] The attraction of skilled Scots to work in the growing industries around Belfast had the unlooked-for effect of making the city a bastion of association football activity.

In Dublin, *émigrés* from Ulster as well as from outside Ireland were important in nurturing the game. The short-lived Montpellier club was founded in Dublin in 1889 by two former players with the Beechmount club of Belfast.[74] A more lasting contribution was made in 1890, when the Bohemian club was formed in the gate lodge of the Phoenix Park. The first chairman of the club was Alexander Blaney, a man later recalled as having 'a huge scrotum and a huge memory'. He was also a former player for Belfast's St Malachy's School team, and Cliftonville. Three Sheehan brothers were also present at the club's inaugural meeting, all of whom were former pupils at the Belfast Mercantile Academy, and one of whom was the former secretary of that school's football club.[75] The Bohemian club went on to dominate Dublin football for the rest of the 1890s and beyond, winning the Leinster Cup, the province's most senior trophy, in the six consecutive years from 1894, and a further seven times prior to the outbreak of the Great War.

It is clear that individual devotees were not the only successful means of spreading and promoting football in Ireland, though. Various youth movements, inspired by the ideology of personal development and improvement, acted as emissaries for the game. Primary among these was the Boy's Brigade. The first Irish companies of the organisation were formed in Belfast in 1888 and in Dublin in 1891, and devoted to 'the development of muscle, mind and heart'. By 1900 the latter city's organisation was the third largest in the United Kingdom.[76] The importance of the Brigade to the game's promotion was recognised in 1892, when at the founding of the LFA it was granted an honorary affiliation. In Belfast, meanwhile, the frequency with which it was noted that the leading players in Ireland had learned the game in the ranks of the Brigade was ample testimony to its importance. The first contest between teams representing the Brigades of the two cities took place in 1895.[77]

Other less likely pioneers of the game also emerged. By the 1890s, touring theatrical companies frequently engaged in sporting contests against local teams as a way of publicising their presence. Thus Sir Frank Benson's Shakespeare Company could be seen taking to the association football field in Cork in 1893, and in Londonderry in 1896. Here, as elsewhere, it was alleged that 'clubs sprang, dragon's-teeth fashion, for the privilege of playing against the Bensonians'. In 1904 the Moody-Manners Operatic Company decided to go one step further, and formalised its footballing status by affiliating to the LFA.[78]

Although comparatively little has been written concerning the history of sports, other than Gaelic games, in Ireland, one apparent shibboleth has emerged, that is the importance of the army and educational establishments in disseminating and popularising certain sports.[79] The perception of association football as inextricably linked to the British military in Ireland has endured to such an extent that the use of the term 'garrison game' to describe the sport has survived long after the departure of the military.[80]

In general terms, there does seem to be some evidence that the military played an important role in the early growth of association football in Ireland. Scottish and English soldiers serving in Ireland provided willing recruits for many early Irish clubs, and also some of the early professional players.[81] At the same time, Irishmen in the British military services took up the game, occasionally returning to Ireland and bringing it with them. The most notable example of this was probably that of Matthew Reilly, who enlisted in the Royal Artillery having played only the Gaelic game in his home city of Dublin. By 1895, at the age of 22, he was the goalkeeper for the Army, Hampshire and Royal Artillery teams. By the end of 1902 he had left the army to play professionally for Portsmouth, and had earned two Irish international caps, before subsequently returning to Dublin to play for the Shelbourne club.[82]

In Ireland military teams played matches against local civilian clubs who were often short of opposition. The fixture list for the Montpellier club in Dublin in 1890/91 gave details of forthcoming matches against six teams, three of which were from the local garrison. In 1893 a tournament in the midland town of Athlone saw two military teams take on those from the town and a local school.[83] One of the earliest games played under the IFA's auspices saw soldiers acting as ball boys. In later years members of the military graduated to filling the often unenviable role of referee.[84]

However, the relative importance of the military in Ireland as association ambassadors varied over both time and place. At the very genesis of the game, military teams were in fact notable by their absence. Only in late 1884 were military clubs formed at the Curragh, the country's largest military station, and no military team had affiliated to the IFA four years later.[85] It was in fact not until the 1890s that army teams enjoyed a brief spell of success and popularity at the highest level.[86] The withdrawal of the Royal Scots from the Irish League, and the King's Own Scottish Borders from the semi-finals of the Irish Cup in 1900, as both were being drafted to the war in South Africa, effectively ended the heyday of military footballing achievement.[87] In that short period, however, something had been achieved, and some damage done.

In 1889 the Army Cup competition, competed for solely by military teams, was reckoned to have 'done an immensity of good' for the game, by providing demonstrations in areas where association football had previously been unknown. A decade later a Leinster FA delegate to the IFA AGM thanked the army 'for the way in which they spread the game throughout all parts of the country'. The IFA's annual report echoed these sentiments, welcoming the affiliation of the Irish Army Association to their own body, and noting that they had 'proved of the greatest service in introducing the game into the South of Ireland'. The first formal game of association football to be seen in the province of Munster had reportedly been that played on Boxing Day 1896, between the team of the 14th Hussars and a local side from Carrick-on-Suir. [88] Though they were not intimately involved in the game's initial introduction to Ireland, military teams had apparently acted as an important means of spreading the game into the country's rural hinterland.

At the same time, however, it is clear that a number of tensions existed between military sides and their civilian counterparts. The comparative success of the former led to several grievances being aired in the press. In 1890 it was suggested that military teams had an unfair advantage in the amount of time they had available to train and practice. The fact that garrisons were equipped with gymnasiums and sports fields was also seen as giving army teams an unwelcome edge over their rivals. Additionally, the fact that soldiers came under military control meant that their players were always available, whereas civilian teams were often handicapped by the absence of players due to business commitments. When the LFA was formed in 1892 it was originally intended to exclude military teams, 'as civilians don't believe in providing a trophy to present it to the soldiers'.[89] Successful military teams were also resented as they were not seen as being representative of the local footballing community: they were not 'the kith and kin' of their rivals in Dublin; nor, it was noted in the Belfast press, did they have any 'interest in the association' which controlled and promoted the game.[90] The fact that almost all the members of the representative Munster side that met Leinster in 1904 were soldiers was seen as tending 'to dishearten the locals', and forcing them to turn to playing rugby.[91]

In a wider context, the nature of the relationship between the Irish garrison and local populations was a complex one. Even the Nationalist press was forced to admit that the presence of the military often provided a welcome fillip to local trade.[92] Simultaneously the officer corps became an integral element in county society, and an indispensable component of the Dublin season.[93] Garrison duty in Ireland had less to offer enlisted men, however. Provincial towns were generally 'bereft of any amusement', and life became 'rather mundane for the common soldier'. According to one civilian resident in the important cavalry station of Newbridge in Co. Kildare, prior to 1914 there was little for troops to do 'but get noisy in a pub or try to lure a girl under a hedge'.[94] It was hardly surprising, then, that relations between troops and local civilians were not always cordial. Additionally, its role in giving aid to the civil power meant that 'the army was sucked into the political morass' that surrounded the Irish land issue from the early 1880s, which made members of the garrison less welcome in rural society.[95] The sporadic clerical and political opposition to army recruiting in Ireland that existed in the nineteenth century crystallised into a more continued and coherent Nationalist campaign against the military with the coming of the Boer War in 1899.[96] Even comparatively moderate Home Rulers felt compelled to harangue the military in Ireland, and their fellow countrymen who enlisted.[97] By 1906 disaffection for the military in the garrison town of Fermoy had reached such a level that the local population refused to attend a concert in the barracks there, even though it was given by an eminent Catholic clergyman.⁹⁸ This situation allowed some activists to decry two targets of the newly vibrant Nationalism simultaneously. In 1896 Michael Cusack, the founder of the GAA and a committed Nationalist, could harangue the association players who came to 'learn their game by fagging the ball for soldiers in the Park'.⁹⁹

Overall, it seems that in the earlier years of association football's development in Ireland the military were indeed important in the game's dissemination, and in setting standards of play. Local civilians, however, resented the success of military teams, and the growing alienation of the military from civil society may ultimately have been reflected in some areas in a rejection of both the army and their pastimes. It was apparently not only members of the Gaelic Athletic Association who characterised military participation in sports as 'a thorough nuisance'.¹⁰⁰

With regard to the role played by schools, colleges and universities in spreading the association gospel in Ireland, regional variations and eventual dichotomies seem to have developed that were not totally dissimilar from those evident in relation to the military.

One contemporary reckoned in 1889 that at least 1,500 boys travelled from Ireland to schools in England annually, a figure that had remained roughly constant for the past 30 years. From there, another observer suggested, too many 'brought home to Ireland proficiency in athletics only'.¹⁰¹ Examples can certainly be found of men who first experienced the association game at schools in England, and who then became prominent in the Irish game. Thomas Kirkwood Hackett, a founder member of the LFA, had learned the game at a boarding school in Dorset. M.F. Goodbody, who twice played for Ireland in the early 1890s, and also represented Dublin University and the elite English Corinthians sides, learned the game at a school in the English midlands. Henry Lockhart from Belfast enjoyed a varied athletic career at the Rossall School in Lancashire, eventually captaining the football team in 1883, and then being capped by Ireland in the following year.¹⁰² As was the case with military service, study could take Irishmen into arenas where association football was a part of everyday routines. A few became convinced converts.

In Ireland itself educational establishments also had some role in promoting the game. Although a national school system had been established in Ireland during the first half of the nineteenth century, it was not until 1901 that any form of physical training was included in the curriculum. Even then, this consisted primarily of drill, rather than team sports or games. The Brown Street School in Belfast, for example, usually accompanied its prize-giving day entertainments with 'several physical exercises in drill'. Although 'suitable games' were to be encouraged by staff at playtimes, these too were to be calculated so that pupils were 'trained to habits of prompt obedience', rather than experiencing teamwork or for enhancing physical development. Neither was the situation helped by a lack of facilities. In 1903 no national school in Dublin had a sports field of any kind, and across the country as a whole, a fifth of all schools lacked even a playground.[103] However, the fact that these schools provided a centre for social interaction between young men and boys meant that they also offered a potential venue for informal games and competitions. At the turn of the century in Kildare Street National School in Dublin, impromptu games with a rag ball took place in the schoolyard. In the 1890s in Belfast the highpoint of Robert McElborough's week was an improvised match between the pupils of his school, with the winning team taking the ball as the trophy. William Greer's memories of his childhood in the same period and place are marked by the fact that 'there was always football'.[104]

In the private educational sector things were quite different. From the mid-nineteenth century 'games were purposefully and deliberately assimilated into the formal curriculum' of the major English public schools. Over the next three decades, 'a passion which grew into an obsession' was nurtured at some, and in many cases sports and games, seen as character-forming and morally improving, came to dominate the preoccupations of boys and masters alike.[105] The cult of athleticism was to take root rather later in Ireland, though here too organised games were eventually to assume an important place in the educational experiences of the nation's elite. In the first place they seem to have been valued primarily for their physical benefits. In 1875 the old boys of the Hillbrook School in Co. Down were allegedly reaping the benefits of their past exertions on the sports field by being 'straight up one side and plumb down the other'. By 1913 games were being encouraged in schools as giving boys the opportunity of practising obedience, co-operation, *esprit de corps*, self-sacrifice, patience, promptness in action, presence of mind, self-control, courage in danger, proper use of physical strength, and, if elected to any office in the club, of using authority without bullying, expending confided money judiciously, disposing of matters in a businesslike way, and debating the pros and cons of success and failures at their meetings. In short, they were 'an excellent apprenticeship for the realities of manhood'.[106]

The potential importance of involving schoolboys in the game was recognised by the IFA in 1884, when a Schools Cup competition was organised. Five teams entered the initial competition, four from Belfast and one from county Monaghan. Enthusiasm quickly waned however, and in 1888 the schools' tournament was abandoned. The trophy was then reconstituted as the IFA Junior Cup, for which any team might enter whose players were not considered of a high enough standard to compete in the Irish Cup proper.[107] Later attempts in Belfast to hold similar schools' competitions were even more unsuccessful. The County Antrim FA, acting initially with the support of the IFA, dropped plans for a Schools Cup in 1910, when after six months of lobbying only two schools expressed any interest in the scheme.[108] Some Ulster schools did take up the game, but their interest was generally short-lived. In 1881 teams representing the leading schools from Londonderry and Coleraine met in friendly competition, though the former had come prepared to play under association rules, and the latter under those of the rugby union. Team games, in the form of association football, were introduced to the Friends' School in Lisburn just after the turn of the century, but by 1905 the boys there were playing rugby.[109] This failure of association football to achieve any measure of lasting popularity in Ulster's leading schools was reflected in a similar lack of activity at the Queen's College in Belfast. No association team seems to have been formed before November

1899, and more than a year later it had still not played a match. By 1902 the College club was regarded as 'a rather mysterious organisation; … [whose] existence is merely a universal tradition'.[110] This lack of success in promoting the game in Belfast was at least in part due to the pre-existence of rugby teams in the city's educational establishments. The Royal Belfast Academical Institution had first fielded a rugby team in 1873, and the Ulster Schools Cup competition was established in 1875.[111] The continued adherence of the city's elite schools to the rugby code, in preference to another deemed by one headmaster to be 'beneath contempt', probably reflected a certain sporting snobbery. Despite the faults that attended the rugby code, 'to reject it wholly as a system, and fall in with Association rules, would be out of "Scylla into Charybdis"'. This situation was in turn reinforced by the Northern Branch of the IRFU itself, when in 1887 it ruled that entry to the Schools Cup should be confined to 'Ulster public schools'. Thus both schools from outside the north of Ireland, and boys from the national schools system, were to be excluded from the system.[112]

In the provinces too the association game largely failed to take root in the public schools and colleges. Despite the fact that the headmaster was a former rugby international, sports played little role in the activities of the Manor School in Co. Cork, and the prospect of competing against other schools was seen as 'outrageous'. In Westmeath the pupils of Farrar School played rugby with some enthusiasm, but allegedly regarded the association game with disdain.[113] At the Queen's College in Cork the lack of sports fields prior to 1898 restricted games of any type, but in later years it was rugby, Gaelic football and hurling at which student teams recorded triumphs, and the caricature of the pipe-smoking rugby player that endured in the academic mind.[114] At the college at Maynooth the combination of a lack of pitches, fears that competitive games might promote unwelcome rivalries or physical injury, and clerical disapproval of the indecorous dress and exertions involved in sport, conspired to make any form of athletic exercise generally unwelcome.[115] In the Queen's College at Galway an association club was formed in 1902, but three years later a lack of competition was noted as severely handicapping any progress. Another three years on, after a series of poor displays, the club was still in existence, though it was noted that there was a general lack of enthusiasm for the game among the student body.[116]

These apparent failures were not reiterated in Dublin, however. A team from the city's Trinity College came into existence in November 1883, making it the second to be formed in the capital. By the following year it had acquired the thirty members necessary for it to become affiliated to the university's Athletic Union, replacing the hurley club in doing so. In the following years, however, the university club had only an intermittent existence, and it quickly faded from the front ranks of the game.[117] By the beginning of the 1890/91 season, under pressure from rugby as the popular pastime, association football had all but disappeared in Dublin.[118] Rather more important to the long-term development of the game in Dublin, though, were three very different educational institutions.

In 1885, just as enthusiasm was beginning to wane elsewhere in Dublin, by popular acclamation the pupils of St Vincent's College at Castleknock on the city's outskirts took up football for the first time, and under association rules. Opposition was hard to find, however, and most games were played internally. A student team representing the Literary and Scientific Society took on 'The Rest' in 1887, while the 'Ecclesiastics' played the lay students. In 1889 an influx of pupils from Belfast led to 'better play and more enthusiasm' for the game.[119] A decade later the College took the extremely unusual step of employing a soldier from the local garrison as a coach, a measure it repeated the following year. In 1901 it went even further, by employing Bob Holmes, a professional player with Preston North End and a possessor of seven English international caps, as college coach. Holmes returned in the two following years, much to the delight of the boys, before being replaced by Archie Goodall, a London-based Irish international, in 1905. Holmes made further visits in 1908 and 1909.[120] Castleknock thus provided a nursery for football in Dublin, from which, it was alleged, many pupils graduated to the Bohemian club in the city.[121]

A similar facility was provided by Clongowes Wood College in nearby Kildare. By 1895 both association and rugby football were being played in the College, though the former was allegedly far more popular with the pupils.[122] Clongowes too provided players to the Bohemian club, notably one Oliver Gogarty, who won a Leinster Cup medal with the latter side in 1897, and went on to develop 'a marvellous facility in goal getting'. The first match between the Clongowes team and the Bohemians took place in March 1895, when it was reported that the College was the *alma mater* of the Bohemian club.[123]

In 1895, however, the relationship between Dublin's football clubs and her educational establishments had been proved to be a symbiotic one, when a number of student members of the Bohemians club had founded the Catholic University Association Football Club. By 1897 the University side was reportedly composed almost entirely of former Clongowes students.[124] This club then enjoyed some success, before temporarily lapsing in 1900. It was reformed early in the following year, this time drawing most of its support, both in manpower and finances, from the colleges at Clongowes and Castleknock.[125]

The essentially confined and interrelated nature of association football in Dublin during the decade that straddled the beginning of the twentieth century is apparent from the nature of the fixtures reported in the press. In 1897 the Clongowes team played just two matches, against sides from the Catholic University and Bohemian clubs. In 1901 the first game in what was to be for a short time an annual fixture took place against a Castleknock team. In 1900 it was still apparently the case that the majority of players in Dublin were students of one kind or another.[126]

This situation, whereby football at the highest level in Dublin was confined largely to a number of elite educational institutions and their members, had severe drawbacks. The fact that the university term started well after the football season was under way, and that most players were not regularly resident in Dublin, meant that competitions involving such clubs and local opposition were difficult to organise. This was also the case in the schools, where there was a persistent problem of teams 'shirking fixtures'.[127] Additionally the association game in Dublin was portrayed by some as essentially elitist and exclusive.[128] Whatever the truth of the situation, it was a perception that lingered on in some quarters.

Overall it seems that the agencies that acted in the dissemination and propagation of association football in Ireland were many and varied. At the game's epicentre in Belfast, the role of the individual migrant and the evangelistic convert seem to have been crucial. The influx especially of Scottish workers gave association football there not only a decided fillip, but also perhaps something of a plebeian edge that it acquired only later elsewhere. In Dublin, the sport's other main stronghold in Ireland, the role of the public schoolboy, who developed into the university student, was crucial. The result was, to some extent, an initial perception of association football in the capital as an elitist concern. Elsewhere in the country, most notably in Munster, a lead was offered by the military. Often this may have been by default, as rugby was already well established by the time the association code was introduced, and some proponents of Gaelic football would eventually wage an aggressive campaign against 'foreign sports'. For whatever reasons it occurred, though, this was an unfortunate development for the game itself, as the introduction of the game coincided with a growing rejection of its main sponsors. Just as popular opinion was moving more generally against the members of the military in Ireland, so they emerged as one of the main emissaries of the association football message.

If a great many factors, both material and ideological, acted to promote and encourage the spread of association football in Ireland, others were present which inhibited its growth, and effectively limited its appeal. Foremost among these was the existence of two other footballing codes. Initially some antagonism came from devotees of the rugby code. Rugby football had been brought to Ireland by former pupils of English public schools who attended Trinity College in Dublin. The Trinity club was formed in 1854, making it the second oldest in the world. Rules for the game were formulated in the college in 1868, and by 1879 a governing body had been formed to regulate the game across Ireland. By the time the IFA was emerging there were already nearly 90 clubs playing the rugby game, including more than a dozen in Belfast.[129] To some extent the two footballing codes initially saw themselves as being in competition. By 1883 it was reported that several of the new association football clubs were drawing many of their players from the second teams of established rugby clubs.[130] By the opening of the 1883/4 season it was reckoned that there were just three clubs left playing under rugby rules in Belfast; at its end, one admittedly rather biased observer could suggest 'that for science, skill and quickness, and for real football in fact ... Association was the true game'.[131]

For the most part, however, such rhetoric was limited in extent, and amounted to no more than good-natured banter. In Dublin the fact that one newspaper had made a number of disparaging remarks about the association game did draw one angry response, but the suggestion that any true animosity existed between the camps was dismissed as mischief-making.[132] Real differences in outlooks and perceptions did continue, though. These were summed up in the 1890s by the *Irish Times*' rugby correspondent in the following tongue-in-cheek description of the various football codes as they then existed in Ireland:

> Football in Ireland may be said to consist of three parts-Rugbeian, Associationist and Gaelic. The rule of play in these organisations has been defined as follows:- In Rugby, you kick the ball; in Association, you kick the man if you cannot kick the ball; and in Gaelic, you kick the ball if you cannot kick the man.[133]

Among the associationists in Belfast the definition was seen as 'very good ... but very Rugby too!'.[134]

Rather more strident and persistent opposition to the spread of the association game came from supporters of Gaelic football. The third form of football to be codified in Ireland, the Gaelic game was first equipped with rules in February 1885, following the founding of the Gaelic Athletic Association (GAA) the previous year. This organisation, formed primarily to govern athletics in Ireland but also intended to promote sports that were reckoned to be indigenous to the country, was from its very beginning closely associated with Irish Nationalist politics and the Catholic church.[135] Its opposition to sports that were not covered by its own remit was most apparent through the various bans and disqualifications that were imposed by the GAA on its members and others who engaged in games other than those defined as 'Irish'. The first hint of a ban on such activities came in February 1886, when GAA delegates voted unanimously not to engage in competition with clubs who operated outside GAA rules. Later that year individuals playing rugby or other non-Gaelic football codes were barred from GAA membership. Though this ruling was rescinded in the 1890s, the 1901 GAA convention called on 'the young men of Ireland not to identify themselves with rugby or association football or any other form of imported sport'. A compulsory ban on anyone involved in association football, among other sports, was readopted the following year. The 1904 convention, actually held in January 1905, upheld this earlier ruling, and imposed a mandatory two-year suspension on offenders. This rule was to stay in place for almost another seven decades.[136]

Attitudes to the ban varied, however. A former vice-president of the GAA's rival body, the Irish Amateur Athletic Association, thought it an inherent contradiction to ban a man from playing association football, 'which may or may not be an ancient Irish game', while permitting him to engage in the distinctly non-Gaelic sport of cycling. It had earlier been suggested by a Nationalist that this 'hampering of a man in the very games he takes part in for his recreation and health' was indeed 'most ridiculous'. Even one man later destined to become a leading GAA administrator, and a fierce opponent of non-Gaelic games, at one time regarded the ban as an unacceptable 'imposition on personal liberty'.[137]

Exactly how effective these measures were in inhibiting the growth of association football seems to have varied with the rigorousness with which they were enforced. The Munster delegates to the GAA were among the most vociferous proponents of the bans, and one would later recall that they were utilised to ensure 'there was not so much as a soccer ball … in Cork County'. In 1908 the secretary of the Waterford Gaelic Sports Field Company actually went to the length of advertising the fact that none of the company's shareholders were connected with 'Rugby or Soccer clubs' for fear of a boycott by Gaelic footballers and athletes.[138] The overall impression is that here at least the GAA ban was an important factor in circumscribing any growth in the association game. By 1907, despite the adverse economic and social circumstances in Munster, there were 270 GAA clubs in the province, but only ten affiliated to the IFA.[139]

In Ulster the situation was rather different. Here the GAA was much slower to organise, and as a consequence by 1905 in some areas of the province, association football provided an entrenched opposition to a resurgent and rejuvenated GAA. This situation, and the nature of the conflict that could result, is illustrated by events in Co. Fermanagh following the final introduction of the ban. At a meeting of the IFA Council in August 1907, delegates from the then Fermanagh and South Tyrone FA sought to extend their area of authority to include much of Connacht, and to obtain a grant from IFA funds. The purpose of both initiatives was 'to enable them to compete against the Gaelic body, who were fighting them'. Combined with the Gaelic League branches in the area, GAA clubs were 'coming in to the soccer territory and doing all they could to kill the game'. This included staging rival attractions at established match times, and banning players.[140]

In some northern areas, though, participation in both sports was possible, and some men did keep a foot, probably complete with studded boot, firmly in both camps. The effect of this eventually became visible on the Gaelic field, as several northern teams resorted to 'a semi-soccer game' of playing the ball from foot to foot along the ground, rather than relying on individual runs or aerial passing. The county Louth GAA team even resorted to employing two Belfast association players as coaches.[141] The growing assertiveness of the GAA in Ulster finally led to a more stringent implementation of the ban on foreign sports, although by 1916 it was reckoned that at least in Belfast the ban was counter-productive. The constant banning of players for participating in the association game meant that the pool of players available for Gaelic teams was too small, while many young men simply opted to give their allegiance to the association game and ignored Gaelic football entirely.[141]

In the Dublin area a similar situation seems to have developed, and at least prior to 1914 a situation of more or less peaceful coexistence emerged. Reports of men who played both the association and Gaelic games appeared in the press with some regularity.[143] Dublin GAA delegates were lukewarm in their support of the ban, and there was a comparable tolerance in association circles. In June 1906 a motion by two Ulster delegates that the IFA ban affiliated teams from playing on pitches 'on which Sunday sports or Gaelic football are held', which would have effectively seen Dublin's Tritonville club expelled from senior competitions, was successfully amended on the initiative of two Leinster delegates.[144]

In a more general context, the case can be made that on occasion the existence of Gaelic football clubs in fact acted in the promotion of the association game. In 1886 the Cookstown Swifts Gaelic Football Club in Co. Tyrone, unable to find any opposition in the area, simply converted to the association game. A similar situation arose at Belnaleck, Co. Fermanagh in 1903.[145] The split that occurred in the Irish Parliamentary Party in 1891 following the fall of its leader, Charles Stewart Parnell, was mirrored in the GAA. To all intents and purposes, outside Cork, Dublin and Galway the GAA ceased to function as a sporting body between 1892 and 1896. Elsewhere, and even in these areas, a number of clubs abandoned Gaelic games in favour of association football.[146] On a personal level, the lack of an overtly professional Gaelic football network meant that in the long term many talented players converted to the more profitable, if less prestigious, association ranks.[147]

It seems, therefore, that the relationships between the association code and its football rivals in Ireland were complex ones. The initial hostility between rugby and association aficionados quickly disappeared, and a relatively peaceful coexistence emerged.[148] The rivalry with Gaelic football was more prolonged and more bitter. While for individuals the choice of game was not necessarily an exclusive one, for the sports' authorities the conflict was very real. By 1914, however, here too the association authorities seem to have become reconciled to limiting their endeavours. In 1910 the IFA decided 'not to interfere in the project' of setting up a Connacht FA to encourage the game in the west of the country. Three years later a motion at an IFA Council meeting to grant £20 to the Munster

FA 'to keep the game alive in Munster' was defeated.[149] Social and geographic spheres of influence had been established, and lines of demarcation drawn. With a few exceptions, rugby football remained the game of the middle classes in Ireland. Gaelic football, with its Sunday play and clear links to the Catholic church and parish system, had established itself as the preferred game of the rural Catholic masses, though it also generated some support in the southern urban centres. The association game had its strongest support in Belfast and Dublin, but with considerable interest in the game being shown elsewhere in Ulster and Leinster, and in isolated pockets around the country.

Another possible factor that prevented a wider enthusiasm for the sport among the Irish was the way in which association football was played in Ireland. Its comparatively late introduction meant that the game came almost fully formed to Ireland. At their second meeting on 30 November 1880, the IFA had decided to adopt 'the Scotch rule book' with one minor amendment, and to refer to the Scottish Football Association (SFA) for clarification on one particular point.[150] In 1882 the International Board was founded, consisting of delegates from the sport's English governing body, the Football Association (FA), and from the Football Association of Wales (FAW), the SFA and the IFA. One of the primary tasks of this body was to ensure a common set of rules for competitions. Thus, from this early date association football in Ireland was governed by the same code as elsewhere in the United Kingdom.[151] In subsequent years, though, Irish legislators and players were to be comparatively active in reforming the rules of the modern game. The penalty kick, whose introduction is reckoned by one historian of the game to be among the most important fundamental developments, was introduced in 1891 at the suggestion of the IFA, following the floating of the idea in the Belfast press. The replacement of umpires, nominated by each team, by neutral linesmen was also an Irish initiative. In later years the style of play adopted by William McCracken, an Irishman playing as a professional in England, was credited with bringing about a major reformation of the off-side law.[152]

But if common rules existed across the United Kingdom, a common style did not. By 1888 it was reckoned that in England there had been 'two ages of Association play, the dribbling and the passing'.153 The initial form of the game, current on its introduction to Ireland, was for individual players to dribble the ball as far as possible, being supported by the presence of their team-mates. By the early 1880s this pattern was being replaced in Britain by the 'combination game' in which passing the ball between team members was the preferred method of carrying the ball upfield.154 In Ireland similar developments took place, but only after some delay. The members of the Linfield club of Belfast were reckoned to be 'the originators of the passing or combination game' in Ireland. This did not occur until 1890, however, when the club hired Nick Ross, a veteran professional with the Preston North End team in England, to act as its coach.155 The conflict between the two styles of play in Ireland was to continue for some time, both between teams playing at the highest level, and between these teams and their junior counterparts. When Bohemians, one of the leading sides in Dublin, played the Belfast team, Distillery, in December 1895, the latter was reported to have played 'with machine-like regularity, the ball passing sharply from man to man, each man being in the proper place to receive his pass'. This 'proved somewhat puzzling to the Bohemians', who themselves relied on the tactic of 'fast rushes'. Distillery won the game by three goals to one. It was not until 1904 that Bohemians decided to employ a Scottish coach and adopt the 'combination game'.156 The following year however, the Shelbourne team, the great rival of Bohemians in Dublin, was still reckoned to be playing 'the kick and rush game'. Four years prior to this the Belfast Celtic side had played its own reserves in a pre-season friendly. The latter 'played a rushing game, while the seniors went in more for the fancy style'.157

From the very beginnings of the game in Ireland, it involved a measure of what was seen by some as rough and brutal play. In the very first Irish Cup competition a player with a Limavady side had broken a leg, while in March 1882 a player with the Belfast side, Avoniel, was banned for life for inflicting a similar injury on a member of an opposing team.158 This trait of the game was certainly modified over time, but examples continued to be cited of teams that relied overly on physical force rather than skill in winning games. The 1892 Irish Cup final allegedly degenerated into 'a war of annihilation' between the opposing players. The following year St Columb's Hall, a senior side from Londonderry, was condemned for a display of how 'brute force can discount the self-restraint, the power of combination, the skill and gentleness the association game is designed to promote'.[159] In 1906 the senior clubs of Belfast went as far as asking the IFA to prevent the Dublin side Tritonville from entering the Irish Cup, at least partly on the grounds that their players were simply too brutal.[160]

Although the game in England was known for its robust nature, the evidence suggests that in Ireland the level of force employed by players, and the importance laid upon physical contact, was even greater. In March 1894 a libel case heard at the Manchester assizes in north-west England saw the Newton Heath Football Club seek damages from the proprietors of the *Birmingham Daily Gazette* over remarks printed in the newspaper concerning John Peden, the Newton Heath centre-half. The plaintiffs asserted that suggestions made by the paper that Peden was likely to 'create an extra run of business for the undertaker' if he carried on in his present style of play were calculated to damage the club's reputation. Peden, already the holder of fifteen Irish international caps, and a recent arrival at Newton Heath from the Linfield club of Belfast, was called to give evidence. He denied deliberately kicking a number of players during a recent match with the West Bromwich Albion club, but was forced to admit that 'in teams against which he had played in Ireland ... several men received injuries, including fractured limbs'.[161]

In a comparative context the Irish game certainly seems to have been not only rather physical, but somewhat lacklustre for much of the period before the advent of the Great War. Matches between Irish club teams and those from England and Scotland were fairly regular occurrences in the early years of the game, with Irish teams even competing in the English Challenge Cup. Only once did an Irish club make it to the first round of the competition proper, though, when in 1888 the Linfield club beat a side from the

English club, Nottingham Forest, by three goals to one in Belfast. However, the home side had already conceded the match as they could not afford to travel to Kent to fulfil their next tie, and had in any case played an unregistered player in the original drawn game in Nottingham. Less edifying but more typical displays were those given by the Cliftonville club, who lost by ten clear goals to a Partick Thistle side in the same competition in 1886, and that of the Distillery team which conceded a similar number of goals against a Bolton Wanderers side in 1890.[162] Friendly encounters against cross-channel opposition, often staged as fund-raising events, rarely saw the Irish clubs fare any better. In November 1894 the Linfield club lost 5–1 to a Sheffield United side in Belfast, though the visitors' team consisted mainly of reserve players. A decade later the Bohemians of Dublin were 'totally outclassed' by their visitors from Liverpool, and in 1909 a team representing the English second division side Manchester City, though it too was composed mainly of reserve team players, beat a Munster Select XI by four goals to two in Cork.[163] The Linfield club did beat the leading English amateur side, the Corinthians, on two occasions in the 1890s, and was congratulated on the first occasion on beating 'a good English team', but all was not what it seemed.[164] The first victory in 1890 was achieved against a Corinthian club whose members were fielding two sides simultaneously; one in Belfast, the other in Lancashire against the reigning Football League champions, Preston North End. By the time of the second victory in 1894, the Corinthians were themselves a declining force in the English game, and their defeat only brought forth the comment from their captain that he did not think the Linfield side 'good enough to hold its own in really first-class company'.[165]

The comparative failure of Irish club teams in competitions with foreign opposition was echoed at the full international level. Following their first international fixture against England in February 1882, when the Irish national side lost by thirteen goals to nil, the tale was initially one of almost undiluted woe. Not until 1887, when the Irish triumphed 4–1 over a Welsh side in Belfast, was there any victory at all. Partial success against England came in 1894 when Ireland secured a 2–2 draw, and a draw with Scotland came two years later. It was not until 1903, however, that the Irish side finally won a game against the Scots, and another decade was to pass before the English were defeated. At the turn of the century the record of the Irish international side stood at played 57 matches, won 6 (all of which were against Wales), drew 5 and lost 46. The Irish had scored a mere 17 goals, while conceding 273. Among the least impressive performances had been two games when 13 goals had been conceded against English opposition, one when Wales had succeeded in scoring 11 without reply, and the conceding of 10 goals against a Scottish side in a match in Belfast.[166]

The failings of Irish footballers in general, and a growing perception that the domestic game was in decline, led to a number of crises of confidence in the sport from the turn of the century. The relative lack of success of the Irish national team was especially galling for the supporters of the game given that 'in every other branch of sport', including rugby, athletics and cycling, despite the small constituency, Irish teams and competitors more than held their own, and were frequently world champions.[167] Additionally, the teams that the Scottish and English Football Associations fielded against Ireland were not generally their strongest. Into the first decade of the twentieth century they employed 'experimental teams' in matches against Wales and Ireland, using these games as trials for the real test of playing each other.[169]

Various reasons were offered in explanation of this sustained failure at international level. In the vogue of the time some observers looked to racial factors. In 1901 a Scottish journalist, 'in keeping with the theory of the racial idea', pinpointed what he perceived to be the key failing of Irish football: it was 'essentially Celtic'. The association code called for 'reasoned action, deliberation in methods, and the union of individual and collective brilliance'. Irish footballers relied on 'impetuosity and torrential courage, not reasoned and scientific tactics'. He found some support in Ireland, though the argument was to some extent reversed. Irishmen, it was suggested, were 'of too frolicsome a nature to be troubled with the finessing pertaining to forward play', though their natural attributes of stoicism and dependability meant they actually made fine full-backs.[169]

Less than a decade later, further popular preoccupations were pressed into use to explain Ireland's failure. A growing concern with the moral degeneration of the nation's youth was translated into the belief that the present generation of Irish footballers were essentially too unruly and ill-mannered to take any notice of their trainers. As a result they failed to improve their standard of play and the national side suffered. This was in sharp contrast to the suggestion made two years before, when it was ventured that the Irish were simply excessively 'good sports', who failed 'to cry and tear their hair out' when they lost, and who were too well endowed 'with the true sporting spirit'.[170]

In the meantime, beyond the purely genetic and the allegedly cerebral, a few more practical suggestions had also been made. As early as 1887 it was suggested that the selection of the Irish team was subject to considerations other than talent.[171] Over the years it was to be regularly suggested that a player's club or his place of residence affected his chance of international selection.[172] On occasion it was fairly obvious that something was awry with these procedures, such as when the son of the IFA's president received a cap for the Irish junior international side after playing the game only once.[173] However, in mitigation of these idiosyncrasies it was claimed that teams were 'built up from a gate point of view', that is Belfast-based players were selected in Belfast, and Dubliners in Dublin, in order to maximise attendances.[174] At the same time, a consideration over which the IFA had only partial control also acted to limit the choices available to the selectors. In 1895, a year after professionalism had been introduced in Ireland, and a full decade after its legalisation in England, the IFA was still not prepared to select Irishmen playing as professionals in England and Scotland to play in the national side. Only in 1899 did they eventually relent, and offer places in the team to professional 'exiles'.[175] However, the situation was now beyond the influence of the IFA. The Irish Association had no authority outside Ireland, and therefore could not demand that clubs in England or Scotland release their Irish players to play for their country. Domestic clubs were dealt with in Ireland by the simple expedient of the IFA declaring a 'closed date', that is one on which no matches were to be played. Once a player crossed the channel he was outside the IFA's jurisdiction, and his club could decide that its fixtures took priority over any commitment to the Irish team. As a result, the migration of top Irish players to professional sides in Britain not only led to a decline in the standard of the domestic game, but on occasion prevented Ireland from fielding the best possible selection.[176] In 1909 the IFA attempted to remedy the situation by voting at its AGM to propose to the International Board 'that clubs must release foreign players for international duty'. The motion was passed unanimously in Ireland, but failed to be accepted by the Board.[177] The improvement and success of Irish football as a whole was paradoxically limited by the growing skill of its individual players.

Given that the various ideological, material and social developments that were taking place in Ireland could in fact have acted to promote almost any sport or game, the question remains as to why some individuals chose association football over its rival pastimes. In fact, it remains particularly acute in Ireland, where the game was eventually faced by opposition and competition from two different codes of football. In part at least, it seems that the nature of the association game itself had certain attributes to commend it above its rivals. In the first place, participation in the sport was possible for most of the population, regardless of their financial or physical condition. Informal association games could be played in the street using a rag ball, or even one of compacted paper. Waste yarn was used by workers at the York Street Mill in Belfast to improvise a ball, though they stood the chance of being fined by the foreman for kicking it in working hours.[178] By 1899 the situation had come to something of a head in Belfast, and a call was made for the police to suppress the practice before a serious accident occurred. This is precisely what happened some years later in Co. Down, when a young man was run down and killed by a cart while kicking a rag ball around the streets of Newtownards.[179]

In the game's early years, even contests at the highest levels required little expenditure on equipment. In 1883 the Hertford team, one of the leading exponents of the new code, took to the field wearing a motley array of tweed caps, moleskin breeches and improvised shin pads. A few years later, teams were wearing uniform shirts, but in at least one case these were accompanied by cut-down formal trousers.[180] Even the coming of greater uniformity did not necessarily mean greater expense. The popular belief that the Distillery club's traditional colours were white because their shirts were made from cast-off flour bags cannot be proved indisputably, but given that these fine white starched cotton bags were in common use for everything from aprons and pyjamas to bandages and bed sheets, the suggestion is far from ridiculous.[181]

Simultaneously, a great stress was put in the early years on the safety of the association game as compared to the rugby code. The initial announcement of the formation of the Cliftonville club in Belfast in 1879 stressed that association football offered players 'a pleasant and invigorating game … without fear of injury to body or limb'. It had already been suggested that 'the old, degrading, dangerous, Rugby rules' raised little popular interest in Ireland.[182] The eventual shift from rugby to association rules in the Bessbrook area of Armagh was apparently hastened by the fact that in 1887 a local rugby player suffered a broken neck while playing.[183] Allied with the general idea of rugby as a physically dangerous game was the perception that the association code offered opportunities for men physically unsuited to playing rugby. 'Training, skill and speed' were the vital ingredients in an association player, while 'in the Rugby game physical prowess [was] the all-important factor'.[184]

As compared to the Gaelic game, association also had advantages for some. In 1895 the chairman of the Co. Meath GAA board compared Gaelic football adversely with the association game, and called for the revision of the former game's rules to make it both more enjoyable for players and more interesting for spectators.[185] Difficulties continued, however. In Co. Fermanagh in March 1906 the correspondents in one Nationalist newspaper reported that spectators had a choice of viewing a Gaelic game in which the players seemed to 'rush aimlessly to and fro in crowds after the ball' or an association game that provided 'ninety minutes of ding-dong play'.[186] Comparatively speaking, Gaelic football had other drawbacks too. The holding of Gaelic matches on Sundays may have been guaranteed to attract the rural labouring classes, but it was also sure to deter participation by Sabbatarian and evangelical Protestants.[187] The provision in the original Gaelic rules of 1885 that a pitch had to measure a minimum of 120 yards by 80 meant that for formal games to take place, an area twice the size of that required for an association pitch was necessary. Moreover, the rough and tumble element of the early Gaelic rules meant they were as likely to result in physical injury to players, as were those of the rugby field.[188] In short, when compared to its rivals, association football was a simple, cheap, exciting and safe sport that offered a measure of satisfaction to those who partook in it with only a minimal risk.

In conclusion, the three and a half decades following the first demonstration of association football in Ireland saw a phenomenal rise in the game's fortunes there. Though its introduction was comparatively late, an administrative body, clubs and competitions were quickly established. By 1914 comparatively large crowds were attending important games, and levels of participation in the sport at all levels were high. Social and economic developments in the country at large provided the essential background for this rapid growth in the game, as they also did for a greater public interest in other forms of sport and leisure activity. Simultaneously, the rise of ideologies that saw sport as essential to the physical, mental and moral welfare of the population acted to encourage and promote sports, not least association football.

The story was not one of universal success, however. Association football remained restricted geographically and, to some extent, socially in Ireland. In part this related to the economic and social conditions that prevailed in the country's various regions, and to the nature of the game as it was played; but it was also due to some extent to class and national prejudices. Yet even if the playing of the game in Ireland left something to be desired, and the international side generally lacked success, the game could still arouse a great deal of passion and attract many devotees. By 1914, in Belfast and Dublin at least, which together with their hinterlands contained up to a third of the country's population as well as the overwhelming bulk of its wealth, power and influence, association football was well on the way to becoming 'the people's game'.

2

Clubs

What Ho, the football season comes apace;
And Sports – to know what combatants will grace
The green arena to command applause –
In breathless silence, view the published draws.

Derry Journal, 4 Sept. 1912

Kesh—W. Cleland, Hilden, Lisburn.
Larne Grammar School—Hon. Sec. School Larne.
Lavinia—James K. Patrick, 17 Lavinia Street.
Ligoniel 1st XI—W. Pedlow, Ligoniel.
Ligoniel Rovers—James Blair, Glenview Terrace, Ligoniel.
Linfield 2nd XI.—John Torrans, 34 Napier Street.
Linfield Wanderers—Oswald M'Murray, 34 Hurst Street.
Larne F.C.—Owen Kettle, 3 Inver Terrace, Larne.
Medical Staff Corps—Corpl. D. Brown, M.S.C., Victoria Barracks.
Milford Reserves—Hon. Sec., W. M'Crum, Milford, Armagh.
Mount Athletics—James Walker, 89 Woodstock Road.

'This extract from a list of junior clubs secretaries from 1890 gives an insight into the basis of the game in Ireland. A military and a school team are listed alongside the Lavinia Street team from south Belfast. The William McCrum shown at Milford Reserves was the originator of the penalty kick.'

Ulster Football and Cycling News

THE CONCEPT OF THE SPORTS CLUB was already well established in Ireland by the time association football was first played in the country. Ireland's first rugby club had been formed at Trinity College in Dublin in 1854, by which time cricket clubs had existed for more than two decades.[1] This situation, along with the relatively formal nature of Irish football from the game's very beginnings, ensured that the football club was an integral part of the sport's structure in Ireland from the earliest days of the game. The circumstances surrounding the founding of clubs, the exact manner in which they were run and the factors that affected their development are not easily discovered, especially considering the complete lack of any club records for the years prior to the Great War. In the following paragraphs, however, an effort will be made to trace the probable origins of clubs, to outline the ways in which clubs functioned, and to assess the wider position of the football club in Irish society.

TABLE 2.1
Number of clubs affiliated to Irish Football Association 1881–1910
(year ending mid May)

YEAR	NO.	YEAR	NO.	YEAR	NO.	YEAR	NO.
1881	7	1889	65	1897	112	1905	278
1882	13	1890	124	1898	103	1906	285
1883	17	1891	not known	1899	104	1907	304
1884	34	1892	78	1900	110	1908	344
1885	37	1893	105	1901	259	1909	373
1886	42	1894	102	1902	199	1910	420
1887	37	1895	101	1903	196		
1888	86	1896	96	1904	222		

Sources: 1881–90, IFA cash book 1880–97; 1898–1902, IFA Committee minute book 1898–1903; 1902–8, IFA Council minute book 1903–9; 1892–3, *Northern Whig* 9 May 1893; 1910, IFA Council minute book 1909–25; 1894–7, *Irish News* 6 May 1895, 3 May 1897.

Exactly how many association football clubs existed in Ireland at any one time is uncertain. Table 2.1 lists the numbers of clubs affiliated to the IFA between the body's founding and 1910. However, these figures should not be seen as a definitive account of the number of clubs playing the game in Ireland. In the first place, more than once accusations were made concerning the actual status of affiliated clubs. An investigation by the IFA and its affiliated associations during the 1902/3 season into the possible existence of 'bogus clubs' failed to reach any very damning conclusions, but rumours proliferated that the Linfield and Cliftonville clubs in Belfast were establishing fictitious clubs, and affiliating them to the IFA, in order to extend their influence in the game's governing body.[2] By 1907 a similar situation had possibly developed in Dublin.[3]

But if the 'bogus clubs affair' of 1902 and the like suggest that the actual number of clubs in Ireland might require revising marginally downwards, the fact that substantial numbers of clubs existed that were never affiliated to the IFA would push the overall total much higher than that provided by the IFA figures. In 1891, of 51 junior clubs reckoned to be active in Ulster, only 18 were affiliated to the IFA. Twenty years later the Munster FA boasted 37 affiliated clubs, though there were reckoned to be at least another seven unaffiliated clubs in the city of Cork alone.[4] The IFA was continually granting affiliated clubs permission to play unaffiliated ones in the years prior to the outbreak of the Great War. For example, in 1909 Bohemians of Dublin were granted permission to play Castleknock Butterflies, while Belfast Celtic's reserve side took on St Malachy's College. The previous year Shelbourne had travelled to play Ballina in Co Mayo.[5]

However, the apparent growing reluctance of the IFA to grant such permission, and the desire of clubs to take part in IFA sponsored competitions, might suggest that the later figures in Table 2.1 may represent a much truer estimate of actual club numbers than the earlier ones. The total of 420 clubs by 1910 was not enormous by contemporary standards, being slightly larger than the number of GAA clubs existing in the country a decade earlier, but given that fewer than a sixth of this number were from the provinces of Munster and Connaught, it is illustrative of the popularity of association football, not to say its dominance, in some areas.[6]

The exact origins of individual football clubs are not easy to trace, and the transient nature of many means they will probably remain no more than a brief mention in a local newspaper, if that. In a few cases, though, primarily those in which clubs endured for some years and gained some degree of distinction, a little of their early history is discernible, and something may be said regarding their subsequent development.

In the first place, it is clear that clubs often had their origins in various existing sporting or social organisations. For example, the Knock Football Club was among the first half dozen to be formed in Ireland, and was composed primarily of members of the Knock Lacrosse Club in Belfast. Similarly, the Cliftonville Club was founded by 'several members of the C[liftonville] C[ricket] C[lub]' who were 'ardent admirers of the Association game'. The Greenwood club from Lisburn was formed in 1880 from the members of an existing harrier club, following a paper chase, and took its name from a house situated next to the team's pitch. In Dublin several original members of the first Bohemians team have been identified as playing for a cricket team of the same name.[7] By 1888 the members of the Catholic Reading Room in Armagh had run an association football club for two years. The following year the Central Presbyterian Association in Belfast, which provided both social and educational resources for the city's Presbyterian population, was also fielding a team.[8] Also in Belfast, the members of the Mountpottinger branch of the YMCA decided in 1900 to form an athletic club 'in connection with our association'. Nine months later the Mountpottinger YMCA Athletic and Football Club was in existence.[9]

If such social institutions centred on the church played a role, so too did the churches themselves. A number of junior clubs existed in Dublin by 1902 which bore the names of the city's Church of Ireland parishes, and which were presumably therefore linked to them. Meanwhile Irish Catholic clergymen were encouraged by one of their number to set up boys' clubs, integral in which was to be a football club. In Dublin even one of the city's synagogues boasted its own football team.[10]

The public house, which by the middle of the nineteenth century allegedly provided 'a controlled and well ordered environment', and by the 1890s was a 'vital part of social and economic life' in Ireland, could also provide a focus for the formation of football clubs. The Crusaders club of Belfast was founded in 1909 following the raising of funds in a pub on the city's York Road. More than a decade earlier the Shelbourne club had been formed in a pub in the Ringsend area of Dublin. Some time before that the Belfast Celtic club had been formed 'on the same lines as the celebrated Glasgow Celtic', and established its headquarters in the Beehive public house on the Falls Road. All were to go on to become notable clubs.[11]

If places intended primarily for the consumption of alcohol could lead to the founding of clubs, so could various elements of the vibrant temperance movement. The 'Catch-My-Pal' organisation, founded in 1909 and so named because members were sworn to total abstinence in groups and then expected to save any of their fellows who fell from grace, was a forward-looking and devoutly modernist organisation. It looked to 'anything that gives a man a healthy interest in matters outside his own narrow groove in life' and might thus 'draw him away from the sordid attractions of the public-house'. The cinema, the car, the telephone and the typewriter were thus welcomed as beneficial influences. By 1911 the net had apparently been widened to include association football, as branches at Downpatrick and Bessbrook established clubs. In earlier years teams associated with the Independent Order of Rechabites had been active in both Belfast and Dublin.[12]

While the exact role that educational establishments themselves played in the dissemination of the game is debatable, there can be little doubt that they provided players and facilities that were vital in establishing some early clubs. Similarly, the military influence on the development of association football in Ireland is open to varying interpretations, but it is irrefutable that the army provided several of the leading clubs in Ireland during the game's early years.[13]

In rural areas some football clubs were founded and fostered by members of the local gentry and their sons. The Moyola Park club, one of the first to be founded in Ireland, operated under the patronage of Major Chichester, who became 'in every respect a worthy patron and supporter'. He provided the club with a pitch in his demesne at Castledawson, Co. Londonderry, and entertained visiting teams at his own expense. Partly as a result he was invited in 1880 to become the first president of the Irish Football Association.[14] Both the Castlerea club in Co. Roscommon and the Athlone Town club in Co. Westmeath were founded in 1887 by Orlando Coote, the younger son of a local landlord, newly returned from schooling in England. The young returnee then succeeded in involving members of his father's tenantry and local shopkeepers in the clubs.[15] Such patronage and paternalism was a long established, if declining, part of life in rural Ireland, which had been present in the sporting arena from at least the eighteenth century.[16] Rural elites had been prominent in the promotion of sports such as hurling during these years, and in the immediate post-famine years Irish landlords continued to provide pitches for play and prizes for competition. In Co. Antrim the Ballymena Cricket Club played on a pitch in the demesne of Lord Waveney, who acted as the president of the club and even provided horses to roll the pitch. On the death of his father in 1886, Waveney's son received a delegation from the club bringing both their condolences and an invitation for him to take over the club's presidency. From the mid-1860s Lord Ranfurly was subscribing annually to the 'cricket field committee' in Dungannon, Co. Tyrone.[17] Such actions were seen as important in creating desirable attitudes of deference and indebtedness among the lower classes, and establishing an image of magnanimity in proprietors. The provision of a hockey pitch for a local team in Co. Cork by Lord Bandon was allegedly made with 'some sort of vague suggestion that we owed a duty in respect to the noble lord'.[18]

If patronage and paternalism were in decline in the countryside, they were alive and well in at least some urban centres. Two clubs that were to become among the most prominent in Ireland have their roots in the industrial heart of Belfast. The Distillery club was originally formed in 1879 from employees of Dunville's distillery in Belfast. By the winter of 1880 its members were playing football. The Linfield club was originally formed in 1885 from the workers at the Ulster Spinning Company's Linfield Mill.[19] In both these cases the clubs seem to have received some encouragement and material assistance from their parent institutions. The Linfield club was originally allocated a ground on company property on which to play its games, and allowed the use of the factory dining hall for changing. The Distillery side was the fortunate recipient of rather more lasting help. Again the club was originally provided with a pitch on company property, and when this was taken over for further building was given a new pitch at 'a purely nominal rent' by Dunville's. A further move in 1900 again saw the club benefit from some 'liberal assistance' from Dunville's, as it had reportedly done in the past.[20]

Such industrial paternalism was not unusual. In 1910 members of the Park Drive club were to thank their employers, Gallahers of Belfast, not only for their help in establishing the club but also for providing Park Drive cigarettes at the club's social functions. Twelve years earlier the engineering company Mackie and Son had given its new works team a pitch, and it was noted 'that the principals of the firm take a personal interest in the team'. In fact, acts of this kind were apparently common enough to warrant parody. In *The Red Hand of Ulster*, his satirical and prophetic account of rebellion in Ireland and the eventual partition of the country, James Hannay included the character of Mr Cahoon, a Belfast industrialist who was to 'devote his spare time on Saturdays to the instruction of young men in cricket and football'.[21] Elsewhere in Ulster, similar patronage was extended by some industrial employers. The Hilden club from near Lisburn was provided with a pitch in 1882 by William Barbour and Sons, a linen company and the major local employer. In the following years various members of the Barbour family acted as patrons and presidents of the club.[22] In Dublin too, industrial patronage of sport was not unknown. At least two major Dublin employers, the Jacobs biscuit factory and Guinness's brewery, fielded football teams. Given the paternalist attitudes of both companies, and especially the fact that Guinness was later to provide substantial playing fields for its workers, it seems likely the Jacobs and St James's Gate clubs profited in some way from the association of their members with these employers.[23]

The existence of this sporting paternalism in some of Ireland's leading industrial concerns both reflected an often unacknowledged aspect of social relationships within the country and located Irish industrial relations in a wider continuity of patronage and affiliation. In Belfast, for example, some employers actively fostered and encouraged workers' benevolent societies, and provided company outings for employees. In Dublin in the 1890s, visiting trade unionists received donations from the city's main industrialists, and even free passes on the city's trams.[24] In late nineteenth century Germany industrial paternalism generally existed as an extension of rural deference and reciprocation, as former landed proprietors became industrialists, and tenants and labourers became factory hands. In Britain – where, as in Ireland, industry came more often under the control of a new bourgeoisie from outside the landed gentry class – a 'new paternalism' was developed, which 'actively complemented *laissez faire* notions of economy and society'.[25]

In other cases, though, while the workplace may have provided the venue for the founding of a club, there is no evidence to suggest that employers offered any encouragement to its members. This was apparently the case in 1884 when a club was founded in Belfast for civil service officers and in 1890 when the Emerald Football Club was formed in Dublin by workers at the General Post Office. 'The High Pressures Football Club' was founded in Newry in 1889 by employees of the Newry Foundry Company without any apparent involvement of management or owners. In Dublin the Pembroke club was formed by bottle blowers from the Ringsend area of the city, all of whom chose to start work thirty minutes early each day, at 5.30 am, in order to finish at lunchtime on Saturdays and thus be able to play football in the afternoon.[26]

Another focus for the formation of many clubs, though one which is largely without any direct proof, may have been simply the street or neighbourhood in which individuals lived. Among the 31 junior clubs registered with the IFA in the Dublin area in 1902 were the Aughrim and Fontenoy clubs. The secretaries of both clubs lived in streets of the same name. Certainly informal street games were common in towns, and the step from these activities to formal competitions was not a great one.[27]

In short, football teams could be formed around almost any institution or entity that brought young men together. These included churches and schools, the pub and the workplace. In some cases they might be offered encouragement by their parent organisations, but in many these acted as no more than an original point of common reference. In these factors, association football clubs in Ireland differed little from those in England.[28]

The relationship that existed between football clubs and existing social foci, and between clubs and patrons, were to become to some extent transposed over time. Football clubs were themselves to become both social institutions and social patrons. The founding of a reading room in Ballymena in 1899 by the local football club is perhaps an extreme example of the growth of the football club as a social centre, but the 'smoker' and the 'club social' had become regular occasions by the first decade of the twentieth century.[29] Simultaneously clubs were also to become the providers rather than the recipients of local patronage. The playing of benefit games, at which spectators' entrance fees were handed over to community-centred projects, was probably begun in the 1890s, and by the following decade it was apparently common. The Masonic and Orange halls in the Ballymacarret area of east Belfast benefited to the tune of £80 and £72 respectively in 1903 from games organised by the local Glentoran club, and in 1909 the St Vincent de Paul Society in Portadown reaped the rewards of a game between the Portadown and Belfast Celtic clubs. Two years earlier the new Catholic church at Ringsend in Dublin had received more than £100 from a match arranged by the Shelbourne and Bohemians clubs.[30] The assumption of such roles by football clubs and their members is a testimony not only to the changing status of these individuals and organisations, but also to their growing importance within Irish life. For some the football club had undoubtedly supplanted other institutions as the primary centre for social interaction and identification. For others it remained subordinate, but clearly still of some importance. The emergence of the club as patron must have reinforced the bond between club and community. A reciprocal relationship of alliance and support resulted in tangible benefits for both.

Although their origins were various, and their number varied over time, it seems from the little evidence available that most football clubs were, at least originally, run on similar lines. A club committee elected by the members was responsible for the handling of all the club's affairs, including team selection. Even with the introduction of paid trainers the situation seems to have remained unchanged, with the club committee choosing team members, and coaches simply advising on the fitness of individuals. On occasion the sports club was actually seen as the model of democracy in Ireland, with 'the debating society or a cricket club' held up by one university student as appropriate icons for any new democracy.[31]

From a financial standpoint, individual members were initially required to pay subscriptions to cover the club's expenses. In 1888 members of the Loughgall club in Co. Armagh paid 2s annually. By the turn of the century the St Columb's Court club in Londonderry was charging its full members 6s., payable in two instalments. Around the same time the members of a junior club in Belfast were subscribing a penny a week each, suggesting a total fee of 2s. each season. In 1901 full membership of the Cliftonville club cost 10s., and that of the Ulster football club 7s. 6d. The Central Presbyterian Association's reformed club demanded 2s. 6d. from playing members in 1907.[32] Such funding could be unreliable, however, and in 1889 the Gilford club apologised for failing to fulfil a fixture, citing the fact that some of its members 'would like sport without paying for it'.[33] Additionally, as the game became more formalised, so the expenses associated with it became greater. The improvisation of clothing and equipment that sufficed for all in the game's early days, and which would continue at the game's lower levels for many years, was increasingly unacceptable for many. In 1888 a complete strip for a player, including boots and shin guards, cost 15s. 2d.: more than a week's wages for a labouring man.[34]

Travelling to compete in cup-ties also placed a financial burden on clubs. The inclusion of clubs from the north-west and mid-Ulster as well as Belfast in the first Irish Cup competition in 1881, and then the decision in 1885 to include Dublin teams in the Belfast section of the initial Irish Cup draw, presented clubs with another potential expense.[35] At this stage gate moneys could only be expected to cover part of this, and subsidy from the IFA was not yet an option.

The most pressing and most financially burdensome consideration, however, was the acquisition of a pitch. Acquiring suitable premises could be an expensive and difficult task. In 1896 the building boom in Belfast was blamed for the difficulties being experienced by one leading club in finding a pitch.[36] Failure to secure a ground could have profound consequences. In 1888 the North End club in Belfast had been forced to disband due to the lack of a pitch. Similar problems compelled the Belfast YMCA club to amalgamate with Cliftonville the following year, despite being granted a £40 subvention by the parent body.[37] Even when a club had secured a suitable ground, continued expenditure on maintenance and improvement was essential. The 'mud, mackintoshes and misery' that spectators were expected to endure at one match in Belfast in 1887 were unlikely to be tolerated for long.[38] A very few clubs that were associated with existing sports clubs, such as the Ulster club of Belfast which was essentially the footballing branch of a club that held regular athletics meetings and fielded a leading cricket side, already had established pitches and facilities for spectators. Most were not so fortunate, though. Over two years in the mid-1880s the Church of Ireland Young Men's Society in Belfast spent £180 simply fencing, maintaining and improving its sports pitches. In 1897 the Distillery club spent £200 erecting a stand at its ground. A decade later the same club spent £500 providing a covered area for 5,000 spectators. By 1904 the St Columb's Court club in Londonderry had carried out improvements valued at more than £1,000 to the ground it rented from the Honourable the Irish Society, including installing drainage and erecting a stand and a pavilion.[39] Still further expenses entered the game with the adoption of professionalism in 1894, and the employment of coaches and trainers by clubs.[40]

The growing expenses incurred by Ireland's leading football clubs therefore necessitated the raising of funds beyond the levels that could realistically be secured through membership subscriptions. The donations and provisions made by patrons and sponsors undoubtedly helped some, and junior sides certainly continued to enjoy such benefits at least up to the outbreak of the Great War, but new circumstances required new methods.[41]

From the late 1880s clubs began to organise raffles, lotteries and prize draws to raise funds. Judging by the prizes on offer, some were considerable undertakings. The total prize fund for the Ulster club's raffle in 1888 was £175. The following year Cliftonville was offering a house as its first prize, while the Linfield club was subsequently to put up a carriage and pair. By the beginning of the 1890/91 season it was thought that 'a football club is nothing without a ballot'.[42] An alternative method of fund-raising was the staging of bazaars and fêtes. In the summer of 1894 three of the most prominent Belfast clubs all held bazaars, that at Glentoran being explicitly 'to reduce the debt hanging over the club'.[43] Such events were to remain common into the 1920s but, as was the case with membership subscriptions, the sums generated were unreliable and unpredictable.[44] A far more dependable method was to launch a club as a limited company, issuing shares in it in exchange for a financial investment.

Prior to the outbreak of war in 1914 at least six Irish football clubs were launched as limited liability public companies. The first was the Cliftonville club in Belfast in 1889. Belfast Celtic and Glentoran followed in 1901 and 1902 respectively. Shelbourne of Dublin followed in 1912, and Distillery of Belfast and Glenavon of Lurgan, were floated in 1913. At least in the latter cases the reasons for taking the step were made abundantly clear. The object of the Belfast Celtic flotation was to establish 'a properly fitted athletic ground in Belfast'. The Glentoran Recreation Company Limited, as the club became, was formed to provide a stadium in the east of the city. The Shelbourne Sports Company intended to erect a 25,000 capacity stadium in Dublin. All three of these clubs were much travelled by the times of their share issues, and had had trouble securing pitches: flotation seemingly offered them security.[45] Such endeavours were neither new nor unique. The flotation of football clubs in England had taken place for various reasons from the mid-1880s, while in Belfast the Ulster Cricket Club had been floated in 1898 in order to raise money for a new ground.[46]

Like much else concerned with the topic of football in Ireland, the reasons how and why individuals became shareholders in companies formed from football clubs are open to speculation. Some shareholders may have been members of the original club, awarded shares as compensation for the existing assets and goodwill of the club. This was certainly the case in Scotland, where flotation was resorted to both much earlier and more frequently.[47] While no explicit evidence exists to support this suggestion, it is clear that some individuals with existing links to clubs and the wider footballing community did become shareholders. By 1921 Olphert Stanfield held seven shares in the Distillery Football and Athletic Club Ltd of Belfast, and Robert Lyttle ten. The former had enjoyed a distinguished playing career with the Distillery club over almost two decades, and between 1887 and 1897 won thirty Irish caps. In 1898 he had been elected a vice-president of the club. Lyttle had been appointed official photographer to the IFA in 1909. Distillery's shareholders also included two men who were described as 'sports outfitters', and at least two other former football internationals.[48] Such links may in fact have been more common than is readily discernible from the surviving records.

If those actually purchasing shares saw clubs as genuine investments and looked for a financial return on their money, they were to be sorely disappointed. The prospectus for the launch of the Cliftonville Recreation Club in 1889 suggested that investors might expect annual dividends of 10 per cent. In fact no dividend appears to have ever been paid, and the club was relaunched as a private company in 1912. By 1918 the football club had re-emerged as a separate entity from the Recreation Company, and both were verging on bankruptcy.[49] In 1939 the historian of the Belfast Celtic club stated with some apparent pride that the club had never paid a dividend in the 38 years of its incorporation.[50] The other Irish football companies seem to have been no more profitable for their investors. The Shelbourne Sports Company was to be finally wound up in 1923, bankruptcy proceedings having been instituted three years before. The Distillery Football and Athletic Club Ltd was necessarily re-floated in 1921, following the acquisition of its stadium for building. By 1921 the Glentoran Recreation Company Ltd owed £700 on the mortgage on its ground that it had taken out in 1904, and that year registered a loss of nearly £350.[51] In all these cases the teams survived as footballing entities, despite the apparent failure of the companies that they had spawned.[52]

Yet if direct profits were not to be made from football clubs there was perhaps the possibility of shareholders benefiting in peripheral ways from a club's existence. Among the original subscribers to the flotation of the Glentoran club, and a member of its original board of directors was 'Mr Tom Mallon, the well-known cycle agent'. A fellow director was W.J. Anderson, who described himself as a 'cycle merchant'. Matthew Marshall and James Armour, themselves shareholders, were also involved in the same business. It was probably no coincidence that by 1906 Glentoran's ground was encircled by a cycle track reputedly regarded as 'the finest in Ireland'.[53]

A not dissimilar situation existed at the Belfast Celtic club. Although gambling on football match results in any form was frowned on by the sport's authorities, it did take place.[54] Additionally whippet racing, boxing and trotting matches, and athletic meetings were to be held at the club's Celtic Park ground, all of which provided much more important events for betting men. Given these developments it is perhaps understandable that the largest shareholder in the club by 1921 was Hugh McAlinden, a 'commission agent' or bookmaker. Six other shareholders listed themselves as being of the same occupation.[55] More indirectly, a successful football team would attract sizeable crowds on match days, and the fact that successful sporting events could provide a welcome fillip for the local economy was recognised by more than one contemporary.[56] This concept may well explain the preponderance of men from commercial and retail backgrounds among the shareholders of the Glenavon club in Lurgan, as detailed in Table 2.2.[57]

Commercial considerations were probably not uppermost in the minds of most potential shareholders, however. Certainly by the beginning of the twentieth century the example set by Cliftonville in Belfast, and by numerous clubs in Britain, must have been enough to damp the enthusiasm of even the most optimistic commercial investor. Possession of shares did not even allow individuals free access to games. The direct benefits of proprietorship were

TABLE 2.2
Shareholders in Glenavon Football and Athletic Club Ltd, 21 June 1921
(total holding 528 shares at 5s. each)

PROFESSIONAL	COMMERCIAL	SKILLED AND RETAIL	SEMI-SKILLED	UNSKILLED
Accountant	News agent (x 2)	Cabinet maker (x 2)	Clerk (x 4)	Labourer (x 2)
Bank manager (x 2)	Publican (x 9)	Mechanic (x 4)	Painter (x 3)	Waiter
Architect	Grocer (x 5)	Blacksmith	Law clerk (x 3)	Billposter
Chemist	Delph merchant	Reed manufacturer	Weaver (x 3)	Postman
Teacher	Draper (x 2)	Boat maker	Tenter	
Solicitor	House furnisher		Barber	
Reporter	Manufacturer		Linen clerk (x 2)	
Designer	Agent (x 3)			
Factory manager	Garage proprietor			
	Farmer (x 3)			
	Pawnbroker			
	Boat merchant			
62 shares	*296 shares*	*39 shares*	*103 shares*	*28 shares*
10 investors	*30 investors*	*9 investors*	*17 investors*	*5 investors*

Source: Glenavon Football and Athletic Club Ltd (Registry of Companies (N.I.), file R.261)

therefore minimal. The probable motivation of many for purchasing shares in football club companies is perhaps revealed more by a comment at the time of the flotation of the Belfast Celtic club than by any possible anticipation of pecuniary benefits. Supporters of the club were encouraged by a local newspaper to 'give practical proof of their earnestness' by purchasing shares in the new company.[58] Acquiring shares in a club allowed men to identify more closely with it, and through the club with their locality. Active involvement in the affairs of a club, through the holding of shares or more conspicuously a directorship, could lend a man a certain prominence within the local community that in itself may have had fringe benefits, but for the most part considerations of local identification, sociability and sporting enthusiasm probably accounted for the bulk of those purchasing shares in Irish football clubs.[59]

As early as 1893 it could be suggested that in Ireland 'the sport [of association football] has risen to a business'. It was a thought that was reiterated in the following years with some regularity.[60] To some extent such suggestions were true. With the advent of professionalism among players, and the employment of administrative staff, football clubs had become means of employment for some. The turnovers of Ireland's leading clubs prior to the Great War, while never on the scale of those in England or Scotland, could amount to considerable sums. The Distillery club had total receipts of £904 in 1896. Four years later this had risen to £1,600, and by 1902 income totalled £2,000. In the last season before the war the Glentoran club's income totalled almost £3,500.[61] But even at this level the description of association football as a business was really a misnomer. Few players made their livings exclusively from the game, shareholders seem never to have been granted dividends, and clubs were often run with rather more benevolence than business acumen. At lower levels, where teams still depended on the generosity of employers and local notables for facilities or subsidy, the description was even less appropriate. For the overwhelming majority of those involved in the game of association football in Ireland, it was to remain just that: a game. For all that, however, it was not to be taken any less seriously than business itself.

Whatever the motivations of individual shareholders for acquiring their shares, it is apparent from the surviving records that they represented a very broad spectrum of society. In the cases of at least the Celtic and Glentoran clubs, the initial demand for shares was brisk. Within twenty minutes of their launch, 358 of Celtic's 3,000 shares had been sold. A week after becoming available, almost a third of the 3,000 shares in Glentoran had been taken up.[62] Due to the destruction of the original company shareholders' returns in 1921, it is not possible to say exactly who purchased shares in the clubs that were floated, though the prices that were set on most suggest that they were unlikely to have been acquired by those who did not enjoy a substantial income. Cliftonville, Celtic, Glentoran and Distillery all priced their shares at £1 each.[63] Shelbourne, however, offered its shares at 10s each, with payment to be made over two months in four instalments of 2s. 6d., while Glenavon priced its

TABLE 2.3
Shareholders in Glentoran Recreation Company Ltd, 10 Oct. 1921
(total holding 1,087 shares at £1 each)

PROFESSIONAL	COMMERCIAL AND RETAIL	SKILLED	SEMI-SKILLED	UNSKILLED
Manager (x 6)	Publican (x 16)	Artisan (x 91)	Linen lapper	Labourer
Doctor	Merchant (x 4)	Tailor (x 4)	Painter	Machine minder
Solicitor	Agent (x 4)	Engineer (x 2)	Clerk (x 11)	
Photographer	Cycle agent (x 3)	Printer (x 2)		
School teacher	Commission agent (x 2)	Carpenter		
Auditor	Grocer (x 3)	Joiner		
Prime minister	Shopkeeper (x 2)	Cabinet maker		
Secretary	Produce broker (x 2)	Blacksmith		
	Butcher (x 2)	Smith		
	Builder (x 2)	Plater		
	Draper			
	Traveller (x 5)			
	Fishmonger			
	Pawnbroker			
	Jeweller			
	Newsagent			
	Brewer			
	Spirit merchant			
	Linen manufacturer			
	Aerated-water manufacturer			
	Car owner			
13 investors	55 investors	105 investors	13 investors	2 investors
520 shares	322 shares	190 shares	53 shares	2 shares

Source: Glentoran Recreation Company Ltd (Registry of Companies (N.I.), file R.263).

shares at only 5s. each.[64] More concrete evidence of the nature of shareholders is provided by the earliest available shareholders lists, which date from the early 1920s. In fact, there is some circumstantial evidence to suggest that these lists probably varied little from those who originally purchased shares at the time of flotation. By 1921 the Glentoran company had issued 1,087 shares: the same number as had been sold in 1912, and only marginally more than had been taken up a few weeks after the initial issue. As later purchasers would more likely have bought shares from the company

TABLE 2.4
Shareholders in Belfast Celtic Football and Athletic Club Ltd, 21 July 1921 (total holding 1,885 shares at £1 each)

PROFESSIONAL	COMMERCIAL AND RETAIL	SKILLED	SEMI-SKILLED	UNSKILLED
Clergyman (x 20)	Spirit merchant (x 74)	Artisan (x 4)	Painter (x 3)	Labourer (x 3)
Teacher (x 4)	Traveller (x 5)	French polisher (x 2)	Postal official (x 4)	Millworker (x 3)
Doctor (x 2)	Commission agent (x 7)	Tailor (x 2)	Pavior (x 2)	Constable
Solicitor (x 2)	Fish merchant (x 4)	Compositor (x 2)	Hairdresser	Storekeeper
Secretary (x 2)	Manufacturer (x 3)	Mechanic (x 2)	Law clerk	Carrier
Artist	Shopkeeper (x 2)	Carpenter (x 2)	Clerk	Cashier
Member of parliament	Fruiterer (x 2)	Cabinet maker		
Magistrate	Draper (x 2)	Bricklayer		
Manager	Waste merchant (x 2)	Blacksmith		
Architect	Wine merchant (x 2)	Baker		
Journalist	Paper merchant			
Accountant	Linen merchant			
	Grocer			
	Dealer			
	Brewer			
	Brewer's agent			
	Tobacconist			
	Agent			
	Contractor			
	Insurance agent			
	Farmer (x 2)			
37 investors	*115 investors*	*18 investors*	*12 investors*	*10 investors*
376 shares	*1,258 shares*	*59 shares*	*58 shares*	*29 shares*

Note: No occupation was given for 13 shareholders, of whom four were women, and the occupation of one further shareholder was illegible. The 85 shares owned by these individuals, and the 20 held in trust for the St Paul's Catholic Social Club, have been excluded from the totals. Source: Belfast Celtic Football and Athletic Club Ltd (Registry of Companies (N.I.), file R.77).

than existing investors, it seems likely these lists show a great deal of continuity with the missing initial issue lists.[65] With this in mind, Tables 2.3 and 2.4 show the occupational background of shareholders in the Glentoran and Belfast Celtic companies.[66]

In truth the shareholding profiles of these three clubs have little in common. In the case of Celtic and Glentoran, small groups of men did hold large blocks of shares. With regard to the former, a fish merchant, a 'commission agent', a brewer's agent and the club's secretary together owned 662 shares, or 35 per cent of the company. At Glentoran 402 shares, or 36 per cent of the club, were owned by two men described as a secretary and a schoolteacher. In Lurgan, however, no individual held more than 25 shares in the Glenavon club, and the leading ten shareholders owned only 210 shares, or 39 per cent of the club, between them. The smallest holding in Glenavon was two shares, with just nine individuals, or 12 per cent of shareholders, holding this number. At Celtic 22 men held only one share, and 37 just two. Together they totalled 28 per cent of the shareholders. At Glentoran 65 men held just one share, and another 52 two shares. They totalled almost 57 per cent of the number of shareholders. However, with respect to the nature of the shareholders themselves, there was perhaps a greater continuity.

In all three cases, unsurprisingly, unskilled men were a very small proportion of shareholders. Only five men at Glenavon were unskilled manual workers; ten may have been in similar occupations at Celtic and just two at Glentoran. In no case did men in this group own more than 6 per cent of a club's shares. Correspondingly, all the clubs saw the ownership of their shares dominated by members of the professions and the commercial and retail groups. In the case of Glenavon these held 358 shares, or 67 per cent of the club. At Glentoran these groups owned 872 shares, or 80 per cent of shares in the club. At Celtic they owned 1,634 shares, which formed 86 per cent of the total. The implication of these figures seems to be that the lowest social groups were least involved in share ownership, while members of the middle classes held the bulk of shares. Given the enormous disparity in the relative disposable incomes of the two groups, this is hardly surprising.

A further similarity among the various shareholders is evident from the addresses given in the registers. The vast majority of those listed were local residents. All but four of Glenavon's 71 shareholders lived in the town of Lurgan; 183 of Celtic's 207 investors were resident in Belfast, with a further 18 elsewhere in the adjacent counties of Antrim and Down. Of Glentoran's 188 shareholders all but seven gave addresses in Belfast.[67] Even the flotation of clubs as public companies did not separate them from their local origins.

Judging by the evidence, shareholding in leading football clubs in Ireland was dominated by men from the upper and middling reaches of local society. However, at least with regard to the two Belfast-based clubs, further consideration of both the occupations and places of residence of shareholders gives fundamental insights into the position of clubs within local society, and their possible relationship to the communities in which they existed.

Of the 188 shareholders in the Glentoran Recreation Company in 1921, the commonest occupational description given was 'artizan'. Almost half of the company's shareholders were so described. Though not absolutely certain, it seems likely these were men who worked in the city's shipyards and related industries. This is perhaps confirmed by the fact that 130 of all those listed were resident in the adjacent Victoria and Pottinger wards of the city, bounded by the shipyards to the north and the Castlereagh Road to the south. Both these facts, a predominance of skilled shipyard workers and of residents in the north-eastern corner of the city, imply that the majority of the club's shareholders were from the Protestant community.[68]

The shareholders in the Belfast Celtic club were spread more widely across the city, but their occupations marked them out as clearly representative of the Catholic and Nationalist community. The second largest occupational description consisted of 20 Catholic priests. The largest was the 74 'spirit merchants' who represented more than a third of the club's shareholders. Not only was the licensed trade 'by far the most heavily Catholic of all occupations' in Belfast, but publicans themselves were the 'key element in the development of lay-controlled Nationalist politics in succession to a clerically controlled Catholic politics'. Prior to partition, Nationalism in Belfast was reputedly 'relying heavily on the co-operation of priests and publicans'.[69] So too, to a large extent, was the Belfast Celtic Football and Athletic Club.

The precise number of football clubs that existed in Ireland at any given time prior to the outbreak of war in 1914 is unknowable.

A growing formality in the game.

Top: The Hertford Football Club *c.* 1883. Note the varied shirts, improvised shin-pads, and fetching headgear. *Bottom*: Roseville FC of Lisburn in 1886. The players' shirts and poses are more uniform even if their shorts are not.

Top: Linfield AFC in 1907. This professional team were
Irish League Champions and County Antrim Shield winners in this year.

However, the numbers provided by the records of the sport's various governing bodies must be seen as providing only a minimum estimate. These institutions had their origins in various pre-existing entities, notably the workplace, the urban neighbourhood, and established social organisations including churches and church-sponsored movements. Eventually some clubs developed to become social institutions themselves, capable of being both patrons and clients of the communities in which they were situated.

Inevitably, the origins of clubs and their assimilation into the local community had wider consequences for the clubs themselves. The often voluntary segregation that existed in employment and housing in some parts of Ulster was reflected in the nature of the football clubs there. The secular division of society was mirrored in confessional social institutions, among which were football clubs. The imposition of a religious template onto the political terrain in turn guaranteed a transference of political identity onto some clubs.

By 1899 the Belfast Celtic and Linfield clubs were already 'supposed to represent opposite principles in politics'. In Belfast, ascertaining which football club a man supported was reckoned among the surest means of discovering his religion.[70] Even the conversion of clubs into limited liability companies did little to alter the situation, but rather reinforced the divisions that existed within the game and the wider society. By 1921 the epitome of the situation was perhaps available among the records of shareholders in the Belfast Celtic and Glentoran clubs. The holder of 50 shares in the latter club, seen as representative of Protestant east Belfast, was Sir James Craig, the leader of the Ulster Unionists and Prime Minister of the newly founded state of Northern Ireland. Among the shareholders of the Catholic and Nationalist Belfast Celtic Football and Athletic Club was Joe Devlin, the *de facto* leader of the remnants of the Nationalist Irish Parliamentary Party and the Member of Parliament for West Belfast.

3

Players

> Now let me sing of the prowess of PADDY the speedy left-winger,
> PADDY the pet of the crowd, PADDY the pride of his pals.
> No one more skilful than he ever scudded along any touch-line,
> Swift as a giddy gazelle, swift as a bolt from the blue;
> Swift as the ready retort of a cabby that's baulked by a 'bus-man;
> Swift as the flash of my brain weaving you verses like these.
>
> *Punch*, 1 April 1908

A player, but not necessarily a gentleman. William McCracken, the consummate professional.

Ireland's Saturday Night

BOTH THE GAME OF FOOTBALL and the clubs that were formed to compete in football competitions depended for their very existence upon the players of the game. Who exactly these individuals were is not easy to discern, however. Precise biographical details of players are rarely available. At least for the early years of the game in Ireland, though, some evidence can be seen as suggestive of the type of individuals who came to play the game.

With regard to religion, association football appears to have drawn a mixed following. The founding of the Schools Cup competition in 1883 saw five teams enter. Four were essentially Protestant institutions, while the fifth was St Malachy's College, the Belfast Catholic diocesan school. In 1886 St Malachy's went on to win the trophy.[1] We have already noted the importance of Catholic educational establishments to the game's development in Dublin.[2] In Londonderry the game was strongly supported and actively promoted by the Catholic clergy, not least as a way of countering what they saw as the subversive political influence of the GAA.[3] Similarly the members of identifiably Protestant organisations, such as the YMCA and the Catch-My-Pals, founded teams that must have been composed primarily, if not exclusively, of Protestants.

But if the sport appealed to men of all religious denominations, at least in Ulster the broader nature of society ensured that the clubs and teams they formed were unlikely to be confessionally mixed. As suggested above, the informal segregation that existed in housing and employment in Belfast meant that clubs based around neighbourhood or workplace affiliations were consequently likely to be composed solely of players of one religious affiliation. The phenomenon of a confessionally based football culture also seems to have taken root in Ulster's other urban centres. One local newspaper editorial noted in 1904 that 'exclusively Catholic' clubs existed across the north of Ireland, and could generally be identified by their assumption of the title 'Celtic'.[4]

With respect to the individuals themselves, association football was originally promoted and played by men with existing sporting connections. For example, Robert Kennedy, who was present at the first IFA meeting in 1880 and was a player with the Cliftonville side, was already the secretary of the Cliftonville Cricket Club and the

Enfield rugby club. Additionally he would later become a noted official of the Irish Amateur Athletic Association.[5] Of the twelve men who played for the Irish national team in 1882, one was noted as 'an old rugby player', while another was 'better known as a lacrosse player'.[6] These observations, along with the fact that players in formal clubs were required to pay membership fees, suggest that most of these early players were drawn from the groups in society who had both the time and money to spare to indulge in such luxuries as sport. Typically these would have been members of the rural gentry and landed classes, and the new urban middle classes. Yet at the same time, almost from the introduction of the game to Ireland there seems to have been a number of rather less socially exalted players. The Moyola Park team which won the first Irish Cup competition in 1881 included not only Arthur Gaussen, a public schoolboy later destined to serve as the Sheriff of Co. Londonderry, but also the brothers William and Thomas Hueston, shoemakers, and Francis McLarnon, a grocer's assistant. As noted above, a number of early clubs were formed by the employees of major industrial concerns in the Belfast area. At the time of his death in 1910, Ireland's first ever international centre-forward was employed as a supervisor in the spindle-turning room of a Belfast foundry. As early as 1884 one Irish periodical could refer to rugby, compared to association, as the 'more noble and manlier game'.[7] In later years it seems to be the case that members of the social elites for the most part chose to abandon participation in association football. In October 1907 the pupils of Clongowes Wood College, whose predecessors had done so much to popularise the game in the Dublin area, voted to drop the association code in favour of rugby. In 1909, following a debate on the motion 'Have games usurped too prominent a place in College life at the present day?', a similar move was made at nearby Castleknock.[8] Dublin's public schools were coming into line with those in Belfast, where the association code was allegedly seen as 'beneath contempt'.[9] In neither city had students at the two main universities ever shown much lasting enthusiasm for the game. In Dublin the Trinity College club may have been one of the first to be formed, but in the following years its existence was intermittent. At the Queen's University in Belfast, although early students could 'amuse themselves kicking a leather ball in a game which was but the germ of the highly developed scientific game of football', their heirs showed a very limited interest in the association game.[10] On a personal level too, the revulsion that some of the upper classes felt towards association football was clearly evident. The son of a Dublin legal official, whose childhood fantasies centred around scoring the winning try for the Irish rugby XV against England, would later recall the 'surpassing humiliation' of having his photograph taken at his mother's insistence 'holding a soccer football'.[11] This apparent retreat of the elites was not total however, and a number of clubs maintained at least the image of being composed of gentlemen. In Dublin, members of the Freebooters and Bohemians clubs were still regarded as approximating to 'gentlemen'. In Belfast it was members of the Cliftonville club that were perceived as the 'snobs' of the game.[12] However, by the turn of the century, perhaps with some justification, the press in both Dublin and Belfast could refer to association football as the game of 'the masses and not the classes', while an English commentator could refer to the game in Ireland as primarily the concern of 'the artisan sportsmen'.[13]

This working-class involvement in Irish sport was something of a novelty. The rules of the Irish Champion Athletic Club, which was still the premier body in Irish athletics at this time, specifically excluded any man who was 'a mechanic, artisan or labourer' from its competitions, and participation in many other sports demanded access to facilities or equipment which were beyond the reach of working men.[14] Given this popular involvement in football it was perhaps inevitable that the issue of professionalism would eventually arise. The IFA had already agreed to pay the expenses of the Irish side that travelled to Wales in 1882, while in the very first Irish Cup competition it was thought necessary to pay a player who suffered a broken leg the sum of £1 compensation. These actions officially recognised both the need of some players to be subsidised to travel, and the fact that others needed to be compensated for the working hours they lost through their participation in the game.[15] Such factors have been seen as influential, if not actually decisive, in the introduction of professionalism into the English game.[16]

Having said that, professionalism was not eventually legalised in Irish football until the annual general meeting of the IFA in 1894. In the context of the game in the United Kingdom this was a comparatively late development. Professionalism had been allowed in England since 1885, though in Scotland the making of payments to players had only become an officially accepted practice in the year previous to its legalisation in Ireland.[17] Moreover, the establishment of professionalism in Irish football was only achieved after something of a struggle. In fact, at their second annual general meeting in May 1883 the IFA had explicitly banned any individual who had taken a professional payment anywhere in the United Kingdom for any form of athletic or sporting activity from playing in the Irish Cup competition. The Wellington Park club successfully invoked this rule the following year, when they objected to their opponents in the Cup, Queen's Island, playing a man who had previously played football as a professional in England.[18]

This early opposition to professionalism in any form was despite the fact that there was already an established, if small, community of other professional sportsmen in the country. The Irish census of 1841 had returned 161 men who made their livings primarily as 'sportsmen'. Forty years later a similar number were employed in 'billiards, cricket and other games'.[19] In the field of horse racing 'a small group of successful professional jockeys' had emerged in Ireland by the second decade of the nineteenth century, while simultaneously prizefighters were regularly competing for purses in excess of £100.[20] In July 1867 a rackets match billed as the world championship had taken place in Belfast for a total prize of £1,000. Even in the country's rural hinterland paid sportsmen, by way of the cricket professional, were established figures.[21] Given this situation, perhaps as surprising as its comparatively late introduction was the nature of the arguments that surrounded professionalism in Irish football. In England the most influential arguments against professionalism had been based on 'the social antipathy of men who considered professional sport ethically unacceptable'.[22] Put simply, the public schoolboys and leisured gentlemen who had codified, fostered and disseminated the game in England baulked at the thought that men should actually be paid for playing, rather than participating in the sport simply for the joys of manly competition. Such attitudes were bolstered by class antagonisms, as the elite recoiled from the incursions that working men were making into the world of formalised leisure.[23] In Ireland, however, perhaps as a result of the plebeian nature of many of those already involved in the sport, such arguments were almost totally absent.[24]

The first annual general meeting of the IFA to discuss the subject of professionalism openly had been held in May 1890. Though it had been thought it was a 'very open question whether it will pass or not', the motion to legalise professionalism was soundly defeated. This was probably not least because the Co. Antrim FA, the largest and most influential regional body affiliated to the IFA, withdrew its earlier support for the measure.[25] In May 1891 another motion to permit payments to be made to players was 'argued at some length', but eventually dismissed.[26] In fact the Association chose rather to crack down on the existing situation in Ireland, where a covert system of payments and 'veiled professionalism' was widely recognised as being in existence. Although genuine expenses and payments for lost time could still be made, players could no longer be paid for grounds work, or even be employed in any capacity by the owner of a club's pitch.[27] This was probably a reaction to a number of incidents that had occurred in the intervening months, and which had resulted in a greater general awareness of the true situation with regards to the illicit paying of players. In October 1890 the Belfast press reported the case of Lizzie McKnight, who was the subject of a prosecution at the city police court for the theft of a £20 note. Her alleged victim was one Robert Hill, a recently discharged member of the Gordon Highlanders. In the course of her defence McKnight's counsel attempted to prove that Hill had never in fact possessed the banknote his client was accused of taking. To counter this Robert Gibson, the chairman of the Linfield club, was called to back up Hill's story. It then became apparent that Hill, who had that year won an Irish Cup medal when the Gordon Highlanders team beat Cliftonville in the final of the competition, had been given £40 by Gibson to buy himself out of the army and to provide for his subsistence until Gibson found him a job. Robert Milne, a former comrade of Hill's, was allegedly in a similar situation, and both were being paid out of the Linfield club's funds. Although Hill was later accused by the IFA of professionalism, a lack of evidence saw the case dismissed.[28]

Two months earlier a hoax advertisement had appeared in the *Belfast Evening Telegraph*, offering work to '5 whitewashers, 2 tar spreaders and 4 handymen' at a football ground in the city. While no experience was deemed necessary, potential applicants were required to 'be expert players' and to give details of their 'age, weight, last club and wages expected'.[29] In December 1890 the Linfield club had taken on the elite English gentleman amateurs of the Corinthian Football Club for the first time at their ground in Belfast. With perhaps less grace than might have been expected from such a genteel organisation, the Corinthians first blamed their defeat on the roughness of the sea passage to Belfast, and then refused to dine with the Linfield team, whom they regarded as professionals.[30] Finally, in February 1891, the Clarence side of Belfast threatened to bring a charge of professionalism against the Ulster team that had defeated them in an Irish Cup tie.[31] Although the allegation was eventually dropped, it further pushed the issue of professionalism in Ireland into the spotlight.

The two months prior to the 1892 general meeting of the IFA saw a debate carried on in the pages of the *Ulster Football and Cycling News*, then Belfast's only sporting newspaper, as to the advantages and drawbacks of professionalism in football. One correspondent suggested that as there was 'scarcely an amateur in the city' playing for a senior club, the legalising of professionalism was a virtual necessity. Others agreed, and further suggested that professionalism would inevitably lead both to an improvement in the standard of the game being played in Ireland and to its further spread. Furthermore, the old argument that professionalism, with its system of win bonuses, would lead to rough play was seen as largely redundant.[32] Only the suggestion that professionalism would see an influx of second-rate players from England and Scotland seeking easy money was seen as a possible objection.[33]

In the event, at the IFA AGM of that year the motion to allow professionalism in the Irish game prompted still further debate. The arguments became centred on the effects that it would have on the game, and the clubs that went to make up the Association. The smaller, rural clubs, it was reported, were opposed to the paying of players on the grounds that the best of them would then inevitably be drawn to the larger, more affluent urban clubs. This, they felt, would lead to a general decline in the standards of the game, and in the interest it generated. Eventually a two-to-one majority of the clubs voted in favour of the *status quo*.[34]

Twelve months later, perhaps cowed by their previous failures, the proponents of professionalism were silent at the AGM, and 'as a consequence everything passed off in peace and quietness'.[35] Yet further developments had taken place that were ultimately to be crucial in the acceptance of professionalism in Ireland. By November 1893 it was reported that the paying of footballers was now a necessity in Ireland, to prevent the best domestic players from migrating to professional clubs in England, or joining the ranks of the newly legalised professionals in Scotland. As early as 1889 a Glentoran player had been approached in Belfast by a Scottish club, and the following year an agent for an English club was rumoured to be recruiting players in the city.[36]

Finally, in May 1894, by a majority of 64 votes to 30, the delegates to the IFA voted to legalise professionalism. The arguments that prevailed on this occasion were many and varied. In contrast to their earlier position, the larger clubs, including Linfield and Distillery of Belfast, opposed the measure, apparently on the grounds that even they would be unable to meet the financial demands that were likely to be made of them. Yet those who had previously had little sympathy with the concept of professionalism now suggested that the move had been made necessary by the need to prevent the best Irish players being lured away to play in England and Scotland. At the same time, while it was inevitable that the sport would be 'degraded through the anxiety of clubs to accumulate money', the demands of supporters for improved facilities and a higher standard of play necessitated the introduction of payments.[37] Finally, the legalisation of professionalism would do away with the existing system of 'veiled professionalism' and covert payments to players that had existed for at least half a decade, and to which many true amateurs strongly objected. With an air of understatement, one Dublin observer had reckoned that in Belfast at least 'some of the proceedings are not quite in accordance with the tenets of amateur football'. Another had already suggested that the 'associationists' in Ireland formed 'a body it would be as difficult to convict of professionalism as it would be for them to prove they are amateurs'.[38] The relative importance of this last factor might be judged by the facts that the eventually successful motion in 1894 was proposed by a member of the staunchly amateur Cliftonville club, and effectively passed on the votes of the Leinster FA delegates for whom professionalism was something of an anathema.[39]

Thus from its very introduction professionalism seems to have been regarded by some simply as a necessary evil. In fact the legalisation of direct payments by the IFA was not the end of the story. The various regional associations that were affiliated to the IFA retained a great deal of autonomy, including setting the rules for the local cup and league competitions that they had established. This situation meant that these subsidiary organisations had in turn to ratify the decision of the central body. In the case of the North West Football Association, which controlled football in the Londonderry area, professionalism was not sanctioned until 1902, despite earlier suggestions that professionalism was the essential 'means to keep the players at home' and prevent the elite migrating to Scotland or Belfast. Despite the action of the Leinster FA in supporting the professionalism motion in 1894, the total acceptance of professionalism in their own jurisdiction was not achieved until May 1905, following a protracted debate that echoed many of the issues of a decade earlier. Professionalism had become necessary in Dublin to advance the popularity and quality of the game, to ensure the provision of a properly fitted-out stadium, and to rid the game of its existing system of covert payments to players.[40]

Despite the prolonged struggle for its establishment, official professionalism was not instantly seized upon by either the players or the clubs. One observer suggested that this was largely due to the players, most of whom wished to carry on receiving unofficial payments, and who were reluctant to tie themselves to a particular club by signing a contract.[41] By the opening week of the 1894/5 season, the first in which professionalism was recognised by the IFA, there were a mere sixteen registered professionals in Ireland. The number had risen to more than forty within a month, but this was still a tiny number compared with those registered in England and Scotland. It was to be more than a year before a team outside Belfast actually signed a professional player.[42]

The effects of professionalism on the game in the short term are uncertain. Within a year the suggestion was being made that the prestige of the Charity Cup competition, whose proceeds were donated to Belfast charities, had been undermined by the appearance of professionals in the final. Rumours also circulated that the Linfield club, one of the first to engage professionals, was being evicted from its pitch by a landlord who was reluctant to make a profit from professional sport.[43]

At the same time, there were also some positive developments within the game. The number of clubs affiliated to the IFA increased over the following decade, as did the areas in which the game was played.[44] In 1903 the Irish national team achieved its first major success, when victories over Wales and Scotland gave it a share in the Home International championship for the first time. Popular interest in the domestic game also increased. An estimated crowd of 4,000 had attended the Irish Cup final in 1889. At the same match in 1905 a crowd of 13,000 paid almost £400 to see Distillery of Belfast beat the Dublin side Shelbourne by three goals. Four years after the introduction of professionalism it was reckoned that 'association football has obtained such a fascinating hold upon the minds of the people in Ireland that almost anything concerning the game is always interesting'.[45] Exactly how much of a part professionalism in Ireland played in these advances is debatable, but changes were occurring, and professional footballers were now at the heart of the Irish game.

The precise extent of professionalism in the game, the nature of those individuals who were registered as professionals, and the conditions under which they operated are not easy to ascertain. Certainly during the early years of professionalism it seems that most of the men being paid to play were in fact semi-professionals who also held down a full-time job. For example, in March 1899

John Lewis, the professional Glentoran and Irish international goalkeeper, petitioned the IFA for the payment of 10s. to compensate him for the time he had lost in being off work travelling to the international match in Wales. Three years earlier the editor of the *Ulster Football and Cycling News* had refuted the suggestion that Irish professionals enjoyed the same conditions as their Scottish counterparts. Rather Irish professionals still had to 'work from morning to night, from Monday to Friday, and noon on a Saturday', while the wages they received 'would hardly pay a car home, or at the heaviest put a decent pair of boots on their feet'.[46] In some cases, as with Robert Hill in 1890, players were apparently still being offered jobs by employers who had an interest in the game, and who paid them additional money for playing football.[47] In other cases men were registered as professionals simply to tie them to a single club, and never received any payment. A player named Harry Murphy was signed under such circumstances by the Distillery club in 1898. In 1901 the same man moved to the reformed Ulster club under similar conditions.[48]

However, the few later details that are available of the wages being paid to some players suggest that full-time professionals were eventually to be found. By 1902 one newspaper already reckoned it was no longer possible to tell professional footballers from their amateur colleagues by their dress, and that professional football in Ireland was now a 'profitable occupation'.[49] The previous year A.J. Hill, an English professional signed by the Linfield club, was receiving £2 a week in season, and half that amount out of season. During the 1901/2 season Belfast Celtic, with 21 registered professionals, apparently had a total weekly wages bill of less than £30. Such a budget seems to have been fairly typical.[50] However, by May 1905 Donald Sloan, the goalkeeper of the Distillery club, who had been offered a contract with several English clubs, was induced to stay in Belfast by being paid £3 a week for 52 weeks of the year. Such terms were seen as unusually generous, though, and almost a decade later £2 5s. was reckoned to be the going rate in Ireland for 'a class halfback'.[51] At the Linfield club some first team members were thought to be receiving £4 a week by 1914, with the rest of the squad 'within measurable distance', and an offer of £6 a week had been made to one player at Belfast Celtic the previous year. Allegedly more usual, though, were wages that 'hardly ever' rose above £2 a week, with even these only being paid during the eight months of the actual season; summer payments were secured for the bulk of players only at the end of the 1913/14 season.[52]

A player's basic wages were not the only form of football-related income available, however. A system of win bonuses appears to have been in place from an early date, though the value of these is uncertain. Some players also received signing-on fees from clubs. In 1911 a player received the sum of £4 for signing for the Belfast Celtic club.[53] For a very few players, representative appearances meant additional payments. Although in 1895 the IFA decided that even professional players appearing for the Irish national side should receive only 'an international cap and the honour', by 1903 they were to receive 10s. 6d. for their trouble. The following year the sum rose to £2 2s., before being fixed at £4 in 1908.[54] The Irish League was paying players in its representative games £2 a game in 1910, though this was cut to £1 1s. in 1913.[55] For even fewer players long and honourable service to a club could mean they would be awarded a benefit game, from which they would receive the proceeds of the gate. Again, precise sums are uncertain, but while in 1899 a sum of over £10 was seen as remarkable, a decade later £145 was collected for a retiring professional in Belfast, and John Darling, a long-serving Linfield player, received almost £300.[56]

Even from these admittedly eclectic figures it is clear that payments to professionals varied greatly both from club to club, and from player to player. Two trends are clear, though. In the first place, payments rose markedly over time. Secondly, despite these increases, payments in Ireland never managed to keep pace with those being made to players in England and Scotland. In November 1896 it was suggested that a weekly wage of £3 was necessary to keep a player in Ireland. Such a sum was on a par with what the best players in the English Football League could expect, and comparable with payments being made to Glasgow Celtic players in Scotland.[57] Yet a decade later, as in the case of Donald Sloan, such terms were still seen as remarkable in Ireland. Even with regard to international appearances, prior to 1908 English players received markedly higher payments than their Irish counterparts.[58] As a direct result of this situation, the best of Ireland's footballing talent continued to haemorrhage away to England and Scotland. By the spring of 1902 it was reckoned that more than twenty Irish professionals had been tempted across the Irish Sea by lucrative offers of employment. Two years later the situation was seen as so acute that the IFA raised the matter of the poaching of Irish players by English clubs at the International Board meeting. Meanwhile a member of the Irish League committee called for a maximum wage to be introduced in Ireland, as the efforts of Irish clubs to match the wages paid in Scotland and England was driving them into bankruptcy. In the event neither suggestion was acted on, and the development of the Irish game continued to be allegedly 'crippled by the advent of wealthy English clubs bent on securing Irish players at any price'.[59]

Even when compared to their professional sporting compatriots in Ireland, Irish footballers were far from generously paid. Irish jockeys were collecting a minimum of £2 for a single ride in 1879; and while the professional at Lansdowne Tennis Club received only £1 10s. a week in 1895, there were substantial tips to supplement this. The same was true of billiard markers in the gentlemen's clubs of Ireland, who acted as coaches to the members as well as performing in the country's regular tournaments.[60]

However, at least in one comparative context professional footballers in Ireland were relatively handsomely paid. From the turn of the century, some were receiving payments considerably greater than those given to members of the country's unskilled labour force, and which often matched or even exceeded the wages paid to skilled men. Donald Sloan's £3 a week in 1905 was more than five times the average wage of an agricultural labourer in Ulster, three times that of a Belfast bricklayer's labourer, and more than half as much again as that of a riveter in the city's shipyards. Even A.J. Hill's average weekly earnings of £1 15s. in 1902 were equivalent to those of a Belfast police sergeant, and only marginally less than those of a qualified shipwright. The £4 a week that it was rumoured the Linfield stars were receiving in 1914 was four times the wage of a plasterer's labourer, and around twice the sum a compositor might expect to be paid. For the elite at least, whose wages were likely to be enhanced with win bonuses and international appearance money, and who might eventually expect some form of gratuity from a benefit game, football provided a prosperous living. For others, whom one contemporary reckoned were paid anything between 5s. and £1 a game, football probably provided a very welcome subsidy to more regular wages from some other form of employment.[61]

Exact details of what professional players in Ireland were required to do for their wages, besides perform on the pitch on match days, are no more easily discovered than rates of remuneration. In the immediate aftermath of the game's professionalisation, one journalist suggested that 'the best training a footballer can follow is to abstain from alcoholic beverages, eat plain wholesome food, … take plenty of walking exercise and a cold sponge bath'. Above all they were recommended to 'avoid fancy training', though in fact few local players were reckoned to take part in any training at all beyond a couple of evenings each week. In later years one former opponent of professionalism would suggest that the paying of players was justified primarily by the fact that it ensured that 'training is more rigidly adhered to'.[62] Four years after those initial suggestions regarding diet, exercise and cleanliness were made, professional players were required to 'walk and run daily several miles', while smoking and 'drinks of an intoxicating nature' were strictly prohibited prior to important games.

By 1902 it was recognised in Ireland that 'coaching and training are two very different things'. While the former was the responsibility of a team coach, the latter was largely for the players themselves to organise. Despite the accusation that club committees looked 'upon the professional as a common slave, and would whip the best out of him', the suggestions that 'a brisk walk of say ten miles twice a week varied by an occasional hundred yards dash will keep any footballer in condition', and that singing practice was a potentially crucial element in fitness programmes, suggest that few training programmes were truly onerous. There were other methods of maintaining an appropriate level of fitness, however, and the necessity of players engaging in practice on the field meant that for some at least football consumed, in one way or another, most of their week. In 1913 three Scottish coaches, one of whom had experience of football in Ireland, outlined their training regimes. The most comprehensive consisted of a four-day programme that included not only deep breathing exercises but also the practising of shooting and heading the ball. There was also an exhortation for players to 'read good literature', and a continuing firm belief in 'cold sponging of the spine'.[63]

The actual duties performed by even the most elite players in Ireland do not therefore appear to have been overwhelming. Similarly, while the contractual obligations entered into between clubs and players must remain something of an area of conjecture, these too seem not to have laid too great a burden on players. In fact it was not until March 1901 that, following a number of disputes between clubs and their players, the IFA insisted that all professionals were to have written contracts. By this time the 'retain and transfer system' had been in operation in England for more than a decade. This system allowed clubs, at the end of each season, to compulsorily retain the services of those players they required for the following season, while those that they did not wish to retain were to be granted transfers to other clubs only on the receipt of a transfer fee from the new club. Players for whom no club was prepared to pay a fee had no option but to 'retire' from professional football, and even players retained by their clubs had only the right to a minimal retaining wage during the close season.[64] In Ireland, meanwhile, players were generally signed only for a single season, with contracts finishing on the 31 May following their signing. This meant of course that players had no security of tenure, but at the same time they enjoyed a mobility that was denied to their English counterparts. This latter aspect of the situation was welcomed by some players at least, as it always offered the chance that they might be recruited by an English or Scottish club, which would have to pay no transfer fee for their services.[65] This anomaly was largely removed, after some long negotiations, in 1914. At that year's annual general meeting of the Irish League the English-style retained system was introduced in Ireland, and the League bodies of both Ireland and England agreed to recognise the validity of players' contracts in each other's jurisdictions.[66]

Overall, it seems that professional footballers in Ireland were perhaps in an enviable position during the years between the turn of the century and the outbreak of the Great War. Compared to many other Irish workers they were well paid, and compared to their counterparts in England they enjoyed comparative freedom of movement. Training commitments were often minimal, and though the number of individuals who warranted such treatment was admittedly tiny, some professionals at least were held in high popular regard. The enormous crowds that professional games drew were testimony not only to the popularity of the game but also to that of individual players. Crowds were known to chant the names of individual players.[67]

In 1900 *Ireland's Saturday Night,* Belfast's leading sports newspaper, organised a poll to discover the most popular player in Irish football. The response flooded the paper's office, and nearly 40,000 votes were cast. The winner was Samuel Torrens, the long-serving professional captain of Linfield.[68] In Dublin in 1906, in its first season as a professional side, Shelbourne succeeded in winning the Irish Cup. It was the first Dublin team to do so, and in celebration bonfires were lit in the Sandymount and Ringsend districts of the city. A huge crowd had already met the team at Amiens Street railway station on their return from the final in Belfast and paraded the trophy and the players through the city. A similar welcome, by a crowd of 6,000 accompanied by a band, occurred the following year when the team again reached the Irish Cup final.[69]

At the same time, however, there were many for whom professional footballers were villains rather than heroes. Perhaps the primary source of scorn was the Gaelic Athletic Association and its members. As noted above, the opposition of these cultural Nationalists to 'foreign sports' culminated in 1904/5 in a ban on the organisation's members taking part in association football matches, or any other non-Gaelic games.[70] Professionalism too provided a focus for hostility. In the introduction to his coaching manual of 1914, the Gaelic football star Dick Fitzgerald noted with satisfaction that his sport was not 'the possession of the professional player', as association was. In fact he went so far as to suggest that the whole nature of association football was anti-heroic. In that game, he suggested, 'combination alone is the only thing commended'. The result was that 'there is no hero – no great individual standing out from the whole field'.[71] The Irish Rugby Football Union, the governing body of Irish rugby, was hardly more sympathetic to professional footballers. Perceiving itself as one of the great bastions of sporting amateurism, it ruled in 1913 that no professional association player was permitted to play rugby in Ireland at any level, even if he had been reinstated as an amateur by the IFA.[72]

More oblique criticism of professionalism had occurred in the IFA's offices in 1898. In November of that year David Drennan, who had recently signed professional forms with the Distillery side, asked to withdraw his registration on the grounds that 'his parents objected to his signing a professional form and also that the fact of him playing as a professional would injure his business prospects'.[73] The attitude of the press was also, in many cases, consistently censorious towards both professionals as individuals and the entire concept of professionalism. In 1901, in an article on Ralph Leonard, an English professional playing in Belfast, *Ireland's Saturday Night* noted that the player was a teetotaller, 'which is more than can be said for most football professionals'. Such a comment seems to echo attitudes in England, where it was thought by some that a professional was likely to be 'a person beneath contempt – a vagabond, who spends the whole of his time in a public house except for an hour and a half when he is called upon to earn his wages'.[74] The following year it was suggested in one Irish newspaper that 'the players of today are but degenerate descendants of the heroes of old'. In another article a lament was made for the 'race of footballers who, practically speaking, ceased to exist with the advent of professionalism'. Even a generally sympathetic observer thought that professionals, though they did 'their utmost for their employers', when defeated 'could not be expected to feel it so acutely as those who play solely for the love of the sport'.[75]

The debate surrounding the eventual legalisation of professionalism by the Leinster Football Association led to suggestions in the press that the professional was 'still looked upon as a hireling and a hooligan in some unenlightened quarters', and that professionalism itself revealed 'a poverty of ideals'.[76] The failure of professional sides, whether representing province or country, was often greeted with almost resigned relish by the press. The defeat of the Ulster side, composed largely of professionals, by the amateurs of Leinster prompted one Belfast newspaper to note with scorn the way the 'Northern professionals … strut about with such an important air'.[77] By 1910, although professionalism in football had been officially recognised for a decade and a half, the Belfast press was still being accused of 'urging on our clubs to amateurism'.[78] In the same year one journalist offered a forthright and unsympathetic assessment of the professional footballer in Ireland, who was fundamentally 'interested in salaries, benefits, transfers and bonuses more than he is interested in the improvement of his play, the welfare of his club, or the improvement of the game'.[79]

Even some of those individuals who were most intimately involved in the game in Ireland seem to have been less than sympathetic to professionalism. In 1909 the 'Improvement Commission' established by the IFA to enquire what measures could be taken to improve the standards of play in the country, and generally to encourage the game's spread, reported that 'it would be in the interests of the game in Ireland if the Association did all in its power to foster amateurism'.[80]

The dichotomy that existed with regard to professional players and professionalism in general can perhaps be seen most clearly through the career of one man: William McCracken. McCracken was born and educated in Belfast, in the street adjacent to the home ground of the Distillery club. He learned to play football in the streets, and in the ranks of various junior sides. In January 1901, at the age of 17, he signed for Distillery as a professional. By 1903 he had acquired three Irish caps and was generally admired both for his footballing skills, and his 'modesty both on and off the football field'. Later that year he was noted as being 'inclined to play to the gallery' but he was not as yet suffering from 'that irritating disease known as "swelled head" brought on usually by the attentions of admirers'.[81] In January 1904, though, McCracken seems to have recognised his own worth, and to the disgust of the press he refused to travel to Londonderry to play in a cup tie. Despite this aberration his success at international level continued to win him praise. In the match against England he was 'the tower of strength in defence', while against Wales he was 'marvellous, for he gave a display which was worth going a long way to see'. In front of a 7,000 crowd in Dublin he was 'head and shoulders above any back on the field' in the final international against Scotland.[82] Such was McCracken's popularity that he was even celebrated in verse:

> Of backs we can offer a charming variety.
> Able to play in class football society;
> Still I'd advise you, without impropriety,
> William McCracken's the king of them all.[83]

At the end of the 1904 season, McCracken took the perhaps inevitable step of leaving Distillery for a cross-channel club. An approach from Glasgow Rangers had already led to Distillery officials registering a complaint with the IFA, but in April 1904 McCracken finally departed for Newcastle United in the north-east of England. The farewell was a sad but fond one, and the Irish sporting press was left to regret that 'there are not many McCrackens nowadays'.[84] Even at a distance McCracken continued to be admired in Ireland. In his first season at Newcastle the club won the English league championship, a feat it was to repeat twice in the next four years. McCracken was widely credited with making an enormous contribution to these victories, as well as a later FA Cup triumph. He also continued to make appearances for the Irish national side when his club commitments permitted, and in February 1906 he arrived back in Belfast 'bent on playing' against England despite a serious ankle injury.[85]

The entire situation changed in 1908, however. At that year's international match against England McCracken demanded to be paid a match fee of £10, the same amount as some of his Newcastle colleagues received for playing for England. The IFA refused, and McCracken spent the entire match in the dressing room. The press, which had been so laudatory over the past half-decade, rounded on the now flawed hero. The fact that McCracken 'preferred his price to his country's football honour' was seen as disgusting. His actions in taking this 'unpatriotic step' and 'putting his pocket before the football claims of his country' caused 'great indignation' in Ireland.[86] Even the tenor of the poetry changed, and the following appeared under the heading 'The football fiasco':

> The exile once longed for the principal part
> To fight that his land may be free
> But now the thought of the patriot heart
> Is, what will the wages be?[87]

At that year's annual general meeting the IFA answered the calls that McCracken be permanently excluded from the Irish side by banning him from playing football anywhere in Ireland, for life. Their annual report recorded that they were scandalised by a man that played 'for lucre not for fame'.

The repercussions of the incident went further, and at that year's International Board meeting the IFA successfully introduced a motion limiting the payment to all professionals for international appearances to £4.[88] The logical end of professionalism was unacceptable to the very body that had introduced the practice. McCracken had gone from being a hero to a villain in one quite easy step: his professionalism had become more obvious than his love of the game.

The estrangement between McCracken and the IFA was a long one. In January 1910 a motion in the IFA Council for McCracken's reinstatement was rejected by 21 votes to 4, despite a comment in the press that his exclusion was 'ruinous to Irish football'.[89] In November the same year McCracken wrote to the IFA requesting a removal of his suspension, but a further motion in his support again failed. Another attempt was made in 1912, with the same results. In 1914 the ritual rejection of McCracken was maintained, with the comment that his actions in 1908 had been 'characterised as lowering the status of Irish football, and even an insult to well-meaning professionals'.[90] In December 1917 McCracken finally sent a 'letter of apology' to the IFA, though it was received with little apparent grace. A fuller rapprochement followed in August 1918 when McCracken attempted, albeit unsuccessfully, to bring over to Ireland a team of English professionals to play in a war charities match.⁹¹ Complete rehabilitation was not achieved until 1920, when McCracken gained his eleventh international cap in the game against England at the age of 37. The man widely accepted as having invented, or at least perfected, the offside trap, and later remembered as 'the grand old man of football', effectively served a twelve-year exile from Irish football for asserting his rights and status as a professional.⁹²

For those who reached the upper echelons of the professional game in Ireland, football could provide a decent living. For those in the lower reaches of the game, the wages they received probably provided a welcome subsidy to their regular wages. Such payments were perhaps more than adequate compensation for the uncertain position in society that they came to occupy. For some at least there was the hope that a move across the Irish Sea would offer them a chance to better both their financial and their social position. Given these circumstances, it seems reasonable to ask exactly who became a professional footballer in Ireland.

For most historians of twentieth-century Ireland two professional footballers may spring readily to mind, though not necessarily for their dazzling ball skills. Oliver St John Gogarty is mainly remembered as a poet, surgeon and politician, and the plaque on his former house in Dublin reminds passers-by of these achievements. It does not, however, remark on the period he spent as a professional footballer in Preston North End reserves.⁹³ One of Gogarty's political contemporaries, though not of his allies, also enjoyed an earlier existence as a professional footballer. Oscar Trainor served as the Fianna Fáil government's defence minister during the Second World War. This was perhaps an extremely fitting post for a man who had previously earned his living as a goalkeeper in Belfast, before becoming the IRA military strategist in Dublin during the Irish Civil War.⁹⁴

Trainor and Gogarty are the exceptions, of course; the majority of professional footballers in pre-partition Ireland are now largely forgotten. However, a major source has survived from which it is possible to glean many personal details of those who were enrolled as football professionals in Ireland. This document takes the form of a register of professional players, giving for each his name, address, place of birth and the club for which he was registered, and covering a period of four and a half seasons at the turn of the century.[95] Using only the complete data for the four seasons from 1899/1900 onwards, it is possible to make a number of suggestions regarding the backgrounds of both professionals and professionalism in Irish football.

In the first place, as Table 3.1 shows, the number of professionals remained small. Even after the practice had been recognised for nearly a decade, barely more than a hundred men were capable of being legally paid for playing each season.

TABLE 3.1
Registered professionals with Irish football clubs, and numbers of clubs registering professional players, 1899–1903

	1899/1900	1900/01	1901/02	1902/03
Players	102	112	113	104
Clubs	11	13	13	14

Source: Register of professionals (IFA).

In total 232 different men appear on the register, of whom 117 are registered for one season only. Of the 102 men registered in 1899/1900, only 34 were still acting as professionals three years later. While the large number of apparently transient professionals may of course include men who were at the beginning or end of longer careers, the overall impression that professional football in Ireland was a business that players drifted in and out of is supported by the few details of individuals' careers that are available to us. For some players a spell as a professional with an Irish club represented a component within a career that might span employment in three kingdoms.

For example, Patrick Farrell, who was a native of Belfast, was registered for the single season 1900/1901 with the Distillery club as a professional. However, he had already played for Distillery in the 1890s before signing for Glasgow Celtic, then moving to the

London-based Arsenal team in 1897. Having 'not yet tired of English professionalism' he moved to Brighton United in 1898, before returning to Belfast in August 1900 when the Brighton club folded. By 1902 he was back in Brighton, playing as a professional for the town's newly formed amateur side.[96]

In November 1898 Ezekiel Johnston was 26 years old. Having started his career with the Ulster and Milltown clubs in Belfast, he had been transferred from Belfast Celtic to Stoke in the English midlands two years previously, before going on to Burnley in Lancashire. He was now returning to his native Belfast, and the Celtic side. The following year he moved to Linfield, before retiring from the game in 1902.[97] Alex McCartney, at one time a professional with Irish clubs Glentoran and Belfast Celtic, and English teams Everton and West Ham, advised would-be Irish *émigré* players simply to 'attend the agents gathering at the Bee Hotel, Liverpool' which was held each May Day. From here a contract was a mere formality.[98] For others a short term as a professional player provided a welcome financial supplement, or a brief moment of personal triumph. In 1909 George McClure was playing as a professional with Distillery in order to earn enough money to cover his indentures as a solicitor. Two years later Leslie Skene, the goalkeeper with the Glentoran club, was reportedly using his wages to train as a doctor.[99] At the heart of the system, though, there seems to have been a resilient core of men for whom local professionalism was probably both a way of life and the means of earning a living.

As for the clubs that employed professionals, there was a similar general lack of continuity tempered with some consistency. Table 3.1 shows the number of clubs registering professionals annually, over our four-year period. These figures make it clear that professionalism was a minority interest among clubs. By the end of the 1901/2 season there were 199 clubs affiliated to the IFA, of which less than 7 per cent were involved in professionalism each season.[100] Once more, though, the bare figures tell only part of the story. Although in any one season no more than fourteen clubs registered professionals, over the four-season period thirty-one clubs enrolled professionals. This apparent dabbling in professionalism can be accounted for by the tendency of some amateur clubs to employ a professional in a coaching capacity, much in the way cricket professionals were already being utilised. This was the case at the Ulster club in Belfast. Professional registration was also used by amateur sides to ensure that their players remained with the club for the duration of the season, a development which worried the IFA as it created a great deal of unnecessary work for its officials.[101]

Not surprisingly, all of the twenty-eight clubs employing professionals whose geographical situation is readily identifiable were located in the province of Ulster. Of these, fifteen were in the city of Belfast; eight were based in the town of Lisburn or in the Lagan valley area between the two urban centres, three in County Down, and one each was situated in Counties Armagh and Tyrone.[102] This situation can of course be seen as prescribed in part by the legislation that prohibited professionalism in some areas of the country, but it is perhaps also worth noting that professionalism had its origins and early practical support in the area of Ireland which enjoyed the greatest level of industrial development. In relation to the rest of the United Kingdom the link between industrialisation and the growth of professional sport of all sorts has been seen as a crucial one, and it should not be discounted in the case of Ireland.[103] In fact even after the legalisation of professionalism throughout the country, the practice was still perceived and portrayed as a northern one. In 1907 one Dublin cultural Nationalist could still note 'the money wasted at present on professionalism' in football by 'the unpatriotic Protestants from the North of Ireland'.[104] There was a grain of truth in such jibes, as by the outbreak of the Great War only one professional side existed in Ireland outside Belfast: the Shelbourne club of Dublin.[105]

Moreover, when the details of numbers of players and numbers of clubs are collated, a further indication is given of an emerging Belfast hegemony in professionalism even at this early stage of the game's development. While there is no evidence that all the players registered were actually active for their clubs, nor that these supposed professionals were actually being paid for their services, if the number of players registered by a club is taken as an indicator of that club's level of activity and financial well-being, the evidence suggests that over these four years professional football was dominated by just four Belfast clubs. Only one club from outside the city, Holywood Swifts from Co. Down, ever registered more than eight professional players. This was in the 1901/02 season, and all the players reverted to amateur status before the end of the season. Only the Belfast Celtic, Linfield, Distillery and Glentoran sides regularly returned large playing staffs. The largest staffs were both of 26 players, registered in the 1902/03 season by Distillery and Belfast Celtic. This predominance in professionalism was reflected in success on the field. During these four seasons the winners and the runners-up in the Irish League competition came exclusively from these four sides.[106]

The final piece of information that can be extracted from the register alone refers to the players' places of birth. On average, each year around 16 per cent of players registered were born outside Ireland. Generally this proportion was evenly split between men of English and Scottish origins. It should be noted, however, that some individuals were inconsistent in their choice of birthplace. Peter Wattie, for example, registered as a professional for the Holywood Swifts club on 17 February 1900 and gave his nationality as Irish. Seven months later, still living at the same address and still registering for the same club, he returned himself as English. Even allowing for such aberrations, though, the proportion of non-Irish-born players is considerably higher than might be expected. The 1901 census report for the city of Belfast, in which most of the professionals lived, gives figures of less than 7 per cent of the male population being born in England, Scotland and Wales.[107]

In part the large numbers of non-Irish-born players can be accounted for by the presence of the children of returned migrants. For example, John Hunter Lyttle, a professional with the Distillery and Castlereagh clubs, returned his place of birth in 1900 as New York. Lyttle had in fact been born in America of Irish parents, who had returned to Belfast when he was a child.[108] This cannot explain the great disparity between the number of Englishmen and Scots in the ranks of the professional footballing community and in the city's population at large, however. One possible contributory factor may have been the nature of the British immigrant community in Belfast. A large proportion of the male element in this group were brought to Ireland by the hope of employment in the shipbuilding industry. It was a happy coincidence that two areas of major shipbuilding activity in Britain, the Clyde and the north-east of England, were also hotbeds of association football. As early as 1885 it was noted that two clubs recently formed near Belfast included 'some ready-made players imported from the Clyde to the shipbuilding yard there'. In 1902 it was noted that the Glentoran club, whose ground was situated in the east of the city near the new yards, was attracting a large number of 'foreign' players because of its location.[109]

Another domestic source of potential foreign footballers also existed in Ireland by way of the military. As noted above, the military were an important factor in the dissemination of the game of association football across Ireland.[110] Until the outbreak of the Boer War and the withdrawal of troops from the Belfast garrison, army teams continued to compete at the highest level there. In 1890 the team of the Gordon Highlanders won the Irish Cup; in 1892 and 1897 respectively the Black Watch and the Sherwood Foresters were runners-up in the same competition. Even before the advent of legalised professionalism, the members of their teams provided more ready-made recruits for the professional clubs. Robert Milne and Robert Hill, as noted above, were bought out of the Gordon Highlanders by the Linfield club, and the former at least went on to enjoy a conspicuously successful career for both club and country. Before this John Reynolds had had his discharge from the East Lancashire Regiment secured by the Distillery club. This 'player of infinite variety' with 'a desire to play to the gallery' uniquely went on to be capped by both Ireland and England. Such practices continued even after military teams had faded from the first rank of the game in Ireland. Fred Barret, a member of the Norfolk Regiment, was bought out of the service by the Belfast Celtic club in 1913, and went on to play professionally in both Ireland and England. In Ireland, as in England, the army provided a ready pool of potential professionals.[111]

In most cases, though, the presence of English and Scottish professionals in Ireland can be explained by much simpler and more direct circumstances. Almost from the initiation of professionalism

Irish clubs actively recruited players from across the Irish Sea. At the opening of the 1894 season, the first in which professionals were to be recognised, a Dublin newspaper suggested that it was unlikely that 'there will be any importation of cross-channel players'. However, in Belfast it had already been reported that a number of former English professionals were in town seeking positions with Irish clubs.[112] By the turn of the century Belfast clubs were regularly advertising in the British sporting press for professional players. In 1902 as the Belfast Celtic club became a limited company, one of the first measures taken by the board was to recruit half a dozen players from clubs in both England and Ireland.[113]

In fact, the continued recruitment of English and Scottish professionals provoked some resentment in Ireland. One correspondent of a Belfast newspaper suggested in 1902 that in general 'the professional senior clubs seem to prefer bringing men from Scotland and England to developing the junior talent of the town'. Four years later, in a speech at an official dinner, a member of the junior branch of the IFA similarly noted the tendency of Belfast clubs to go 'across the water for played-out old crocks' rather than train up local players. As late as 1914 Irish clubs were accused of being 'quite too fond of cross-channel players'.[114]

Despite such criticisms, it appears that the majority of professional players were actually Irish-born. In fact a great many seem to have been men from the immediate vicinity of the clubs for which they played: the infamous William McCracken was not the only player to have been born and raised within a stone's throw of his eventual employer's premises. For example, John Darling, who was by 1899 a professional with the Linfield club, had begun his career with Glentoran, whose ground was then situated in the Ballymacarrett area of Belfast where he had been born. Samuel Swan, a Linfield professional whose death from influenza was reported in May 1903, had been born in an area of west Belfast adjacent to the club's original ground. The same area was home to Joseph Dorrian, of Distillery and then Belfast Celtic.[115]

From the evidence so far, it appears that at least during the years at the turn of the century professional footballers in Ireland were small in number, and largely confined to a few Belfast clubs. They were mainly locally recruited, but were supplemented by a considerable minority of 'mercenaries' from Britain. However, a great deal more can be discovered about individual players by comparing the manuscript census returns for 1901 with the IFA register of professionals. The former detail the age, occupation, marital status, religion, and level of literacy of individuals, as well as confirming their place of birth.[116]

In the first place, it is notable that of the 164 players registered for the 1900/01 and 1901/02 seasons, only 55 are easily identifiable from the census returns. As well as perhaps providing further proof that the footballing fraternity was a transient one, this gives us a 33 per cent sample which, if not exactly scientifically selected, may be large enough to be in some way representative of the group as a whole.[117]

TABLE 3.2
Ages of professional footballers in Ireland, 1901

Age	No. of players	Average age
18	3	22.7 years
19	3	
20	6	
21	8	
22	10	
23	6	
24	7	
25	5	
26	2	
27	2	
28	0	
29	2	
30	0	
31	0	
32	1	

Source: Register of professionals (IFA); 1901 manuscript census returns.

Table 3.2 details the ages of the group identified. The impression is that professional football in Ireland was certainly a young man's game. More than half of the players found were aged 22 or under, while more than three-quarters were 24 or under. This observation is confirmed by a press report of a game in 1901, when the 32-year-old captain of Linfield, Samuel Torrans, was referred to as 'the old war horse'.[118]

In fact most players could reckon that their footballing careers would take them no further than the age of 30 or so. 'Ten years or at the very utmost fifteen' was the estimate of a professional's playing life made by one English contemporary in 1896. In 1902, at the age of 24, Robert Rea of Belfast Celtic was reckoned to be 'good for another ten years' first class football'; yet at 26 the Irish international goalkeeper's career was reckoned to be nearly over.[119]

With such limited prospects in the long term, it seems reasonable to consider what became of players once their footballing days were over. The little available evidence suggests that post-playing careers varied greatly from one player to another, with a man's exploits in the game counting for little once his playing days were over. A very few players could find employment as club trainers, coaches, or officials; the number of such opportunities was always tiny.

By 1898 the role of the trainer was seen by some as crucial to a team's prospects of success. Perhaps with this in mind, in the same year the Distillery club appointed as its trainer the former centre-forward of an English club. In 1904 the Bohemians club in Dublin signed John Divers, a former Scottish international, as its coach. He was to hold the post for two years. The employment of 'foreign' coaches and trainers was to be continually seen as essential up to 1914.[120] Even for the few Irishmen who achieved such positions, the longer-term prospects were not always rosy. Jack McCandless won five Irish caps and scored three goals in international matches, during a career that extended both sides of the Great War. His playing career blossomed with Bradford City in Yorkshire, though his first venture into management was with Ebbw Vale in Wales. Eventually he returned to his native Coleraine to run the local side, and a small shop. The Depression and the effects of a gas attack in the trenches bore down heavily on him, however. He died in 1940 leaving a wife and young family in straitened circumstances.

Unsurprisingly he never encouraged either of his sons to take up the game.[121]

Some former Irish players undoubtedly found their feet in other ways. The much travelled Patrick Farrell had 'settled down in comfortable circumstances' in Brighton by 1927. A decade earlier one former Distillery professional had established himself as a dentist.[122] Some simply returned to their old professions full-time. A former Belfast Celtic goalkeeper was back in the shipyards as a boilermaker in 1914, and William Creevy, formerly of Glentoran and Linfield, returned to his trade as a fitter.[123]

It seems likely that the fame a player might have accrued on the field could prove an asset. By 1917 two former Irish professionals had joined the music hall circuit: John West, late of Glentoran and Cardiff City, was a singer; while Archie Goodall, capped nine times by Ireland and a former coach at Clongowes School, was giving 'a sensational performance entitled "Walking the Hoop"'.[124] Others perhaps used their football fame to some extent in the licensing trade. The Belfast Celtic star and Irish international Mickey Hamill eventually became a 'spirit merchant' and the landlord of the 'Centre Half Bar' on Belfast's Falls Road.[125] For others, neither the material nor the character benefits of their footballing days proved of any lasting worth. By 1924 John Kirwan, capped seventeen times by Ireland and an FA Cup winner with Tottenham Hotspur in 1901, had become so desperate that he sought, and obtained, a grant of £10 from the IFA to help his situation.[126]

Perhaps the ultimate example of the fleeting nature of the fame and fortune that football could bring to a man is provided by Jack Reynolds. Despite his five Irish international appearances, a further eight for England, three FA Cup winner's medals and two League Championships, which included a double-winning performance with Aston Villa in 1897, by 1899 Reynolds was playing for a semi-professional side in Barnsley and appearing in court for failing to pay for the maintenance of his illegitimate child. He finally died in 1917, aged 47, while employed as a miner in Sheffield.[127] Even the greatest achievements on the football field could count for little in later years.

The relative youth of the players in the sample probably accounts for a number of other personal circumstances. Only nineteen men (35 per cent) were married, and just one, Samuel Torrans, was widowed. The remaining thirty-five (64 per cent) were bachelors. There was also a 100 per cent literacy rate, which was perhaps to be expected in a country in which a national school system had existed since the 1830s. Less believable is the claim that four players spoke only Irish. These included John Campbell, a 22-year-old foundry labourer, who had been born in Co. Antrim and was now a registered professional with the Glentoran club. It seems likely that this may be an enumerator's error due to the way in which linguistic abilities were to be registered.[128]

With regard to the declared occupations of the group, it is most noticeable that not a single player returned himself as a 'professional footballer'. This could be indicative of several things. In the first place it is confirmation that some professionals were such only in name, and were not actually paid for playing football. Others were undoubtedly being paid, but football did not represent their main source of income. Finally, it is at least possible that some men preferred not to return themselves as professionals because of the comparatively low status that the job enjoyed. The most prominent case of this may be that of Robert Milne of Linfield. By 1901 Milne had been a registered professional at the club for five years, was the captain of the first team and the coach of the reserves. Although born in Scotland he had collected fifteen caps for the Irish national side, and would go on to earn a dozen more. In 1904 he was to be given a 'purse of sovereigns' as the proceeds of a benefit game. Yet in the 1901 census he described himself as an unemployed clerk.[129] The employment details returned by the 55 men identified, as detailed in Table 3.3, possibly reveal something of the socio-economic background of players though. If nothing else they reveal how these men viewed themselves.

As Table 3.3 shows, more than a third of Irish professionals at this time were drawn from the unskilled sector of the labour force, with around half being skilled men or craftsmen. These figures contrast markedly with similar assessments of professional footballers in England at the same time and later. Of a sample of 51 English professional players employed over the years 1884–1900, none were described as labourers, and only a maximum of nine (18 per cent) were from the unskilled sector. By the period 1907–10, from a sample of 114 professionals in England, only fourteen (12 per cent) were reckoned to be unskilled men, and again none were returned as labourers.[130] Small as the statistical base is, there is still a great disparity here. It seems unlikely that it can be attributed solely to a substantial difference in the employment patterns of the two countries. As the centre of Ireland's shipbuilding and textile industries, Belfast was home to a large general labouring population, but it also had a good many skilled men.

At least two related factors may explain why skilled men made up a significantly smaller proportion of professional footballers in Ireland than in England. In the first place, it may have been the case that at this particular time Irish labouring men were more likely to be attracted to the wages offered by professional clubs than their skilled counterparts. For the labouring classes payments for playing football could provide a substantial supplement to the weekly wage

TABLE 3.3
Employment backgrounds of professional footballers in Ireland c.1900

Labourers and unskilled (20, 36.4%)	*Artisans* (7, 12.7%)	*Skilled* (21, 38.2%)	*White collar* (7, 12.7%)
Labourer (x 3)	Cabinet maker (x 1)	Brass finisher (x 1)	Draper's assistant (x 1)
General labourer (x 4)	Carpenter (x 2)	Iron moulder (x 4)	Telephone inspector (x 1)
Bricklayer's labourer (x 1)	Shoemaker (x 1)	Iron turner (x 4)	Railway clerk (x 1)
Shipyard labourer (x 3)	Tailor (x 1)	Riveter (x 3)	Clerk (x 2)
Factory labourer (x 1)	Butcher (x 1)	Shipwright (x 1)	Linen salesman (x 1)
Ironworks labourer (x 1)	Plasterer (x 1)	Caulker (x 2)	'Private means' (x 1)
Foundry labourer (x 1)		Boilermaker (x 2)	
Crane driver (x 1)		Painter (x 1)	
Smith's helper (x 1)		Wire worker (x 1)	
Carter (x 1)		Silk printer (x 1)	
Boxmaker (x 1)		Mechanic (x 1)	
Machine man in works (x 1)			
Riveter's holder-upper (x 1)			

Source: Register of professionals (IFA); 1901 manuscript census returns.

or, if employed by a club full-time, a notable increase. For the skilled man a move to full-time professional football in 1900 possibly meant exchanging one job for another with a comparable income, but certainly less security. At the same time, the comparatively low accommodation costs in Belfast, and greater availability of employment for female dependants there, meant that real domestic incomes in Edwardian Belfast were potentially higher than elsewhere in the United Kingdom.[131] This may have reduced the need of skilled men in Belfast to take part in paid sport. In short, skilled men in Ireland probably had less need of subsidising their wages through football than did their English counterparts, and were less likely to take up the paid game, with its uncertain employment potential, than their unskilled colleagues.

TABLE 3.4
Religious affiliations of professional footballers, c.1900

	Number	Percentage	Percentage for Belfast as a whole
Presbyterian	24	43.6%	34%
Roman Catholic	14	25.5%	24%
Episcopalian Protestant	10	18.2%	30%
Methodist	5	7.2%	6%
Others	2	3.6%	6%

Source: Register of professionals (IFA); 1901 manuscript census returns; 1901 census report on Belfast.

The final tranche of information that can be extracted from the census returns concerns the religious affiliation of players (Table 3.4). Although, generally speaking, the religious balance of players is comparable with the religious complexion of the city as a whole, it is noticeable that the most under-represented group is members of the Church of Ireland. Exactly why this should be so is again uncertain, though the explanation may be more directly related to class, and employment and habitation patterns, than religion. One study of Edwardian Belfast has shown that Protestants in general were over-represented in the skilled employment sector, while

Catholics dominated the unskilled and labouring sector.[132] If we are correct in suggesting that skilled men were less likely to become professional players because of the limited rewards that were offered, this may account for some of the apparent aberrations. Even if this is true, however, it does not account for the preponderance of Presbyterians in the professional ranks, nor for the failure of Catholics to dominate professional football alongside the unskilled labour market.

Alternatively, the lack of members of the Church of Ireland may be explained by the fact that at least some of this church's members were likely to be of a higher social standing, and may well have been engaged in more elitist sporting activities. Rugby, for example, with its roots in the public school system and the Irish middle classes, still enjoyed a large following in Belfast. Allied with this were the sporting pastimes that were encouraged by the social bodies allied to the two main Protestant churches. The Boys' Brigade, noted above as a nursery of association football talent, was dominated in Belfast by the Presbyterian church. Additionally the Central Presbyterian Association, which provided the social focus of the city's Presbyterian community, fielded various association football teams, but did not have a representative rugby side. In contrast, the Church of Ireland Young Men's Society in the city had a very active rugby side, but no association team.[133]

Once more, though, this explanation can only be seen as partial, at best. A further contribution to the lack of episcopalian Protestants may have been the patterns of recruitment of professionals. It is suggested above that the bulk of professional players were recruited from the direct vicinity of clubs' grounds. For the most part these grounds were situated in areas of the city where members of the Church of Ireland were in a minority. In the three electoral wards which contained the grounds of the four leading professional clubs, Presbyterians made up a third of the total population, Catholics marginally less, and episcopalian Protestants only a quarter.[134] Once again these circumstances do not fully explain the situation, however, as while they do cast the three main religious groups in the same numerical order as in the returns for the individual players, they again fail to explain fully the Presbyterian dominance in the professional ranks. It is perhaps most likely that all these factors played their part: definitive answers may have to await further research into both the social structure of Belfast and the wider situation of football in Irish society.

By and large it seems that at least with respect to their religious affiliations, professional footballers reflected the society from which they came, and which they eventually came to represent. In fact, the relationship between the religious groups to which professional players belonged, their clubs and the wider community was often a distinct one. The fourteen Catholic professionals identified as being registered between 1899 and 1903 were affiliated to just five clubs. Glentoran, Distillery and the incongruously named Belfast Amateurs all registered one Catholic professional player; of the remainder, three were signed to Belfast Hibernians and the rest to Belfast Celtic.[135] The latter two clubs shared not only the same ground and the same chairman, but also a common Catholic identity within the city of Belfast. Celtic registered only one player, international Isaac Docherty, who was an identifiable Protestant. The Linfield club registered eight players of known religions: three were Anglicans, three Presbyterians, one a Congregationalist and one a Jew. None was Catholic. This club, with its roots in the overwhelmingly Protestant area of Belfast's Sandy Row, and which continued to hold its general meetings in that area's Orange Hall, perhaps saw its Protestant identity as reinforced by the nature of its professional playing staff. By 1912 Celtic and Linfield were simply identified in the English press as Belfast's Catholic and Protestant teams.[136]

In conclusion, prior to the Great War, professional footballers were a rare breed in Ireland. The practice of paying players was confined almost wholly to Belfast and the surrounding area. For the individuals so employed the game provided either a good living or a useful financial supplement, which probably more than made up for the dubious position that they occupied in society, and the limited long-term prospects that professional football offered.

The practice of legalised professionalism was almost forced on the game's authorities in Ireland. The exodus of the game's best exponents to clubs in Britain, where they could receive what they regarded as a just reward for their efforts, was probably the main cause of the professional debate. Ultimately it was this issue, and the demand of truly amateur clubs that 'veiled professionalism' should cease, that led to the legalising of professionalism.

The introduction of professionalism was accompanied by both hopes and fears. For the most part, the former were to be disappointed and the latter realised. A small group of professional clubs based in urban areas did indeed come to dominate the major competitions, just as the smaller clubs had argued. In the two decades between 1895 and 1914 the Irish Cup travelled outside Belfast on only three occasions, and on each of these no further than Dublin. Over the same period only five clubs won the Irish League competition. All of these were based in Belfast, and only one was wholly amateur.[137]

At the same time, the wages that Irish clubs could offer were never enough to keep the very best native players at home. Ireland's last international match of the 1913/14 season was played by a team with only four Irish-based players. Of the seven others, two were playing in Scotland and five in England.[138] It might therefore be suggested that professionalism ultimately failed the pre-war game in Ireland. Moreover, it might also be seen as having failed the wider community. Even the paying of players did not wholly break down the sectarian barriers that existed between the different clubs and their members in Belfast. By and large Catholic players continued to play for Catholic clubs, and Protestants for Protestant ones.

4

Crowds

> Hurry up in battalions,
> But bring your medallions,
> (I mean the bright coins for the man at the gate).
> The turn-stiles are clicking,
> Your paces must quicken,
> For if you're not early bedad ye'll be late.
>
> *Ireland's Saturday Night*, 5 Feb. 1910

Crowd problems at matches in Belfast reached a hiatus in the two years before the outbreak of the Great War. Distribution of handbills like this one, produced for the Glentoran club in the east of the city, were part of the measures taken to counter the disturbances.

Irish Football League

DISORDERLY CONDUCT
AT FOOTBALL MATCHES.

The Committee have been instructed by the Irish Football League to draw the attention of Spectators to the injury done to football by the unsportsmanlike conduct of a section of the crowd at matches, whereby the field of play is invaded after the game, and revolvers and explosive material used to intimidate players and referee.

It has been decided that Spectators found guilty of these practices will be INSTANTLY EXPELLED from the grounds and GIVEN INTO CUSTODY, as it is imperative in the interests of the game generally that disorderly conduct of this nature be stopped.

The Committee, therefore, appeal to the Members, and those who have the welfare of the game at heart, to assist them in preserving good order, and in stamping out the unseemly conduct which is bringing our winter pastime into disrepute.

By order, Glentoran F.C.,

September, 1913.

J. E. DAWSON, Secretary.

Wm. Brown & Sons, Printers, Belfast.

FROM THE VERY BEGINNING of association football in Ireland, the crowd was an integral part of the game. The ruling of the IFA in 1884 that every team entering its competitions should have access to a pitch to which entrance could be controlled, and thus an admission fee charged, meant that paying spectators were even at this time seen as an essential component of the sport.[1] With this in mind, the purposes of the present chapter are threefold. First it will attempt to estimate the numbers of individuals who attended matches as spectators, and thus offer an assessment of the game's level of popularity in Ireland. Second, it will examine the evidence concerning the nature of those individuals who made up the crowd. Finally it will consider the ways in which spectators behaved at games, and attempt to draw some conclusions concerning the ways in which football crowds affected the game itself and its perception in Ireland.

Any attempt to calculate the numbers of individuals who attended football matches in Ireland prior to the Great War must entail a great deal of circumspection. No records exist for this period that explicitly detail match attendances. As a result, as with so much else concerning the game, we are forced to rely on the reports of the press. Estimates of the number of spectators at games were regularly published, but these could vary enormously from publication to publication. For example, estimates of the attendance at an international match in Dublin in 1913 varied from 'at least 12,000', to 'around 10,000'.[2] Even different correspondents writing for the same newspaper could give wildly varying estimates as to attendances.[3] While for the most part there is no possible way of testing the reliability of these figures, in two cases some measure of objectivity is possible through a comparison of gate receipts and crowd estimates. All international matches played in Ireland were directly under the control of the IFA, and the gate moneys collected were recorded in their accounts. Similarly, each year's Irish Cup semi-finals and final saw a proportion of their entrance fees given over to the IFA. These figures, when compared to the ticket prices and the various estimates of attendances, have allowed Figure 4.1 to be drawn up, detailing probable attendances at Irish Cup finals between 1881 and 1914.[4]

FIGURE 4.1
Estimated attendances at Irish Cup finals 1881–1914

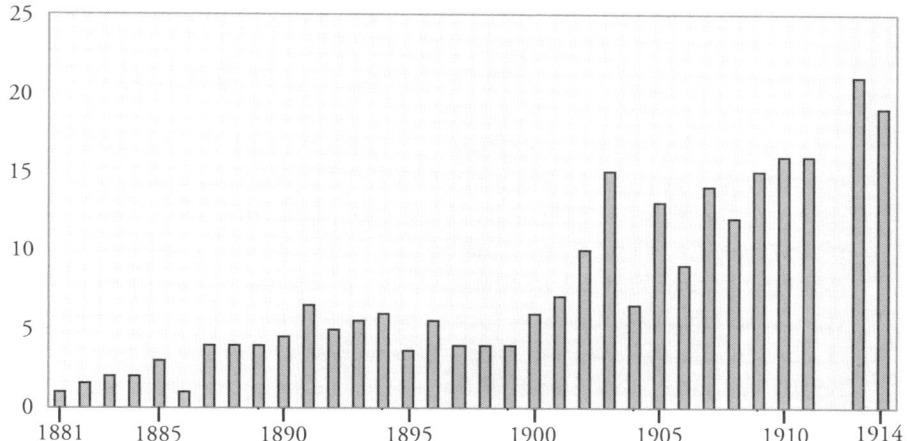

Notwithstanding the inaccuracies it may include, Figure 4.1 serves to highlight a number of factors and trends relative to attendances at football matches in Ireland, which become apparent from a wider reading of the surviving contemporary evidence. First, it seems to have been the case that certain clubs had larger followings than others. As early as 1892 two clubs were thought to be almost monopolising crowds in Belfast.[5] It also seems that the prospect of a truly competitive game was likely to bring in more spectators. The relatively poor attendance at the 1898 final between Linfield and the St Columb's Hall Celtic side from Londonderry was put down largely to the perception that the match would be a walkover for the Belfast side.[6] In more general terms, the widespread downturn in attendances at matches in the 1891/2 season was attributed to the continuing dominance of the Linfield club in all the major competitions. A later spectator stressed that the overwhelming attraction of the game for many was 'the chance that something extraordinary will happen', and the inherent 'uncertainty' that the game offered.[7] Finally, it seems that over the period between the establishment of the game on a regular footing in Ireland in 1880 and the outbreak of the Great War, the numbers of individuals attending football matches in Ireland grew enormously. This growth was not a constant one, though, nor was it remarkably rapid. Attendances remained small for the first five years of the game's history, but then experienced a marked upturn. These levels were maintained and slowly improved until around the turn of the century. Rapid increases then followed, reaching a peak in the years directly prior to the outbreak of war.[8]

At the same time it is important to realise that the figures provided by the analysis of the Irish Cup final attendances do not reflect all the realities of the general levels of attendance. In the first place, the Irish Cup final came to be regarded as the premier domestic fixture, and as such drew a disproportionately large audience. Irish League games were often played in front of much smaller crowds, such as the estimated 1,500 who saw Cliftonville beat Belfast Celtic in 1897 (although by 1913 a League game between Linfield and Belfast Celtic could draw more than 10,000 spectators).[9] On the other hand, even cup finals tended not to draw as large crowds as games involving 'foreign' opposition. This was true both during the game's early days with respect to visiting club teams, and in later years with regard to international fixtures. For example, in 1886 an exhibition game between the Cliftonville team and a Glasgow Rangers team from Scotland attracted an estimated 3,000 crowd, a figure three times that which attended that year's Irish Cup final.[10] Probably the largest gate at any game in Ireland was the international match against Scotland in 1914. The Cliftonville club declined the offer of the IFA to stage the game at their stadium, as the 25,000 capacity was likely to be exceeded. It subsequently appeared that this had been a wise decision, as a crowd in excess of 30,000 attended.[11]

The levels of attendance at even the most important games therefore varied greatly. For the most part, as noted above, these variations were probably due to the anticipated nature of the game itself. However, a number of more general factors also acted to affect possible levels of attendance, including the conditions that spectators were expected to endure. Bad weather, in the form of excessively wet or cold conditions, was frequently cited as reducing crowd numbers.[12] Even as clubs managed to improve their facilities, providing grandstands and covered areas, most spectators were still expected to stand, and mainly in the open.[13]

The awareness of the public as to the arrangements that were made for games was dealt with at an early stage. The IFA arranged for the details of the first semi-finals of the Irish Cup to be advertised in all the major Belfast newspapers, and to be displayed on sandwich boards around the city. By 1910 the Co. Antrim FA was publicising its matches not only in the press, but also by the means of 'wheelboards', that is mobile hoardings that were pulled around the city.[14]

Perhaps most importantly, the gathering of large crowds, even in urban centres, to some extent depended on considerations of transportation. Spectators needed to be able to travel to games cheaply and with ease. In Belfast and Dublin this meant the use of tram systems, while elsewhere spectators travelling any distance came to rely on trains. The first Irish 'football special' was apparently provided by the Co. Down Railway in 1882 to take spectators to the international match against England in Belfast. It was to be another eight years before a domestic fixture warranted such arrangements.[15] By 1895 it was viable for the Great Northern Railway to run a special excursion train from Belfast to Dublin to take supporters to an Irish Cup quarter-final match. The following year the Irish Football League arranged a number of cheap day-trips to Belfast from 'the country towns' for those wishing to attend the game between its team and that of the Football League. By 1910 the Great Northern was running a regular football special service from Lurgan and Portadown each Saturday during the season, to take spectators to matches in Belfast.[16] In Belfast itself, as early as 1889 special tram services were being laid on for important matches. The comparative importance of the transport network to the game is illustrated by the attitudes displayed by football's supporters to it. Clubs eventually came to arrange excursions to games specifically for their teams' followers. In 1912 it was seen as a crucial attribute of the Shelbourne club's new ground that it was just 'a penny tram fair' from the centre of Dublin.[17]

Although it is clear that association football matches were capable of attracting large crowds, it is also true that other sports drew considerably larger ones. Most notably this was the case with Gaelic football. An estimated 10,000 crowd watched the All-Ireland final in Dublin in 1895, while in 1905 a county match in Tralee, which has been cited as the turning point in the development of the GAA as a modern sporting organisation, was reckoned to have attracted twice that number.[18] In the same years the Irish Cup finals in Belfast attracted only 3,500 and 13,000 spectators respectively. But such direct comparisons are perhaps essentially flawed. The close ties between the GAA and Irish Nationalist politics meant that for many attending Gaelic games was a convenient way of making a political statement; for others it was perhaps a national duty.[19] The spectacle provided at these games was also considerably different from the 90 minutes of play that a football fan could at best expect. Major Gaelic contests, such as county finals, often had programmes that included more than one match, while the sports could be alloyed by the inclusion of band parades, Irish dancing displays, or even the recitation of Gaelic poetry.[20]

The holding of sports meetings on a Sunday, the day of the week when Gaelic games were usually played, had additional advantages. In the first place, the choice of Sunday ensured the largest possible availability of potential spectators. Even after the 1904 Shop Hours Act was passed, few Irish workers were guaranteed more than the one traditional day of rest. Secondly, the Irish Sunday Closing Act of 1878, extended and made permanent in 1906, required public houses in rural areas and most towns to shut on the sabbath. However, 'bona fide travellers', those who had travelled a distance of more than three miles, could be served.[21] Even the trip from one parish to the next might satisfy this legislative need, and thus the appetites and thirsts of spectators. Despite the official banning of alcohol from GAA meetings, the rejection of sponsorship from publicans, and claims that the GAA was in some cases marked by 'a certain puritanism', players continued to be entertained with drink after games, and unlicensed beer tents, known as shebeens, continued to be erected at matches for the use of spectators.[22] The overall effect, according to one English observer, was that Gaelic games were held amid 'an atmosphere more akin to a race meeting than a football match'.[23]

This was in stark contrast to the situation regarding association games. Despite the staging of unofficial games on Sundays, and occasional moves to introduce general Sunday play, the IFA remained staunchly opposed to any games being played on the sabbath.[24] As for the intrusion of alcohol into the major stadiums, this too was officially opposed on moral grounds. Suggestions in 1923 that a 'spirit bar' was to be erected at an international game outraged the IFA Council, and were unreservedly condemned. Only in 1907 was it agreed that alcohol should be available at post-international match dinners.[25] The best that a spectator at an Irish association game might expect was a cup of Bovril (served for the first time at a match in 1892), and even the provision of this nutritious and unintoxicating beverage initially required specific permission from the footballing authorities.[26] As for gambling, the other major attraction that might make a football game comparable to a race meeting, this too was seen as totally unacceptable by the association code's officials in Ireland. A bookmaker attempting to shout the odds at a Belfast game in 1896 was 'promptly … sat on' by members of the club's committee, while the IFA stoutly opposed any form of gambling based on the results of games.[27]

In effect there was little to attract a crowd to an association football match in Ireland beyond the game itself. The provision of a band to perform during the half-time interval was usual at the more important games in Belfast, but as late as 1912 the practice was almost unheard of in Dublin.[28] A more valid comparison of crowd size might therefore be made with the estimated attendance at the other similar attraction for large-scale sports crowds: rugby matches. Here too the game itself seems to have been the central, and perhaps only, feature drawing in spectators, with only an occasional musical accompaniment to supplement the primary sporting attraction. Again we must realise that by and large any crowd figures are only estimates, but once more these are our only source of information.

For the most part, crowd figures were neither reported nor recorded for local club games. This was not the case with international games, though, and therefore it is these that must form the basis of any comparison. In 1891 the IRFU arranged for the printing of 3,500 tickets for the international rugby match between Ireland and Scotland in Belfast. In the same year the Irish association team played Wales in front of an estimated crowd of 6,000. In 1906 around 12,000 spectators, who paid £850 for the privilege, watched the unique spectacle of an international rugby match against the South African touring side in Belfast. This was an attendance figure of around the same level as that for the association international against England in the same year.[29] However, the relative attractiveness of the two codes to the Belfast public was highlighted by an incident in 1904. Despite some rather hurried, and eventually very public, negotiations between the Northern Branch of the IRFU and the IFA, in March of that year there was a clash of international fixtures in Belfast.[30] The Irish rugby XV were to play Wales at the Balmoral grounds in the south of the city, while the association XI were to take on England at Cliftonville in the north. Both opposition teams had already beaten the other two home nations, so each represented a real sporting attraction. In the event the association game was watched by an estimated 16,000 crowd, while the rugby match was seen by 'at the outside 5,000'.[31] At least in Belfast, it appears that association football matches provided perhaps the most popular sporting events of the pre-Great War period. A slightly later observer was perhaps right when he suggested that when it came to the people of Belfast, their 'chief idea of happiness lay in drink, football matches, and the hot gospel'.[32]

In Dublin football crowds were initially much smaller than those in Belfast, though this must be seen in the light of the comparative delay in the establishment of the game in the capital, and the differing social and economic circumstances of the population there.[33] By 1904, however, a crowd of 6,000 was reckoned as having attended the Leinster Cup final, a figure comparable to that year's attendance at the Irish Cup final in Belfast.[34] During the first decade of the twentieth century, crowds at international games and Irish Cup finals staged in Dublin could be practically on a par with those that gathered at similar matches in the north.

The first association international to be held in Dublin was a match against England in 1900, played at the Lansdowne Road rugby pitch. An estimated 5,000 watched the game. The international game against Scotland in Belfast in the same year was witnessed by no more than 6,000 supporters.[35] With regard to the Irish Cup, the Dublin final of 1906 attracted around 9,000 fans, only 1,000 fewer than the following year's game in Belfast.[36] However, with only two senior clubs in Dublin, Bohemians and Shelbourne, the matches between local sides did not always draw large crowds. A match between the Freebooters and Bohemians sides in 1906 was witnessed by only 282 paying spectators. Even the top attractions could draw lower gates in Dublin than might be expected in Belfast. International contests in 1904 saw estimated crowds of 7,000 in Dublin and 14,000 in Belfast.[37] Additionally, association games in Dublin had stiffer competition for patrons than was the case in Belfast. Gaelic games were better established in the capital than in Belfast, and direct competition from rugby games was also evident.

With regard to comparative attendances at rugby and association matches, a clash of fixtures is again revealing. In February 1906 the two leading Dublin association clubs met in a local cup semi-final on the same day that the Irish rugby team entertained Wales at Lansdowne Road. The former fixture attracted around 4,000 spectators, and the latter more than twice that number.[38] In short, it seems that while individual association football games in Dublin could attract very large crowds, the rival footballing codes could attract larger ones, and could do so on a more regular basis. Dublin crowds for comparable matches tended to be smaller than those that assembled in Belfast. In 1914 three Irish League games in Belfast saw average receipts of £91, while the single game in Dublin yielded only £36.[39] Association football could be a great attraction in Dublin, but it was not the primary popular sporting interest, nor was it the draw it was in Belfast. In both cities, however, the crowds that gathered at games were large enough, and generated enough revenue, to attract peripheral private enterprises. By 1906 privately published programmes were being sold outside football grounds in Dublin. In Belfast, a number of forged tickets were presented at that year's international match against England.[40]

As must remain the case with levels of attendance, a definitive assessment of exactly who made up the crowds at football matches in Ireland is similarly impossible. Once more, however, a qualified use of press reports can give us some insight into the probable socio-economic and gender groups of the crowds.

The fact that admission was charged to matches from almost the very beginning of the game in Ireland must have excluded the very poorest members of society from the most important games. However, those who wished to could still witness some games without paying. Junior games, played in the parks and on areas of waste land, drew considerable crowds in Belfast. For the more ambitious there was the prospect of viewing even the best local talent without paying for the privilege. In 1888 the Glentoran club was forced to erect a screen around its ground to prevent onlookers from avoiding the entrance fee; in 1895 the Distillery club went so far as to smear tar on the railings around its ground to deter non-paying guests. In Londonderry both the main football pitches in the city were overlooked by higher ground, which proved irresistible to many.[41]

For the most part, though, those who actually gained admission to grounds were required to pay some sort of fee. In fact it was frequently suggested in the years before 1900 that admission prices were too high for many who wished to attend games. In 1889 it was reckoned that the prices for standing at games were generally too high, while those for seating were too low. This was followed by a call for 'popular prices' of 3d to be brought in, rather than the 6d usually charged at the time. The situation had not changed two years later, however, when 'An Artisan' wrote to a Belfast newspaper noting that the current charges of 6d and 9d were 'a great deal to any workingman', and calling for gates to be reduced to 3d as they were in England.[42] Despite such suggestions that they were being effectively excluded, there is ample testimony in the Belfast press that it was in fact the working classes of the city who made up the bulk of those attending football matches there.

The description of Belfast crowds, even by largely sympathetic newspapers, as 'the great unwashed' probably reflected social prejudice and impatience with occasional unruly behaviour rather than any real attempt to categorise spectators.⁴³ However, later testimony, both direct and indirect, seems to confirm the dominance of the lower social orders among football's spectators in Belfast. The Ulster press may well have been taking their lead from developments in association football elsewhere in the United Kingdom when they described it as 'the people's game' and 'one for the masses', but this is no reason to dismiss such observations out of hand.⁴⁴

In the mid-1890s two incidents were reported which certainly give weight to such observations. In 1893, faced with large-scale trade union meetings in the city, all matches in Belfast were postponed as 'there would have been a very poor attendance'. Two years later a strike by engineers in the city's shipyards was reported as 'having a very bad effect on club returns'.⁴⁵ An explicit relationship between the game of association football and the working classes of Belfast had been acknowledged in late 1891, when the Linfield and Distillery clubs played a benefit game for the Linenlappers Strike Fund. Members of this 'deserving and ill-used body of men' were employed in Belfast's linen mills, folding the cloth into the various shapes required before final packaging, and inspecting the material for faults. Though reckoning themselves to be skilled workers, their trade was apparently under threat from mechanisation and suffering a decline in status. The offer of support by the clubs was seen as especially fitting as the lappers themselves provided 'a tolerable number' of those who regularly paid to attend these clubs' matches.⁴⁶

This reciprocal relationship was to prove a rather durable one. In 1907, at the height of the general strike in Belfast, a trade union delegation approached the IFA and was given permission to stage a benefit match for its members. Later beneficiaries from such patronage included not only the 'Children of the Unemployed' but also the city's Coal Fund.⁴⁷ Rather than being part of the remaining vestiges of industrial paternalism which were so important in the early development of the game in Ireland, such actions can be seen as a confirmation of the growing affinity between the city's working classes and the association game, and also as a mark of the growing self-reliance and assertiveness within the lower orders of Irish society. Football had come a considerable distance in a very short time.

In Dublin too the association game was eventually alleged to be emerging as the preferred game of the lower social orders. In 1904, with the game possibly at the peak of its popularity in the capital, a crowd of 6,000 at the Leinster Cup final prompted one journalist to suggest that Dublin football had 'no pretensions to be considered the pet game of the highly respectable, but it rejoices in the fact that it is the chosen sport of the democracy, and is mainly of a plebeian nature'. Two years later it was suggested that 'the Dublin trades people … form the main support of the game in the Irish capital'. In 1913 the Irish Transport and General Workers' Union strike was reportedly having much the same effect on Dublin's football crowds as the less widespread Belfast dispute of 1895 had had there. [48]

At the same time, the evidence suggests that football crowds were not solely composed of working men. In 1890 members of the crowd at the Irish Cup final were noted as being 'individually different in appearance', with men wearing all modes of dress 'from the high collar to the muffler'.[49] 'Many of the leading residents of the town and district' of Belfast had been present at the Charity Cup final in 1886, and in 1892 the competition came under the patronage of the city's mayor.[50] In 1906 the decision of the IFA to charge boys the same admission prices as adults prompted one disgruntled minor to write to the Association informing it that although many of 'the lower class of boys' attended games, so too did some 'respectable' ones, like him.[51] Certainly the prices being charged to some games were regarded as too high to allow 'the average worker' to attend, and members of the 'non-artisan class' were reportedly unable to afford the minimum 1s. admission being charged for international games by 1913.[52] Such sums had been regularly charged for admission to the reserved and covered areas of grounds during cup games from around 1900. Thus it seems that at least to the turn of the century, football matches could attract a fairly broad social spectrum.

It should be noted that women were also sometimes to be seen at matches. The fact that women were generally admitted free to games during the early years of the sport may account for the presence of some. The decision to charge women for admittance to the Charity Cup final in 1890 was seen as the primary reason why fewer than expected attended. Prior to this the attendance of women at games was frequently noted, and with some satisfaction. 'A very large concourse of ladies' were among the 3,000 spectators who attended the exhibition match to celebrate the opening of the Cliftonville club's new grandstand in 1886. The following year 'the fair sex' were 'well represented' among the crowd who attended a game in Ballynahinch, Co. Down. 'A very large number of ladies' saw the Linfield club beat a Bolton Wanderers team in an FA Cup tie in 1888.[53] Even after women were charged admission fees, special efforts continued to be made to attract them to games. At the Leinster Cup final in Dublin in 1894 a special area was set aside 'for the large number of ladies who have signified their intention of being present', and seating provided.[54] As late as 1905 members of the Cliftonville club were requesting extra tickets for international games to be played at their club's ground, to enable them to 'take in a lady friend'.[55]

If the size of crowds ultimately came to depend on the nature of individual games, and of the teams involved in them, so too did their composition. The impression is that the higher social orders and women spectators were far more likely to be drawn to prestigious games, such as charity games or cup finals; and also that they would more probably attend the matches involving the leading amateur teams than those of professional teams. Such matches could in fact take on a certain air of gentility and respectability that in turn attracted more of the nation's elite. The Charity Cup final in Belfast consistently drew a crowd that included many women, and some in the middle classes warmly welcomed matches between the amateur Bohemian club of Dublin and Cliftonville of Belfast, as they guaranteed 'plenty of excitement if not too much real football'.[56] The deliberate transformation of a sports event into an elite social occasion was most clearly, and successfully, accomplished by the Northern Branch of the IRFU in 1905. Eager to make its charity competition more profitable, the trustees of the trophy arranged for the attendance of Lord Londonderry at the final tie, and for the presentation of 200 ladies from the crowd to him. Afternoon tea with the Lord Mayor of Belfast was a further attraction. The result was a near doubling of the receipts.[57]

For the most part, however, although the lack of evidence prevents it from being indisputably proven, association crowds seem to have been made up of working-class young men. As time progressed, women and gentlefolk became less common spectators. The former may have been deterred to some extent by the imposition of admission charges; growing domestic responsibilities and the imposition of new gender roles may also have played their part.[58] The latter were perhaps more likely to have been dissuaded by the nature and demeanour of their fellow male spectators. It seems that by the turn of the century the gentlemen and their ladies who attended matches probably mainly confined themselves to the stands that the leading clubs now provided. The unreserved areas became the domain of the plebeian, male masses. By 1902 an incident in which a male spectator was manhandled on the terraces by a woman with a child at her breast was an amusing memory of a bygone era.[59]

The random observations on which these deductions have been based can be seen as rather subjective. The treasurer of the IRFU was perhaps typical of his class in regarding spectators at association games as not really meriting any great analysis as to class or social origins.[60] Hard evidence as to exactly who attended football matches in Ireland is not easily come by. Occasionally individuals have left testimony as to their interest and involvement in the game. James Nevin, a councillor and medical doctor in the north Antrim town of Ballymoney, attended a junior challenge match in the town on St Patrick's Day in 1905, while William Greer's father, a downwardly mobile Presbyterian mangle salesman, once visited a game in Belfast. Neither man made a habit of the practice, however. In Belfast, the proletarian playwright and one-time dock crane-driver Thomas Carnduff was a life-long supporter of the Linfield club that had been founded near his childhood home in Sandy Row. C.S. Andrews, the son of a small Catholic Dublin shopkeeper, was just as enthusiastic in his following of the local Bohemian club in Dublin.[61] Such individual reminiscences, while of great interest, are too small in number to provide any broad picture of the nature of football crowds.

In one case, however, it is possible to collate a small amount of hard data concerning the age, gender, and occupational backgrounds of some of the individuals who made up the crowds that paid to attend football matches in Ireland. This information is supplied by the casualty lists from a disturbance at a game in Belfast played in September 1912, between Belfast Celtic and their local rivals from Linfield. Whether the crowd at this match was truly typical is debatable. Estimated at up to 20,000, it was thought to have been boosted by the attendance of many casual watchers who were hopeful of also seeing the air display at nearby Balmoral. One local football correspondent noted that 'the beautiful weather and the prospect of ... viewing the flying at the same time' as the football had tempted many individuals to Celtic Park who would not normally have attended the game.[62] It was also later suggested that some individuals had attended the match solely with the intention of causing trouble, and with little or no interest in the game.[63] The implication is that this crowd, and especially the individuals hurt in the ensuing disturbances, were far from truly typical; but at the same time the details that can be culled from the returns represent the only source of hard evidence concerning the nature of Irish football crowds prior to the Great War, and as such they deserve some analysis.

First, it is noticeable that all the injured were male. Although it is perhaps less likely that women would become directly involved in such large-scale disorders than men, the complete absence of female casualties, even as bystanders, may be seen as confirmation that most spectators were indeed male. Table 4.1 details the ages of those injured. Again these figures seem to confirm earlier observations that young men made up the bulk of crowds. A majority of the available examples were under 30 years of age.

Using the same sources, and street directories for the years 1912 and 1913, Table 4.2 details the occupations of the injured individuals. In this case our small amount of quantitative evidence is to some extent in conflict with the existing contemporary observations and our earlier deductions. According to the former, almost a third of the crowd consisted of unskilled men and labourers, while the latter might have suggested that the unskilled, with less security of employment and financial power, were in fact unlikely to be paying spectators at all. In this case we would perhaps do well to remember both the very small size of our sample and the fact that the disturbances in which these individuals were injured overflowed the grounds where they began. However, all the evidence seems to agree in that the overwhelming majority of those present were from the city's working classes. Their status as skilled or unskilled men is perhaps less important than their probable position within the lower strata of society.[64]

TABLE 4.1
Ages of injured spectators, Belfast Celtic v. Linfield, 1912

Age group	Number	Average age
18 and under	10	28.4
19 to 29	22	
30 to 39	16	
40 to 49	4	
50 to 59	2	
Total	54	

Source: IN and *NW* 16 Sept. 1912. The details of the police officers injured on duty are excluded.

TABLE 4.2
Occupations of injured spectators, Belfast Celtic v. Linfield, 1912

	Labourers and unskilled	Artisans	Skilled	White collar
	Labourer (x 4)	Butcher	Riveter	Bookseller
	Yarn drier	Bricklayer	Compositor	Overseer
	Bottler	Joiner	Painter	
	Coachman	Blacksmith	Iron turner	
		French polisher	Fitter	
		Plumber	Plater	
			Beetler	
Total	7 (32%)	6 (28.5%)	7 (32%)	2 (9.5%)

Source: As for Table 4.1, and *Belfast and Province of Ulster Directory* 1912 and 1913.

In short, the evidence suggests that the majority of the spectators at leading Irish football matches were young, working-class men.

Further to this, the addresses given by all the 56 civilian injured were essentially local.[65] Despite the expansion of interest in the game, and the forced migration of clubs away from the neighbourhoods in which they had originated, a club's following was still probably drawn primarily from the immediate vicinity of its original home ground.

Mass movements and collective action have proved to be extremely popular areas of study and research for Irish historians. The sports crowd, however, has largely escaped their attentions. This seems to be due to the lack of interest in sports history in general rather than either a paucity of evidence or any excessive banality on the part of such crowds. In fact it appears that football crowds in particular displayed patterns of behaviour that were both uniquely interesting and marked by a broader continuity with comparable groups in Ireland and elsewhere.

There seems little doubt that supporters at football matches were eager to display their enthusiasm, appreciation and approbation of their favoured teams and players. The wearing of team colours and badges was noted from an early date. In 1890 supporters of the Limavady team playing at Londonderry sported badges and cards in their hats bearing the legend 'Play up Limavady'. In 1903 Distillery supporters visiting Dublin for a cup-tie displayed green shamrock badges and a similar banner, also inciting their team to 'play up'. In 1906 a Belfast Celtic fan was seen sporting a green umbrella, emblazoned with the motto 'Celtic for the Cup'. The following year free badges were given to those buying their Irish Cup final tickets in advance in Dublin, and the Shelbourne supporters who travelled north for the game were noted as wearing these and other 'favours'.[66] Others employed more conventional methods of displaying their allegiances and appreciation. Members of the crowd at an Irish Cup semi-final in 1882 reportedly 'exercised their lungs freely'; and while few spectators probably applauded harder than the gentleman who snapped his walking stick at a Belfast game in 1888, 'the shouting, stamping, hat-waving, oscillating enthusiast' whom 'the grave and sober citizen' became was allegedly a common sight on the terraces and in the stands.[67] It was perhaps inevitable that such enthusiasm should take on aspects that those in authority, and the press, thought unacceptable.

As early as 1884, 'hooting roughs' using 'language which can only be described as beastly' were present at matches in Belfast, and in 1888 a crowd in Armagh were thought to be 'much too free with their tongues'. A decade later the use of the 'choicest Billingsgate' by supporters was said to be lowering the tone of the whole game, and driving 'a good many of ... the more respectable people' away from matches. Yet more than once the press noted that abuse was just as likely to emanate from the 'respectable class of spectators' as from the lower orders. Nor was the nature of the game a bar to such conduct. In 1905 a military referee complained to the Co. Antrim FA concerning the language used by the crowd at a juvenile game, presumably because the swearing had been rather harder than that expected of the proverbial trooper.[68] But the shouts of the crowd could be more than simple expletives, or mindless abuse. A spectator with a 'quick eye for technique and a ready wit' actually added to the enjoyment of one journalist at a Belfast game in 1900.

At the same time, focused verbal assaults on individual players, sometimes with unexpected results, were not unknown. A player for the Ulster club of Belfast, who was 'possessed of a hasty temper', was frequently baited by opposition fans, in the hope he could be incited to foul play. In 1885 the Irish international goalkeeper was so perturbed at the abuse that his own fans heaped on him following a drubbing by the Welsh side that he gave up all forms of sport immediately afterwards. In 1911 a Dublin crowd's chants at a Belfast player were offered by him to the IFA as a possible mitigation for his being sent off in a League game there.[69]

The use of threatening language by spectators was frequently cited as a component in the creation of an intimidatory atmosphere, though usually by defeated teams appealing to the IFA or another body to overturn a result.[70] But real disorder, in some cases incorporating a genuine measure of violence, also occurred.

When exactly the first violent incident connected with an association football match occurred in Ireland is uncertain, but in November 1888 a report that a referee had been attacked at a game in Scotland was greeted in Ireland with thanks that 'we have not learned that portion of the game here'. Within a week, however, representatives of the Linfield club were complaining to the Co. Antrim FA that the fans of their opponents in a Co. Antrim Shield match had been prone to 'systematically interfere with play'.[71] By the end of that season even more overtly violent actions were being reported. When the members of the Oxford team walked off the field following some excessively rough play by their opponents in Lisburn, they were confronted by members of the crowd who 'called them cowards, called on them to stand and fight them, and shouted they would kick them up and down the field'. A year later the final of the Co. Antrim Shield ended prematurely as the crowd invaded the pitch and smashed the goalposts.[72] Such incidents apparently remained isolated, though, and it was not until October 1895 that the first major disturbance occurred at a match in Belfast. Even then it was reported that 'we have not much of that sort of thing in Belfast'.[73] During that season, however, a string of disorders were reported at games across the north of Ireland. In Londonderry a game in September was accompanied by 'two or three lively skirmishes' in the crowd, and a Cup quarter-final was later abandoned due to crowd trouble.[74]

In the following years football matches across the country came to be marked by reports of disorder and violence. In March 1899 disorder followed the final of the Intermediate Cup in Dublin. In 1904 'rough work by the crowd' stopped a game in Bundoran, Co. Donegal; and in the same year the Resident Magistrate in Portadown, Co. Armagh fined a man and a woman a total of £1 5s. for two separate offences of riotous behaviour at football matches in the town. By 1910 the problems had even spread to Munster, as a crowd there invaded the pitch at a match between the Bandon club and the Black Watch Reserves.[75]

Such reports in the press should not, of course, be taken at face value. Political and class prejudices seem to have coloured reports not only of games, but also of all the attendant activities. For example, the report of the middle-class, Liberal *Northern Whig* that one Belfast game 'culminated in a free fight' amongst spectators, and that the police 'had to intervene to quell the riot', was rubbished by the more populist *Ulster Football and Cycling News*, which subsequently noted that the disturbance was actually the result of the ungentlemanly conduct of a single drunk. The previously mentioned incident in Portadown that led to the prosecution of an elderly drunken woman was not even reported in the local north Armagh press. Meanwhile the Nationalist *Fermanagh Herald*, which encouraged its young readers 'only to play Irish games', made the most of an incident it described as reminiscent of 'South Sea Islanders at war!'.[76] Unfortunately the records of the IFA, which might have provided a rather more objective view of such events, have not survived for the period 1887–97: the years in which crowd trouble first emerged in Irish football. Thus we are forced to rely for the most part on the possibly coloured reports of journalists and other observers, and should therefore treat their testimony with due caution.

Given these caveats, any estimation of the frequency of crowd disorder, especially prior to 1898, must remain speculative. The impression, however, is that the various forms of socially unacceptable crowd activity that went beyond the use of offensive or provocative language became more common from early 1895 in Belfast and Londonderry. Elsewhere in Ulster incidents were at least more regularly reported from about 1904.[77] In Dublin, the other major centre of the sport, sporadic incidents were certainly reported from around the same date, but only after 1912 were these seen as serious. It is important to realise that the overwhelming majority of games in Ireland were played in front of comparatively well-ordered crowds, and any form of disturbance was the exception rather than the norm. For example, in the 1906/07 season the IFA was called upon to deal with only one incident of crowd trouble, which followed a match between the Glentoran and Cliftonville sides in Belfast. The previous season no incidents at all were brought to the Association's notice.[78] Over these two seasons Ireland's senior clubs took part in more than a hundred Irish League games, and more than twice that number of games in the various cup competitions. Additionally the numerous Junior and Intermediate clubs, some of whom also drew large crowds, may have played ten times this number of games between them.

Yet if disorder in itself was rare, it is clear that it could be sparked by a variety of factors. A pitch invasion and a number of scuffles in the crowd at a match between a representative team from the Irish Football League and their English counterparts in 1896 was put down to simple overcrowding. While such problems were apparently uncommon in Ireland, the Ibrox disaster in 1902, when the collapse of terracing led to 25 deaths and around 500 injuries, gave rise to some concern regarding grounds in Belfast.[79] A rather more common suggestion was that disorder was a reaction to incompetent refereeing. This was the assertion of the Dublin press following a cup final match in the city in 1899 which saw stones thrown and the pitch invaded at the game's close. A decade later a similar accusation, that a referee was 'incompetent or prejudiced', was offered by a Belfast club official as the reason why the home supporters had chased the referee from the field four minutes before the end of the game against a visiting side from Dublin.[80] The frustration or disappointment that supporters could feel if their team under-performed or suffered an unexpected reverse was also cited as a possible cause of crowd disorder. In 1905 this was suggested as the reason behind the stoning of the Cliftonville team at a match in Dublin, and a similar fate befell the referee after a match in Belfast in 1898, allegedly for similar reasons.[81] In some cases such actions, which could force a game to be abandoned or make a replay necessary, were allegedly premeditated. This was the implication of one report of the Co. Antrim Shield final in 1890, when supporters of the losing side invaded the pitch three minutes before time, and broke up the goalposts.[82]

In general, it seems that any unruly or disorderly conduct among spectators was generally related to events on the field of play. It was even suggested in 1889 that this relationship was a reciprocal one, with 'rough play' on either the pitch or the terraces likely to inspire the same behaviour in the other quarter.[83] Before the turn of the century, however, it was being suggested that at least some of the disturbances that were occurring at football matches in Belfast were wholly unrelated to the game itself. In the spring of 1899 the 'disgraceful riot' at an Irish Cup semi-final replay between the Belfast Celtic and Glentoran sides was seen by one local newspaper as marking the entry of 'the curse of party bigotry' to football, and thus 'threatening to destroy not only the reputation of footballers, but the peace of the community'. How accurate this report was is uncertain. The match itself had been stiffly contested, and was in its third replay, so a great deal of tension surrounded the contest. Other reports did not stress the alleged politico-sectarian nature of the violence, and the IFA seem to have put the disturbances down to the fact that Celtic had just conceded an unexpected goal.[84]

However, the spectre of sectarianism among the game's followers in Belfast had arisen, and was not easily to be laid. At the beginning of the following season fights in the crowd and a pitch invasion at a match involving teams from Belfast Celtic and Cliftonville, prompted the secretary of the latter to write to the press clarifying the situation. He stressed the good relations that existed between the two clubs, and suggested that 'those who occasioned the disturbances were not supporters or followers of either club'.[85] Allegations that incidents of disorder at football matches were politically inspired continued, however. In 1902 fans from the Linfield and Belfast Celtic clubs were chased down Belfast's Donegall Road by the police after throwing stones and exchanging 'party tunes' rather than blows. More overtly political, and more serious, disturbances were to come.[86]

The concern that was generated by crowd behaviour led to various measures being taken by clubs, and the football and civil authorities, to prevent and control potential disorder. By late 1889 the Distillery club had posted notices at its ground prohibiting the use of bad language, and was employing 40 stewards to deal with offenders. A year later the Linfield ground was similarly adorned with posters warning against 'profane language etc.'. Such initiatives were apparently of limited use, however, as both 'ear-grating cat calls and grossly offensive language' continued to be heard, alongside demands for further action.[87]

A less direct method of averting such conduct was the increasing of admission prices. This was done by the IFA at the 1891 Irish Cup final, when it was thought that the increasing of prices from 6d. to

9d. for the unreserved part of the stand effectively excluded the lower social orders, who were blamed for the conduct which was 'outraging ordinary ideas of decency and propriety'. Two years later the prices were raised again, making the cheapest ticket 1s. This was done 'to keep the attendance as select as possible', and to exclude the 'rough element'. The implication of one report was that this was now a standard practice.[88] However, as disorders became more serious, so did the measures employed for their control. In May 1893 the police were reported as being on duty at a football match in Belfast for the first time, a fact that one observer thought 'quite a slur on the game'. But the attendance of the RIC at matches was not without its problems. In 1899 two policemen on duty at a Belfast game refused, perhaps wisely, to wade into a crowd and arrest a man who had knocked a linesman unconscious with a stone. Instead they requested that the club's officials retrieve him from the terraces, and only then would they arrest him.[89] The situation was shortly to become even more confused. With a number of clubs becoming limited companies, and purchasing their own grounds, the police in Belfast held that they now needed a warrant, or express permission of the club's board, before they could enter a ground. The situation was seen as so anomalous that an Irish Nationalist member raised the matter in parliament.[90]

This being the case, though, it became largely the prerogative of the game's authorities and supporters to ensure that good order and discipline were maintained at matches. With this in mind, the IFA decided at the beginning of the 1899/1900 season that it would fund the prosecution of any spectators deemed 'guilty of disorderly conduct'. This was in stark contrast to the stance taken a year before, when the Association had taken no action beyond an expression of regret when supporters of the Belfast Celtic club had allegedly stoned opposition players and threatened the referee.[91] An earlier threat to close a club's ground had been taken seriously, but such measures were condemned from an early date as draconian, and potentially damaging to the game's progress in Ireland.[92] In consequence the IFA looked not only to its own resources, but also towards its member clubs and affiliated associations, and their officers, to shoulder their responsibilities.

They were not always as successful as they might have hoped. Within six weeks of the IFA's pledge to prosecute disorderly fans, an incident occurred at a match in Belfast between the Distillery and Belfast Celtic sides. Although the Distillery officials employed a number of stewards, and informed the police of possible violence, the Celtic linesman was struck by a number of stones thrown from the crowd. When questioned about the event the secretary of the Distillery club said that 'it would pass the wit of man to make any other arrangements to preserve order'. Two years later, at a match between the same two teams, an assault on the referee by a supporter led the IFA to give the Celtic club fourteen days in which to prosecute the offender. In the event no action seems to have been taken.[93]

Fears that a lack of effective action would result in football getting 'into the hands of a rowdy, disorderly and unsportsmanlike mob' were somewhat exaggerated, but they did mark out the effective impotence of the authorities.[94] The IFA at least was not to be totally thwarted, however. In August 1909 the 'Improvement Commission' convened under its auspices reported that the disorderly conduct of spectators remained a problem in the game. One possible solution was renewed prosecutions, both by the Association itself and its member clubs. It was possibly this decision that prompted a court action at Antrim petty sessions in December of that year, when a spectator at a local game was prosecuted by the IFA for an assault on a referee. The resultant £1 fine, with the same amount in costs, was perhaps not a great deterrent.[95]

Whatever the actual effects of these initiatives, by 1911 at least one observer in Belfast thought that football crowds there were more orderly than before. To some extent this is reflected in the records of the IFA, whose minute books record only two incidents of reported disorder between 1905 and 1911. The raising of the issue of the role of the police in Belfast in parliament in 1908 had been met by the response that 'no disturbance of moment has arisen at any football match in Belfast for a considerable time past'. In April of that year, and again in March 1910, the Linfield and Belfast Celtic clubs – the two teams most clearly identified with opposing religious and political parties – played benefit games for a number of Celtic players. In the last instance Joseph Devlin, the Nationalist Member of Parliament for West Belfast, actually kicked off the match. All these games were carried off without any reported trouble.[96]

In September 1912, however, the most serious disturbance to date at any match in Ireland occurred at the ground of the Belfast Celtic club. The occasion was provided by the first Irish League game of the season between the Belfast Celtic and Linfield teams. At half time the visiting team led by a goal to nil after a closely fought but fairly played first forty-five minutes. During the interval a number of fistfights broke out on the terraces. The intervention of the RIC heralded an escalation of the violence, with spectators stoning each other and the police. The fighting spilled over onto the pitch, with the teams still in the pavilion. Eventually gunfire was heard, and among the fifty or so casualties later admitted to the city's hospitals more than one was suffering from gunshot wounds.

The exact acts that precipitated the riot were disputed in the press, but the Unionist newspapers had little doubt about the real motivations of those involved. The *Belfast Newsletter* portrayed the Celtic supporters as the aggressors. Flourishing a flag in the green and white colours of the Celtic team, and a banner with the slogan 'Play up Celtic', the home supporters had rushed the visitors. They in turn unfurled an Orange Order bannerette and a Union flag, and the two parties met under their respective colours. The *Northern Whig* largely agreed with this report, but added that shouts of 'Home Rule for Ireland' had precipitated the inevitable escalation of violence. The *Irish News*, the Belfast Nationalist newspaper, played down the political aspects of the disturbance, but admitted that the rival fans had indulged in singing 'party songs' before the game.[97]

Others more distant from the action had little doubt as to the context of the riot. The Dublin press dismissed it as a 'political riot, pure and simple'. The elderly Nationalist historian Alice Stopford Green wrote to *The Times* from her London home, stressing the fact that the display of the Union flag 'was for party purposes', and asking whether 'every scrap of green was regarded as treasonable'.[98] Two rather more neutral witnesses suggested that the riot had little connection with the game, and more to do with external tensions.

The referee, an Englishman from Stockport, wrote to the IFA to explain his abandoning of the game. He confirmed that 'the disturbance had nothing to do with the game' and that previous to the riot he had 'had no trouble on the field with players or spectators'. The RIC Commissioner for Belfast reported to the authorities in Dublin Castle that 'the followers of these clubs belong to different parties', and that this was the primary reason for the conflict.[99]

It is also important to realise this unprecedented outbreak of violence at a football match took place at a time of growing political tension and militancy in Ireland. The third Home Rule bill had been introduced in April that year, and, with the loss of the House of Lords' veto the previous year, seemed to be inexorably making its way towards the statute book. Two days before the riot Edward Carson, the increasingly militant leader of the Irish Unionist party, had arrived in Belfast *en route* to visit friends in Co. Antrim, and received a rapturous welcome from members of the city's Unionist Clubs.[100] Belfast had a long and dishonourable tradition of intercommunal disorder, stretching back to the early nineteenth century.[101] Central to this conflict were the inhabitants of two areas in the west of the city: the Pound, later known as the Falls, and Sandy Row. Politico-sectarian, and to a lesser extent sporting rivalries, had been evident between these two groups for more than half a century.[102] It was also these two areas that provided the bulk of the support for the Linfield and Belfast Celtic clubs. An early Celtic game in 1895 saw 'the inhabitants of the Falls Road district turned out to a man' to support their team. The Linfield club, meanwhile, despite moving its pitch almost a mile to the south of its original location off Sandy Row, maintained close links with the Protestant community there that had given birth to it.[103] On this particular occasion, the venue of the match had additional significance. Six months before the riot, Celtic Park had been the scene of an important political rally in support of Home Rule. Winston Churchill, then a Liberal supporter of Home Rule, was the key speaker. On this occasion too there had been a measure of disorder. Prior to the meeting rumours circulated that Loyalist workers had been armed by their employers, and Churchill's car was jeered and rocked as he travelled to the stadium. Later, as he left his hotel, Churchill was mobbed by a hostile crowd.[104]

Essentially it seems that the football match at Celtic Park provided a convenient venue for a clash between two groups of young men of differing religious and political views, but a possible common sporting interest. Given that football crowds in Belfast apparently consisted largely of young, working-class males, drawn at least in part from areas inured to sectarian conflict, it was perhaps inevitable that such a disturbance as that which eventually occurred at Celtic Park should take place. In fact, it is perhaps more surprising that it was not until late in 1912 that it did finally occur.

After the 1912 riot at Celtic Park, new measures for the control of spectators were called for, and taken. Within a week of the riot the Irish Football League produced a handbill signed by its own officials and the secretaries of all the League clubs, for distribution to supporters at matches in their competitions. It stated that 'under no circumstances will any banners, flags, or other emblems of any kind be permitted inside our respective grounds at football matches'. A week later a notice appeared in the Belfast press, similarly signed, promising the prosecution of any offenders. A week after that the League produced 350 stewards' badges for distribution to its member clubs, in the hope that such volunteers would be able 'to preserve order during games'. In December 1912 a motion was passed at a League Management Committee meeting to the effect that 'in all future League and City Cup games where revolver firing is resorted to by spectators, such game or games [are] to be immediately abandoned, and further, that the replay of such game or games [will] take place on grounds closed to the public'.[105] The RIC Commissioner for Belfast, who later informed Dublin Castle that future games involving Belfast Celtic were 'likely to prove a source of trouble', had already called for discussions on crowd control at Belfast games.[106] In the direct aftermath of the riot, troops were sent to the city's shipyards to contain any violence that might erupt there.[107] Yet despite the evidently serious nature of the disturbance, and the arrest and trial of six men, the civil authorities refrained from making any examples. At the Winter Assizes at Londonderry, the judge suggested these were matters that should more properly have been dealt with at the petty sessions. The jury failed to agree on a verdict, and the accused, who 'belonged to different schools', were awarded their train fares home from public funds.[108]

Faced by such apparently ineffective counter-measures, it is perhaps no surprise that disorders continued up to the outbreak of the Great War and beyond, even if they were not on the same scale as that which had occurred at Celtic Park. A month after the Celtic Park riot, a further meeting of the Linfield and Celtic teams saw further shooting, although there were no casualties. That season's Co. Antrim Shield final, in which Linfield defeated the amateur club Cliftonville, was accompanied by 'the inevitable demonstration of revolver music'. The Irish defeat of England in Belfast in March, the first such victory in 21 contests, was remembered by the secretary of the FA as being accompanied by pistol shots and 'such pandemonium ... that even the tall and stolid men of the RIC looked on the crowd with anxious eyes'. The start of the following season saw Linfield supporters invade the pitch at their club's first League game, while once more 'the revolver idiot was present'. In fact by this time the practice of firing warning shots and *feux de joie* at matches was apparently becoming so common that not only was the football correspondent of one Belfast newspaper claiming to be able to identify the type of weapon used by its report, but the captain of one opposition side claimed that he was less worried by the shooting than by 'the hooting and jeering remarks'.[109]

Attempts at controlling disorder also remained largely unchanged, even though the disturbances had taken on a sinister new bent. A handbill produced at the request of the Irish League in September 1913 went rather further than that of the previous year. It requested the crowd to refrain from 'unsportsmanlike conduct', which included bringing along to games 'revolvers and explosive material used to intimidate players and referee'. This was on the grounds that such 'unseemly conduct' was 'bringing our winter pastime into disrepute'. Before the end of the season 'it was unanimously agreed to recommend the clubs to prohibit singing and such like at games as being offensive to spectators'. In the meantime the Co. Antrim FA successfully prosecuted a man for an assault on a referee, but it was perhaps wider events than the actions of any individual or body in Ireland that would solve the problems of association football with respect to its supporters.[110]

In conclusion, it seems that the leading association footballmatches in Ireland were capable of drawing enormous crowds. In Belfast they attracted perhaps the largest crowds of any sporting events staged there. In Dublin too large crowds attended the most prestigious games, though they were probably sometimes exceeded in numbers by those at rugby or Gaelic football games. Over the country as a whole, by 1914 an international association match against England was capable of attracting a crowd of similar proportions to the All-Ireland Gaelic football final.[111]

For the most part the crowds at football matches were made up of young, working-class men. The overwhelming majority of games were conducted in front of comparatively orderly and disciplined gatherings, though disorder and violence could erupt. The majority of such actions were related to the proceedings on the pitch, as the disappointment or frustration of supporters became manifest in their behaviour. In Belfast, however, football crowds came to represent not only rival sporting factions, but also religious and political ones. As political and sectarian tensions in the city rose, they found their expression on the terraces. The best efforts of the sport's clubs and authorities were only partially successful in controlling them.

Perhaps surprisingly, in both their composition and their behaviour football crowds in Ireland had a great deal in common with those elsewhere in the United Kingdom. While it is true that in absolute terms the crowds attending matches in England were much larger, if the 120,000 crowd that attended the 1913 FA Cup final is put into the appropriate contemporary demographic context, the 21,000 crowd that attended the Irish Cup final in the same year was just as large.[112] In both England and Ireland spectators were drawn largely from the male working classes.[113] In both countries crowds were prone to outbursts of disorderly conduct. Contrary to many modern perceptions, football-related violence is not a new phenomenon in England. One study of the game in England over the two decades before the Great War has concluded that 'spectator disorderliness was a recurrent and relatively frequent feature of soccer'. The sport's controlling body in England took action in response to spectator disorder on more than a hundred occasions between 1895 and 1915. Over a similar period, in a single English county, a local newspaper reported nearly 60 incidents of disorderly and riotous conduct at football matches.[114] Yet in at least two crucial aspects the nature of such actions in Ireland and England differed markedly. In the first place, an analysis of the causes of disorders in England has suggested that the political or 'remonstrance' disorder was totally absent.[115] This was patently not so in Ireland. Secondly, the severity of the violence that could occur in Ireland, notably in Belfast in 1912, was much greater than that experienced in England. The number of casualties resulting from the Celtic Park riot was far in excess of anything that occurred in England prior to the Great War.

Across England's northern border, though, more comparable incidents did occur. Largely as a result of Irish immigration, Scotland too experienced politico-sectarian conflict between supporters of rival football clubs. Supporters of the identifiably Irish and Catholic Glasgow Celtic club, and those of the aggressively Protestant Glasgow Rangers, were reportedly engaged in violent confrontations from the mid-1890s, with suggestions of sectarian motivations following a decade later. The supporters of these two clubs also provided perhaps the most violent incident in British football prior to the excesses of the 1970s. In 1909 Celtic and Rangers met in the replayed final of the Scottish Cup. As the game finished in a draw, and the crowd's expectations of extra time went unsatisfied, they invaded the pitch, set fire to the stand and attacked the attendant firemen and police officers. More than a hundred casualties resulted.[116] Yet even in comparison to this event, those in Belfast remained unique. The discharge of firearms at games, notably by the city's 'revolver idiot', marked out the singular nature and frightening potential of football-related violence in Ireland.

The effects of such behaviour and the potential threats it posed were fourfold. In the first place, as we have already suggested, the threat of disorder allegedly deterred some from attending matches.[117] Secondly, although Gaelic games were not totally immune from such activities, crowd violence at association games provided cultural Nationalists with an additional reason for rejecting the game. In 1904 one Nationalist newspaper used its editorial column to highlight what it saw as an innate sectarianism in the game in

Ulster, and the damaging effect that even watching the sport might have on national morale. By 1912 the *Gaelic Athlete* could rather smugly suggest that association crowds were 'rougher' than those at GAA games, while 'sparring exhibitions' both on and off the pitch were a prevalent feature of the game.[118]

Thirdly, crowd disorder at international matches threatened to alienate Irish football from the game elsewhere in the United Kingdom. Following a riot at a match against Scotland in Dublin in 1913, the Scottish Football Association demanded that the IFA instigate prosecutions against those spectators involved, and issue an official apology. Rumours also circulated that the Scottish team would refuse to play in Ireland in the future. A decade earlier the stoning of the English team in Belfast had led to similar demands by the FA.[119]

Finally, despite the existence of crowd disorder in Dublin and elsewhere, the greater prominence that was given to reports of incidents in Belfast, as well as the unprecedented levels of violence that these could incorporate, led to the perception that football violence in Ireland was a uniquely Belfast-based phenomenon. The stoning of two visiting northern teams in Dublin in 1914 prompted one of the capital's newspapers to suggest that there was a danger that Dublin spectators might 'descend to the level of Belfast football crowds'. The Celtic Park riot in 1912 had led the same newspaper to note that Belfast 'had its own way of doing things'. The sporting memories of one Munsterman formerly resident in Belfast were dominated by recollections that 'at hotly contested football matches a goal would be greeted by a salvo of revolver shots from the spectators, which sent mud and gravel spurting up almost under the feet of the players'.[120] If Belfast's political and religious tensions were being vented in the city's football grounds, the repercussions would possibly be felt both in the city at large and within the game itself.

5

Football and politics

> I stood with a vote prepared to reward
> The man who was worthiest deemed,
> But so many, alas, were morally barred,
> More than I'd ever dreamed.
> 'I've been managing football clubs for 20 years', said one,
> 'So I ought to know the local pubs
> Where the signing on is done.'
>
> *Nomad's Weekly*, 16 Jan. 1909

A satirical view of William Kennedy Gibson, international full back, solicitor and Belfast politician. His initial election campaign in 1909 benefitted from the entreaty to 'Vote for your old football friend'.

Scottish Referee

THE LAST DECADE OF THE NINETEENTH CENTURY, and the first of the twentieth, saw association football in Ireland establish and consolidate its position as a popular pastime. By 1914 it was a major gate-money sport, with an administrative structure that spanned the entire country and thousands of regular players, both amateur and professional. The wider background of this period was one of political, social and cultural development and change. Political Nationalism, though still dominated by the constitutionalist Irish Parliamentary Party, also witnessed the emergence of Sinn Fein as an eclectic grouping of radicals aiming for Irish self-government. From 1907 a rejuvenated Irish Republican Brotherhood also began to re-establish itself as the primary organisation aiming for the creation of an independent Ireland.[1]

At the same time, attempts were made to initiate and reinvigorate a non-political cultural Nationalism, by providing common areas of concern in which men of all political persuasions might involve themselves. The Gaelic League, which sought to revive Irish as a spoken and literary language, was foremost among such organisations.[2] Within Unionism ideologues such as Horace Plunkett and Gerald Balfour sought to reconcile Irish public opinion to the Union through a series of measures that have been seen as constituting a policy of 'constructive Unionism'. Government and educational reforms lay at the heart of a programme that fell short of promoting full self-government, but which entailed the creation of new and unique institutions in Ireland.[3] Additionally, economic and industrial developments seemed to offer the chance of providing some form of class-consciousness and common working-class identity in Ireland. Both Dublin and Belfast were to experience rapid growths in unionisation, and an attendant growth in Labour politics, in the years before the Great War. In conflict with such ideals, however, notably around Belfast and the north-east, were deep religious divisions within the working classes.[4] In essence, a plethora of influences and ideologies existed from which contemporaries could mix and match components almost at will. Sectarianism could exist alongside an acceptance of imperialism, and calls for working class solidarity. Cultural revivalism was not incompatible with constitutional politics, or even attachment to the

Union. Violent rhetoric could be coupled with a call for economic regeneration, but remain distinct from any desire for political separation. A desire for an independent Irish republic need have no inherent component of cultural separatism or de-anglicisation.[5] Thus association football was seeking to establish its identity in Ireland at a time of political development and cultural redefinition. The situation was in many ways a very fluid one, in which allegiances, affiliations and identities waited to be claimed and established.

The image that association football was to assume in Ireland was not therefore immediately apparent upon the game's introduction to Ireland. Perhaps inevitably, though, its identity was eventually to be defined by some in terms of the national and political. Within Irish sport the Gaelic Athletic Association, founded four years after the Irish Football Association, relatively quickly succeeded in defining for itself and the games it controlled an identity that interwove the threads of Nationalism, Catholicism and rurality, which themselves underpinned an emergent Irish identity.

Perhaps the most obvious manifestation of this stance came with the choice of the GAA's patrons. The three original patrons of the GAA represented the three great pillars of the broad Nationalist movement in Ireland. Charles Stewart Parnell, the leader of the Irish Parliamentary Party, was joined by Michael Davitt, the founder of the Land League, and Archbishop Croke of Cashel, the youngest and most political of the Catholic hierarchy. Later they were to be joined by John O'Leary, the Fenian hero of the 1867 rising. The choice of the Catholic parish as the basic unit of administration reinforced the religious identity of the association, as, to some extent, did the reliance upon Sunday play.[6] The prominence of members of the Fenian movement in the GAA's administration from its very founding provided further damning evidence, especially as far as the Dublin Castle authorities were concerned, that the GAA was perhaps as much a political organisation as a sporting one.[7] At club level, the religious and political preferences of individual members were made apparent through the choice of team names, and the selection of playing colours. For example, GAA clubs dubbed Sarsfields, Parnells, and even the rather less likely

Gladstonians could all be found in Mayo before 1900, while some teams at least seem to have had a pronounced tendency to wear green uniforms, a colour occasionally later supplemented with white and orange.[8] For the leading historian of British sport, the GAA in Ireland thereby provides 'arguably the most striking instance of politics shaping sport in modern history'.[9]

The existence of the GAA as an overtly Catholic and Nationalist body, not to mention its 'intensely, even obsessively … anti-British' stance, and its rivalry with other sporting bodies in Ireland, led some GAA members to criticise other sports and their adherents on religious and political, as well as sporting, grounds.[10] For example, Michael Cusack, the founding father of the GAA, railed in 1896 against 'the foreign faction, the Orange Catholics [and] the West Britons' who played association football in Dublin's Phoenix Park. It was a view shared by the author and culturalist D.P. Moran and others. Arthur Griffith's *United Irishman* dismissed the game as simply 'racy of the land of Infallible and Almighty England'.[11] The implication of more measured criticism was also that football was an inherently English and Protestant game. This was clearly a massive over-simplification of the situation. Where the conditions allowed, Catholics as well as Protestants enjoyed both playing and watching the game. Moreover, in some areas of the country clubs became as closely identified with, and as integral parts of, the Catholic community as they did the Protestant.[12] Yet the question remains as to the extent to which the IFA itself, as a corporate sporting body, remained an apolitical and secular institution.

At its founding in November 1880, the IFA was a predictably informal body. Although a number of officers were immediately appointed, exact rules governing the constitution of the Association were not rapidly forthcoming. The small number of clubs playing under association rules at the time meant that at subsequent meetings each club seems simply to have sent along up to two delegates to represent it. In August 1881 a meeting at which only four delegates attended was abandoned as lacking a quorum; the following year a suggestion that another meeting was invalid as not all the Association's clubs had delegates present was overruled.[13]

A greater measure of formality was apparently not long in emerging. During the 1890s the growth in the overall number of clubs playing the game meant that the system as it existed became unwieldy, and the general business of the Association came to be managed by a general committee that was elected at each year's annual general meeting, by the representatives of the clubs. Each club cast eight votes for potential committee members. By 1894 this committee consisted of a dozen members.[14] A number of permanent sub-committees also seem to have been formed within the IFA to deal with particular duties, such as finance and international team selection, which had previously been carried out by the full IFA committee.[15] By this time the IFA had already in part become a federal body, with various regional Associations affiliating to the IFA in Belfast, on behalf of their own member clubs, from 1887. By 1890 county Associations were affiliated from Derry, Down and Antrim, while the Mid-Ulster FA was formed from clubs in Armagh and Tyrone.[16] In March 1901, the IFA committee was reconstituted as the IFA Council. The Council's membership was then to be elected each year at the IFA AGM, with each affiliated club allowed just a single vote. [17] By 1904 the Council consisted of fifteen members.

Two years later, an entirely new constitution was proposed under which the Council members were again to be limited to twelve in number, and nominated by five new regional 'districts'. Five members were to be nominated by a new Belfast and County Antrim Association, and one by Munster. Two each were to be delegated by the Leinster; Londonderry and Donegal; and Armagh, Monaghan, Fermanagh and Cavan Associations. The whole proposal created a measure of uproar, not least from the Dublin clubs, who saw themselves as grossly under-represented.[18] Eventually though, following the redefinition of the Fermanagh and Western FA as a separate district returning its own representative to Council, the renaming of three of the other regions, and the defeat of a proposal that the existing regional Associations should be allocated Council members in proportion to the number of clubs affiliated to them, the new federal constitution was adopted.[19] Further changes would come in 1908/09 when the IFA became a limited company, but these were essentially minimal, and the game would continue to be administered under a similar system for the foreseeable future.

While some details concerning the evolution of the structure of the IFA are unclear, two general movements seem to have been occurring in the first three decades of its existence. In the first place, there was a growing formalisation in the administrative structures of the game. This was reflected in a growth in sub-committees and more regular procedures, and was at least in part necessitated by the growing number of clubs joining the Association. At the same time, at least in theory, the IFA moved comparatively quickly away from being a body composed and representative of individual clubs, towards one in which regional Associations were effectively the real power bases.

However, behind this apparently egalitarian, federal constitution was a system in which an immense amount of power actually rested in the hands of a few men, and even fewer clubs. The possibility certainly existed that individuals associated with the leading clubs in the district could dominate the regional associations. For example, of the ten men to chair the Leinster Football Association between its founding in 1892 and 1909, at least half were active members of the Bohemian club of Dublin.[20] In addition, the fact that most ordinary meetings of the IFA Council were held in Belfast encouraged the provincial associations to nominate men who were resident in the city as their Council members. In this way Thomas Moles first secured a seat on the IFA Council in 1911 as the representative of the Fermanagh and Western Association, although he was in fact a member of the Linfield club, and a journalist with the *Belfast Telegraph*.[21] Finally, the Belfast bias of the constitution from 1907 guaranteed not only a disproportionate level of influence for Ulster delegates, but through this a greater level of power for the professional clubs that dominated the sport in Belfast.

Returning to the relationship between football and politics, judging the IFA by the same criteria that have generally been used to highlight the political nature of the GAA, it becomes clear that religion and politics may well have played some part in the Association's make-up and decisions. The protocols of the day meant that any body, sporting, charitable, or merely social, seeking a place in Irish society required at least one patron. Several football clubs were to benefit considerably through the patronage of individuals or institutions with which they became associated.²² The IFA was to be no different in deciding to appoint a number of honorary officials to act as apparent figureheads, with the probable hope that they would reflect at least some of their personal stature or glory on the Association.²³ The first honorary official appointed by the IFA was Major Spencer Chichester, the third son of the Marquess of Donegall, who was appointed Honorary President in 1880. He was elected to the office at the IFA's first meeting in November of that year, and continued to serve in that capacity for nearly seventeen years. Although his grandson was to be the last Prime Minister of Northern Ireland, and the Chichesters were among the most prominent Protestant and Unionist families in Ulster, Chichester himself seems to have had no particular political interests nor to have been politically active in any way. Neither was he a man of particular wealth or influence outside his local area. His obituary in a local newspaper in 1901 stated simply that 'he bore without abuse the grand old name of gentleman'. His appointment as president of the IFA seems to have been for sporting rather than any great symbolic reasons. Chichester had in fact founded the Moyola Park club, allegedly acted as its trainer, and provided it with a pitch in his demesne that had formerly been used for the playing of cricket and the practice of archery.²⁴

In fact, the potential for offending the political sensibilities of those playing association football in Ireland was recognised at an early stage, and the IFA seems to have consciously avoided any overt political actions for some time. In 1886 the suggestion that the English FA Cup be re-named the 'National Cup' as Scottish and Irish clubs competed in it was thought unsuitable in Ireland. There, it was suggested, 'the latter term would convey a wrong impression ... particularly in Belfast, where the word has become a party war cry with one section of the people and a term of reproach with the other'. For some 'the word "National" savours of Home Rule, green flags, evictions, boycotting and other political associations'. Six years later an attempt to install Thomas Sexton, the then Nationalist MP for West Belfast, as an IFA vice-president was rejected as too political.²⁵

A change in direction apparently occurred at the IFA's AGM in

May 1897, when Chichester was replaced as the IFA's president by the Marquess of Londonderry. Londonderry was allegedly regarded even by some of his own family as being a trifle dim, and was described by one contemporary as one of 'the two stupidest men in Britain', but he was also a major political figure within Irish Unionism. Despite the suggestion on his entering the House of Commons in 1879 that he had 'no excessive amount of application, and none of that devouring ambition which wears men out before their time', he served as Irish Lord Lieutenant in the late 1880s.[26] In 1893 he was prominent in the opposition to the second Home Rule bill, and he was later credited with facilitating the ratification of a number of agreements between Ulster's Tories and Liberal Unionists.[27] This apparently overtly political move by the IFA was followed up in 1900 by further appointments of a similar nature.

As has recently been pointed out, the advent of the Second Boer War had deep repercussions in Ireland.[28] Although it may be an overstatement to say that it was 'the first in a series of increasingly dramatic occurrences which led to the establishment of the Irish Free State',[29] the Boer War certainly split Irish opinion even more sharply along Unionist/Nationalist lines. Putting it simply, Nationalists supported the Boers, while Unionists supported the British military intervention. One Belfast Nationalist later recalled events in just this way, as the city's Nationalist population recoiled from the jingoism of the music halls. Raising the subject in any conversation and awaiting your companion's reaction, suggested one Dublin periodical, was the surest way to tell a man's religion and politics.[30] The world of Irish football did not remain unaffected. The fact that in late 1899, as tensions mounted in the Cape, Belfast Celtic entertained a team known as the Kaffirs from the Orange Free State is probably a coincidence.[31] A number of actions of the IFA were clearly not, however. In January 1900 the Association's Finance Committee donated £20 to the Transvaal War Fund and established its own fund to buy comforts for the troops in South Africa. In May of that year at the Association's AGM, Field Marshall Lord Roberts and General Sir George White were installed as the body's senior vice-presidents.[32] Roberts was at the time the British Commander-in-Chief in South Africa, while

White had secured his own military reputation as the commander of the besieged garrison of Ladysmith.

The extent to which these actions should be seen as motivated solely by political considerations is of course questionable. At the time of his appointment in 1897 the Marquess of Londonderry was very much a major figure in Belfast society, as well as being a politician. He already held a number of honorary offices in the city, including President of the Malone Protestant Reformatory, as well as acting as patron of the non-sectarian Belfast Hospital for Sick Children and the Ulster Hospital for Children and Women.[33] The IFA, as a Belfast-dominated organisation, may have looked naturally to Londonderry as a potential patron. It is perhaps noteworthy that the appointment went largely uncommented on in the Irish press.[34] In the same way, it should be remembered that both Roberts and White were actually Irishmen. White had been born in Co. Antrim, while Roberts was raised in Waterford.[35] Additionally, Irish troops were heavily involved in the fighting in South Africa. In March 1900 the decisive charge in the Battle of Pieter's Hill had been led by the Royal Irish Fusiliers and the Royal Dublin Fusiliers. Their victory and bravery was noted even by the anti-war Nationalist press in Ireland, and the action led to the eventual forming of the Irish Guards.[36] Thus the IFA's actions might be seen as an expression of Irish patriotism, albeit within an imperial context, rather than as expressly political.

Such patriotism, which drew upon some of the same rhetoric and iconography that was eventually to become more common in relation to Irish Nationalism than Unionism, is evident from other actions of the Association. One of the first acts of the IFA in December 1880 was to order headed stationary. It was emblazoned with the Association's new crest, consisting of a stylised, stemless Celtic cross. Admittedly the Association refrained from adopting green as the national colour, opting instead for 'Royal blue jerseys and hose and white knickers', but even the most extreme Nationalist press had to admit that blue was 'regarded by some as the Irish flag'.[37] In September 1911 the specifications for quotations for shirts for the Irish international team included the provision that they be of Irish manufacture. In 1913 the

Association sanctioned the awarding of special medals to the Irish team that had become the first to beat England.[38]

However, the extent to which White's involvement in the South African War, rather than solely his Irish connections, led some to support his candidacy for his post within the IFA is perhaps revealed by a later incident. At the same time as White was elected to the vice-presidency of the IFA he was also elected to a similar honorary position in the Co. Antrim FA. However, at that Association's annual meeting in 1903, a mere fortnight after the government had revealed that the Boer War had cost almost a third of the nation's annual budget, a motion was broached to remove White from his honorary office. It was suggested by the proposer that as the delegates 'had got over the war fever, and the rate payers were now paying the piper, and were not as excited as they were', White should go.[39]

It does seem therefore that the IFA, or more particularly the delegates of the affiliated Associations and clubs that constituted its membership, were quite capable of using the administrative structures of association football for political purposes. However, the reconstitution of the IFA in 1909 as a limited company brought an end to the appointment of honorary officers, and therefore the brief interlude of the IFA as a body with overt political affiliations.

That is not to say that religion and politics were no longer to intrude into the upper echelons of the world of Irish football. There may have been a certain inevitability about the situation. The creation of an elected local government structure in Ireland from the turn of the century meant that men from the same social groups that provided Ireland's sporting administrators were for the first time now involved directly in local politics. For example, in January 1911 both the Honorary Secretary and Treasurer of the Fermanagh and Western FA were elected to Enniskillen Borough Council, the former as a Nationalist councillor for the town's north ward and the latter as a Unionist member for the east ward.[40]

If some football devotees could apparently work happily together in the name of sport despite their political differences, both religion and politics were to continue to be evident in Irish football, and to foment division. At this stage, however, it is important to note that, contrary to some modern speculation, the major disruption that occurred in pre-Great War Irish football was neither politically nor religiously motivated.[41] This was the split between the majority of the senior clubs and the IFA that occurred in 1911/12. This dispute led to the collapse of that year's Irish Cup and Co. Antrim Shield competitions, and ultimately created a new structure within the IFA.

The potential for problems first became apparent in May 1911, when at that year's IFA AGM a dispute began between the senior and junior clubs on one side and the IFA on the other over the allocation of gate monies collected at the Junior international game between Ireland and Scotland in Belfast. Essentially the Senior clubs resented the small amounts they received for the hire of their grounds.[42] The situation took a new twist a few days later when the Irish Football League set about creating a second division for its competition. Several months later this was approved by the IFA, whose Council then proceeded to draw this competition's entrants in the Irish Cup as though they were Senior sides.[43] This ultimately proved unacceptable to the majority of the clubs involved in the two divisions of the League. The established Senior sides were unhappy about the decreased revenues that would be generated by matches against the new sides, while the second division sides were concerned that they would then be permanently classified as Senior sides and therefore unable to enter the Junior competitions that they usually patronised. The result was the refusal of all the clubs concerned to play in the Irish Cup, and the seceding of the Senior clubs from the IFA entirely.[44]

The IFA was now in something of a predicament. Its income was derived primarily from two sources: its proportion of the gates in the final ties of the Irish Cup, and the takings at full international matches played in Ireland.[45] The former competition had now folded for the year, while the IFA had no stadium of its own, and ultimately relied on the Senior clubs to rent it their grounds for internationals. In fact the IFA had earlier agreed to rent the Windsor Park ground in Belfast from the Linfield club for that year's match against Scotland. The context of the dispute then widened, as the Linfield committee, in line with the stance now taken by the other

Senior clubs, seized their chance and demanded an increased rent for the use of their ground.[46] However, a boardroom coup then seems to have taken place at the Linfield club; along with the Bohemian club from Dublin, they recanted and settled for the previous terms of hire. Meanwhile the IFA barred the dissenting Linfield committee members 'from taking any part in football or football management' for two years, and expelled the seven senior clubs, other than Linfield and Bohemians, from the IFA.[47] In some ways the latter was an empty gesture as these clubs had already withdrawn from the IFA to establish the 'New Football Association'. Among their first actions were the playing of a benefit game for the funds of the Shelbourne club in Dublin, and the acquisition of a new trophy for competition. The result by the end of February 1912 was that Irish football was 'in a chaotic state'.[48]

Various reasons were offered as to why the situation had deteriorated to such a degree. One journalist suggested that too much power had been delegated to the IFA's Emergency Committee, which lacked the tact and skill to solve the problems. Another, of contrary political convictions, condemned the IFA for using 'the prescriptions and methods of a third rate Latin-American state'. Delegates to the Irish League, which adopted a position of neutrality in the dispute, thought that at least one club representative had acted in a way that 'had not improved the state of affairs'. The Co. Antrim FA called for those involved to display a 'spirit of moderation all round' that had previously been lacking.[49]

Whatever the cause of the escalation of the problems, their origins were obvious, and lay in the financial situation of both the clubs and the IFA. 'The financial responsibilities of the Senior clubs' had become burdensome over the years, especially with the growth of professionalism and the need for clubs to secure private grounds with better facilities. This necessitated that clubs maximise their incomes, including those sums raised from renting out their grounds. At the same time, the IFA was far from financially secure in 1911. With the advent of this dispute it even had to go as far as seeking a £100 loan from the Co. Antrim FA, and dispensing with the services of the Association's office boy.[50]

Essentially this was a financial dispute, not one based on political or religious divisions. It was clearly not a division on north/south lines, as has been suggested by one later observer.[51] In fact it was the Glentoran club of Belfast and the Shelbourne club of Dublin that were subsequently seen as 'the stalwarts of the new FA', while the only two senior clubs to eventually side with the IFA prior to the full resolution of the problem were the Bohemian club from Dublin and the Belfast-based Linfield side. One Belfast newspaper had even gone so far as to note that the nature of the 'new FA' actually showed 'the friendly terms that exist between Dublin and Belfast sportsmen'. Meanwhile, during the dispute the IFA received letters of support from all the regional associations, including the Leinster and Munster bodies.[52]

In the event the split was healed in time for normality to be resumed the following season. That year's international programme had not been disturbed, though, as the two Irish home games were played on the pitches belonging to the Bohemian and Linfield clubs. There were longer-term repercussions, however. Although ground rents payable by the IFA were pegged at 10 per cent, the terms on which the dispute was resolved allowed for the Senior clubs to have specific individual representation within the IFA structure, the establishment of a new Senior Clubs committee to deal with most disputes involving players and clubs, and a new constitution for the IFA itself.[53]

However, if 1912 saw the satisfactory resolution of one dispute, another, with more clearly sectarian and political undertones, was still to come. This conflict came to the notice of the IFA on 3 December, when a letter was received from the North West FA complaining that the IFA had granted permission for the formation of a Junior Alliance competition in Londonderry. This competition, it alleged, 'had been formed out of spite' and 'to produce political feeling'. However, the IFA Council concluded there was little it could do beyond outlining the respective responsibilities of the regional associations and the clubs in their areas.[54]

A point of origin for this dispute might be located at a charity match between teams representing the Institute and the Derry Guilds clubs in May 1912. The former club was based around the Presbyterian Working Men's Institute, while the Guilds was formed from members of the Derry Catholic Young Men's Society. According to the Unionist and Protestant *Londonderry Sentinel*, following a foul on a Guilds player, a fight broke out between two players from each side which eventually spread to the large crowd present. The players fled the field and the Institute team were eventually pinned in their changing rooms by a crowd singing Nationalist songs. The account offered by the Catholic and Nationalist *Derry Journal* accepted that a fight between players had been the initial catalyst for the incident, but suggested that the main reason for its escalation had been the refusal of the Institute players to continue the match. The crowd of Guilds supporters around the pavilion had not been the singing and chanting mob suggested by the *Sentinel*, but merely 'a group of youths … indulging in chaff and horse-play'. It specifically denied there was any violence or any political banter: in fact, this had only come later when a Protestant mob had arrived from the Fountain area of the city, complete with shouts of 'No Home Rule' and a volley of stones.[55]

The recriminations rolled on. The *Sentinel* later referred to the 'Presbyterian team of football players, besieged for two hours by a howling mob' in its editorial columns, and noted that Catholic children cheered the funeral cortege of an Institute player's wife.[56] The *Journal* consistently accused the *Sentinel* of making political capital from what was essentially a minor sporting incident.[57] Whatever the truth of the matter, there were further footballing repercussions in the city. Towards the end of June the Institute club held its annual social event, to which members of half a dozen other clubs had been invited. They were welcomed as 'showing their sympathy with Institute' and the idea of launching a new local competition was floated. The event closed with the singing of the national anthem.[58] By September the *Journal* was reporting that the new competition would result in football in Londonderry being played 'on sectarian lines', as the city's Protestant clubs had broken away to form their own Alliance competition. The following month reference was made in the paper to the 'City of Derry and District (Protestant) Alliance'; while a month after that the phrase 'the holy sectarian Alliance' was mooted.[59]

On New Year's Eve, despite the IFA's original reluctance to become involved, the situation had reached such a level that a subcommittee of the IFA Rules Revision Committee travelled to Londonderry to hear submissions from the interested parties in the city. The delegation heard testimony from representatives of the North West FA and the recently established City of Derry Junior Alliance. The latter organisation had by this time seceded from the former, and was seeking to affiliate to the IFA directly rather than through the local Association. Its clubs had also effectively mounted a boycott of the competitions sponsored by the NWFA. One of the NWFA delegates outlined the situation as he saw it in simple terms. The new Alliance had taken all the local Protestant clubs out of the established league competition, but would not 'let a Catholic club in'. The resulting lack of competitive games had meant that the local league had collapsed, and half a dozen Catholic clubs had taken up Gaelic football. An official of the Alliance countered this view by stating that they had simply advertised for competitors for their competition and accepted all those who applied. The conclusion of the IFA adjudicators was that the Alliance should continue in existence, though accommodations should be made on both sides.[60] A great deal of damage had clearly been done to the game in the city, however, and the local press had made the most of the incidents that had surrounded the formation and continuation of the Alliance.

This incident, although it was unrepresentative in the extreme of general relations within the sport, was not a totally isolated one. Two years before the Londonderry débâcle, in May 1910, the IFA AGM descended into something like chaos. The newly limited Association and its leading members came under severe criticism, not least for their inept handling of the Association's finances. Attempts were also made to introduce two motions that were considered rather controversial. The first was an attempt to confine the venue of the IFA AGM to Belfast, rather than allowing it to rotate around the country as had become the custom. The second was to bar any journalists from seats on the IFA Council.[61] Neither was successful, but at the same time neither was generally regarded as what it at first appeared to be. The result was an investigation by the IFA Emergency Committee into exactly who and which clubs had been responsible for initiating the motions. The general perception of the latter motion had been that it was intended to ensure that James McAnerny, a Catholic journalist with the *Irish News* and a representative of the Belfast Celtic club, was excluded from the IFA Council. The former was allegedly an attempt by 'Protestant Belfast to stop the meetings going to Roman Catholic Dublin'. The implication was that both represented the efforts of a number of predominantly Protestant clubs to ensure that Catholic influence within the IFA was kept to a minimum. Although the inquiry cleared most of those involved of any intentional religious or political motives, the impression remained of a body wracked by internal dissension.[62]

At the core of such a view was the perception held by some that the IFA failed to deal impartially with clubs perceived as Catholic or Nationalist in complexion. The longest lasting and most resilient of such grievances was held by supporters of the Belfast Celtic club. As early as 1895 a correspondent to the *Ulster Football and Cycling News* implied that the existing senior clubs within the IFA were effectively excluding Celtic, and frustrating their efforts to improve their status.[63] Once the club had secured Senior status in 1896 the situation did not improve. An outbreak of violence at a game involving the Celtic club in 1898 led the IFA to 'express regret' over the incident, but take no other action. The following year, further crowd violence in an Irish Cup semi-final tie resulted in the Celtic team being ordered by their committee to refuse to play extra time, and the club forfeiting the tie as a consequence. In 1901 an assault on a referee by supporters at Celtic Park, and the refusal of the Celtic stewards to assist the victim, resulted in the IFA demanding that Celtic prosecute the offenders within a fortnight.[64] Such actions were seen as unnecessarily harsh, especially when compared to measures taken against clubs that were not seen as in any way associated with the Catholic community. For example, in 1899 an attack on a linesman at the Distillery club's ground had seen the IFA 'exonerate the committee' of the club rather than take any punitive measures whatsoever. In 1908 the IFA went as far as temporarily suspending the Celtic club, along with fellow Belfast club

Cliftonville, from football altogether following accusations of rough play and more crowd trouble.[65]

At the same time, the Celtic club and the IFA differed on the contentious issue of Sunday play. In late 1898 Celtic was censured by the IFA for permitting its ground to be used for a sports meeting on a Sunday. Six years later the club proposed, and then withdrew, a motion at the IFA AGM that all clubs should be permitted to make use of their grounds for any purpose on Sundays. This was, according to one opponent of the proposal, a clear attempt 'to introduce … religious matters into their national game'.[66] The situation came to a head in 1910 when James Entwhistle, an Englishman refereeing an Irish Cup match between Celtic and the Bohemians side at Celtic Park, was chased from the field by Celtic supporters four minutes before the end of the game. The IFA decided to suspend Neal Clarke, the Celtic player whom Entwhistle had sent off directly before the ensuing riot, for ten months for foul play. It also demanded that Celtic Park be shut for a month, and gave a warning that further disturbances would be 'severely dealt with'. James Clarke, the Belfast Celtic representative on the IFA Protest, Appeals and Reinstatement Committee that made these decisions, stormed out of the meeting saying 'that there was some underhand work, and he would not sit on this b___y Committee'. He was subsequently suspended for seven months.[67] The directors and shareholders of the Belfast Celtic Football and Athletic Company then voted to withdraw from association football completely due to their 'unfair treatment' by the IFA. In the event a compromise was reached, but niggling grievances had been aired, and a worrying precedent had been set.[68]

Overall it seems that association football in Ireland was both influenced and affected by the politics of the day, and in some areas by allied sectarian considerations. On one level the sport, with its roots outside Ireland and involving competitions between representative teams from the Home Nations, was liable to be portrayed as inherently British, and therefore Protestant and Unionist. Despite such accusations, however, the game enjoyed a large measure of support from men of various religious and political persuasions.

Paradoxically, this situation ultimately had a detrimental effect on the game and its administration. The situation was most acute in Ulster. It was here that football was most popular, but also here that the population was most divided. This was reflected in the creation of confessional clubs, which in turn encouraged friction between opposing players and supporters. The further result of this situation was the conflict within the game's administrative structures, as these came to be convened from those individuals nominated by, and representative of, the clubs. Ironically, men in authority, along with many others, had predicted that this sport would result in greater social cohesion, but it proved on occasion to be fundamentally divisive.

If politics came to exert some influence over Irish football, it was also the case that football could have some influence and importance within Irish politics. More than once prior to 1914 matters pertaining to association football in Ireland were discussed in the House of Commons. In 1906 the matter of the provision of football fields in Dublin's Phoenix Park was twice raised in the House; in 1908 the issue of crowd control at games in Belfast was discussed.[69]

On a more practical level, as political tensions rose in Belfast with what appeared to be the inexorable approach of Home Rule from 1912, Belfast's football clubs, or at least their stadia, became key components in the political struggle. In 1912 visitors to the ground of the Glentoran club in Protestant east Belfast could witness 'the formation of a living Union Jack … by 1,000 Unionists'. In the Catholic west of the city Celtic Park became the venue for the drilling of the Nationalist Irish Volunteers, and mass political rallies in support of Home Rule.[70]

This is not to say that football in Dublin, the sport's other main centre, was immune from the intrusion of politics. During the drawn-out industrial disputes of 1913 the violence that developed between strikers on the one hand and employers and the police on the other at least once found its way into the sporting arena. On 30

August 1913 the *Irish Worker*, the official newspaper of the Irish Transport and General Workers' Union, denounced two Dublin players – Jack Millar of the Bohemian club and Jack Lowry of Shelbourne – as 'scabs'. The next day these two sides met in a charity game to inaugurate Shelbourne's new ground at Sandymount. The result was that the game became 'mixed up in the labour troubles'. Trams going to the game, which the trade union leaders had urged their members to boycott, were stoned, as were spectators entering the ground. In the end it allegedly took the firing of a revolver by a tram passenger to prevent further disorder in the area. It was apparently this incident, however, that catalysed two days of sporadic rioting across the city, during which two men died.[71]

In the same year a less sanguinary but perhaps more powerful political demonstration took place at another Dublin football match. The international match against Scotland at Bohemian's Dalymount ground was attended by the Lord Lieutenant, the earl of Aberdeen. The expected pomp and ceremony of the occasion got off to rather a bad start. According to one account he was 'received with but a moderate degree of enthusiasm' by many in the crowd, while others displayed a marked 'indifference'. The 'Ireland's Own' band, hired to provide the pre-match entertainment, complicated matters by refusing to play 'God save the King'. Only the hurried arrival of a military band from the nearby Marlborough Barracks saved the occasion.[72]

In Dublin, as in Belfast, politics and association football almost coincidentally came into close and intimate contact. At the same time, the popularity of football in some areas made it a potential vote-winner for politicians. If during the game's early years its followers had sought to associate it with men of standing in the hope of broadening its appeal, so in later years men seeking power and influence were not slow to use the game's popularity to enhance their own images. In 1892 one Belfast newspaper, commenting on the ubiquitous Michael Davitt kicking off an association football match in Glasgow, thought that it was 'bad taste to give any club a political tinge'.[73] However, such populist tactics were eventually to become evident in domestic Irish politics too. In 1901, in what was described as 'a new departure in Dublin', the Bohemian club's new ground at Dalymount was opened by Timothy Harrington, the Member of Parliament for the city's Harbour constituency, and the serving Lord Mayor. Wearing his mayoral chain of office, Harrington raised the club flag and kicked off the game against Shelbourne.[74] Some years before Harrington had been the originator of the campaign of agrarian protest known as the 'Plan of Campaign'; the following year he was to be a leading member of the Irish Land Conference as a tenant's representative. He was also allegedly given an extended term as Lord Mayor to ensure that a royal visit in 1903 was not given municipal recognition.[75] In Londonderry in January 1910, a few days prior to the general election, the Marquess of Hamilton, the prospective Unionist Member of Parliament for the city, kicked off a game between the Institute and St Columb's Court teams in the city.[76] In Belfast Joseph Devlin, the city's only Nationalist MP, could be seen more than once kicking off matches at the Celtic Park ground in his West Belfast constituency. Two months after the 1910 election, for example, he patronised a benefit match between the Belfast Celtic and Linfield clubs, being played for an injured Celtic player. This was despite the fact that Devlin had been instrumental in founding one of the earliest GAA clubs in the city.[77] However, events in the previous year in Belfast had perhaps thrown into sharpest relief the potential importance and utility of association football in Belfast politics.

The political situation in Belfast during the first decade of the twentieth century was in a state of flux. The Franchise Act of 1884 and the Redistribution Act of the following year had quadrupled Belfast's parliamentary electorate, and established the West of the city as a marginal seat. Between 1885 and 1892 the constituency was represented first by a Conservative, then by a Nationalist, then by a Liberal Unionist. In 1906, after fourteen years as a Liberal Unionist seat, the West Belfast constituency was taken with a sixteen-vote majority by Joseph Devlin, the leading Nationalist figure in Ulster. He was to hold it for more than a decade and a half. In a by-election in 1902, T.H. Sloan, a radical, militant Protestant evangelical, was elected as the Belfast Protestant Association member for the South Belfast constituency against official Unionist opposition. With the defeat of the second Home Rule bill in 1893 the way had been opened for the emergent Ulster Party, based in Belfast on the existing Conservative Association, to be faced by a number of populist candidates playing on their protestantism or espousing labour values. At the municipal level the Belfast Corporation Act of 1896 gave the city the widest franchise of any urban centre in Ireland. Partly as a result of this, and due to the general dissatisfaction with the existing Conservative hegemony, the 1897 election saw the first Labour representatives elected to the city's council.[78] By and large, though, the enduring sectarian pattern of Belfast politics, and the overwhelming importance of the national issue, had been established. A Unionist/Nationalist dichotomy, buttressed by the Protestant/Catholic division of the community, provided the fundamental basis of Belfast politics. The 1896 act, which had been drawn up with the agreement of the Belfast Catholic Committee, not only enlarged the franchise but also divided the city into fifteen wards. Two of these, Falls and Smithfield, were almost exclusively Catholic, while the remaining thirteen had guaranteed Protestant majorities. Meanwhile, complete revolt by Belfast's Protestant majority against their established political leaders could still be effectively 'restrained by a sectarian leash'.[79] It was against this background that a new factor emerged in Belfast's political life.

The annual municipal elections, at which a third of the Corporation's councillors were required to seek re-election, were held in mid-January each year. On 9 January 1909 Belfast's leading sports newspaper, *Ireland's Saturday Night*, headed its front page with an appropriate cartoon, and announced that 'two gentlemen, well known in football circles' had been nominated for council seats.[80] In fact, three men were involved in the election who had close connections with association football in the city. One of these was Joseph Donnelly, a Catholic Nationalist solicitor. With the backing of the United Irish League, the main Nationalist constituency organisation, Donnelly was almost assured of taking the vacant councillorship in the Falls division.[81] He was a director of the Belfast Celtic club, and occasionally attended Irish Football Association meetings. Unsurprisingly Donnelly won the seat, which he then retained until 1915. In fact the Celtic boardroom seems to have provided a sanctuary for a number of men who were significant figures in the west Belfast Nationalist organisation. These included Daniel McCann, the man credited with engineering Devlin's parliamentary victory in 1906, and who served as the managing director of the club for two decades.[82] Hugh McAlinden, an active chairman of the club, was also a prominent member of Devlin's political entourage.[83]

The second football-related candidate was Brice McIlroy, a prosperous building contractor and a sitting councillor for the Victoria Ward. McIlroy had first been elected to the city council at a by-election in February 1902, as a reformist 'independent conservative' candidate, having earlier left the Belfast Conservative Association's ranks.[84] The following month he acted as one of the seven original subscribers to the flotation of the Glentoran Recreation Company Ltd, which was based around the existing Glentoran Football Club. He then became a director of the new company, a position he was to hold into the 1920s. The club's new stadium lay at the heart of the Victoria ward, amid a mass of newly built terraced housing designed for the use of the artisans employed in the nearby shipyards.[85] Like Donnelly in the Catholic- and Nationalist-dominated Falls ward, by 1909 McIlroy's victory in overwhelmingly Protestant and Unionist Victoria was seen as 'a foregone conclusion'.[86]

Rather more interesting than Donnelly or McIlroy was the other footballing candidate, William Kennedy Gibson. Like Donnelly, Gibson was a solicitor, and like McIlroy he was a well-known figure in the city. Unlike either though, his political potential was perhaps far from obvious.

Gibson had been born in Glasgow in 1877. His father, Andrew, had come to Belfast from Scotland in the early 1880s to act as a shipping agent. Over the next three decades the elder Gibson established himself a secure place in the city's commercial, intellectual and sporting elites. By 1910 Andrew Gibson was the Belfast agent of both the Burns and Cunard Lines. He was also a governor of the Belfast Library and Society for Promoting Knowledge, colloquially known as the Linen Hall Library. In fact, in 1901 he had been responsible for providing the library with a collection of works by and on Robert Burns that was unrivalled in the world. He was also regarded as an authority on the Irish poet Thomas Moore, and had been elected a fellow of the Royal Society of Antiquaries in Ireland. Under the auspices of the Linen Hall he also became involved in the 1903 Belfast Harp Festival, and joined the Irish Folk Song Society.[87] On the sporting front, Gibson served for three years as the president of the Belfast Bowling Club, and as early as 1892 was both president of Cliftonville Football Club and a vice-president of the Irish Football Association.[88]

From this background the younger Gibson emerged as a gifted scholar and footballer; it was perhaps the latter distinction that was to prove most useful and enduring. William made his debut for his local senior team, Cliftonville, while still at school, and went on to have a distinguished career for club and country. His international debut, at the age of 16, was a memorable occasion for both Gibson himself and Ireland. On 3 March 1894, playing at left half, and in front of his home crowd at Cliftonville, Gibson scored a late goal for Ireland in their match against England.[89] It was the first time in thirteen meetings that Ireland had avoided defeat against England, and also the first occasion on which Ireland scored more than a single goal against an England team. Although he never scored again for Ireland, Gibson went on to become a stalwart of the national side and, despite a number of injuries, made thirteen appearances over an eight-year period. These included the game against Wales at Llandudno in February 1898, when, having adopted his more usual position of left back, Gibson captained Ireland to their first-ever international victory outside Belfast. Even when Ireland were comprehensively defeated, as they frequently were, Gibson could be depended on to play 'his usual sterling game at back'. The extent of Gibson's talents was recognised outside Ireland. In 1902 rumours circulated in Scotland that he would be invited to play in that country's team, as he was qualified to do by birth. An invitation was also received from Sunderland, the English League champions, for Gibson to sign for them. In his memoirs published in the 1930s, Sir Frederick Wall, who spent forty years as the secretary of the Football Association in England, remembered Gibson as among the three finest players ever to appear in an Irish side.[90] In a less than glorious period for Irish football, Gibson secured himself an enviable reputation.

Gibson's club career coincided with amateur side Cliftonville's golden age. Gibson's team won Ireland's premier club competition, the Irish Cup, on three consecutive occasions from 1895. In 1894 and 1898 Cliftonville lifted the Co. Antrim Shield, for which all the major Belfast clubs competed. In the latter match Gibson twice cleared off the line as the Linfield club, the hot favourites, were defeated by the odd goal in five.[91] Even the eventual end of his playing career did not mean the end of Gibson's involvement with Irish football. Following in his father's footsteps, he went on to become the president of the Cliftonville club, and in 1906 was reportedly 'still a leading man in the management of the club'. In the following year Gibson was elected a vice-president of the Irish Football Association. As a solicitor he also offered legal advice to the Association, and was widely credited with overseeing its establishment as a limited company. As the press reminded the electorate in 1909, Gibson had become, at different times, an indispensable component of Irish football as both a player and an administrator.[92]

Gibson's prospective candidature in the Clifton ward of the city had been rumoured before his nomination was received, and the prospects of the 'well-known and popular Irish international fullback' were seen as good.[93] The ward, situated in the north of the city, was socially and religiously mixed. It included a large number of new suburban villas in prosperous, predominantly Protestant areas, such as Cliftonville, where Gibson himself lived; but it also contained the 'almost exclusively Catholic' enclave of Ardoyne. The population as a whole was around one quarter Catholic, making it arguably the ward that best represented the religious balance of the city as a whole.[94]

Gibson was to stand for election as an independent candidate, as was his opponent William G. Turner, a Protestant fruiterer from the Shankill Road. However, from the beginning of the campaign it was evident that Turner was receiving the backing of the Belfast Conservative Association and other powerful interests in the city. On 8 January he was joined on a platform by Councillor Dunlop, the Conservative candidate for the Aldermanship in the same ward. A few days later Turner and Dunlop held a joint public meeting in Clifton Street Orange Hall, complete with Orange flute band. One

Orange Lodge even went so far as to publish its promise of support for Turner. Similar endorsement of Turner came from the Belfast Temperance Voters' Executive.[95]

Gibson's campaign was rather less conventional. He too acquired established political allies, by way of the Citizens' Association. This was an ostensibly non-sectarian, non-political grouping, concerned primarily with competence and economy in the city's management.[96] Gibson also recruited a number of less orthodox allies. On 10 January he convened a meeting in the Cliftonville club pavilion, following a City Cup match between Cliftonville and Linfield. It was chaired by James Barron, Gibson's former partner in the back line of both Cliftonville and Ireland. The first speaker was Hugh Hegan of Portadown, the chairman of the IFA. He stressed 'Mr Gibson's capacity not only as a footballer in the past, but as a rising young public man'. Hegan was followed by John Warwick, the president of Linfield, who similarly endorsed Gibson.[97] Gibson had already addressed groups of workers in the ward from the back of a brake as they left the mills in the area, and went on to organise a number of street meetings. The members of the Cliftonville club had earlier convened a meeting 'to arrange for a thorough canvass of the division'.[98]

Municipal politics in Belfast were generally a rather dull affair, but the Nationalist *Irish News* now suggested that Gibson had 'taken the issue from the old lines of party, or inter-party rivalry and controversy, and given a certain vigour and breeziness to the campaign'. A speaker at one subsequent meeting would compare Gibson to the then President of the United States, Theodore Roosevelt, 'one of the finest all round sportsmen'.[99] Turner, perhaps sensing that he was losing ground, stressed that although he was not a labour candidate he would ensure that 'the working man had a fair crack of the whip'. He also suggested at one of his own meetings that 'Mr Gibson asked to be supported on the ground that he was a good footballer'.[100] This was not wholly true, as Gibson had published a detailed list of his priorities if returned, but he was certainly making the most of his footballing prowess, and connections.[101]

In the event both Turner and Gibson placed advertisements in *Ireland's Saturday Night*, in an apparent attempt to attract the football vote. The situation was perhaps best summed up by their respective slogans: Turner was 'the representative candidate', while Gibson was 'your old football friend'.[102] In the event Gibson was returned to the city council with the second largest majority, and the largest individual vote of any candidate. One football correspondent noted that his return was testimony to 'both the popularity of the new councillor and his association with the game'. The Conservative and Unionist *Belfast Newsletter*, which had supported Turner, put Gibson's victory down to both the support lent by the Citizens' Association and 'the enthusiastic support of the members of Cliftonville Football Club'.[103] The relative importance of each might be judged by the fact that the following year the same ward saw another election, this time for a vacant aldermanship. In a comparable turnout, John Tyrell, the official Citizens' Association candidate, was the eventual victor, but by fewer than 200 votes (see Table 5.1). His defeated opponent had wished to know whether Tyrell's recent application for membership at Cliftonville had been made 'as a sportsman or for municipal purposes'.

TABLE 5.1
Comparison of election results in Clifton Ward, Belfast, 1909–10

	1909 Councillorship	1910 Aldermanship
	W. K. Gibson 2,535 (Ind/Czn Assn/CFC)	J. Tyrrell (Czn Assn) 1,952
	W.G. Turner (Ind/Con) 1,146	T.E. Alexander (Con) 1,755
Majority	1,389	197
Total vote	3,681	3,707

Source: *Irish News* 16 Jan. 1909, 17 Jan. 1910.

Gibson himself had felt grateful enough to his football colleagues to write to them thanking them for their help. The Irish Football Association responded with a letter of congratulation. The motion to send it was proposed by Joseph MacBride, who many years later would chair the Association, and seconded by Daniel McCann of Belfast Celtic.[104]

In Gibson's case it seems that association football could be utilised, both in a practical and an ideological sense, to motivate and influence a sizeable proportion of the electorate.[105] While his example is of course an extreme one, it was not a totally isolated case. The frequency with which politicians of various creeds sought to associate themselves with the game is proof of the political potential of association football in Ireland. If politics was to affect Irish football, so too could football influence politics.

Prior to the outbreak of the Great War, association football in Ireland was occasionally affected by the country's politics. Despite its portrayal by some Nationalists as the preserve of Protestants and Unionists, it was actually the fact that it attracted men of all religious and political beliefs that presented the sport and its authorities with many of its problems. At one very prominent level this led to crowd violence as groups of young men with a common interest in football, but opposing views on politics and religion, clashed on the terraces and the pitches. On another it had repercussions for the sport itself, as administrators interpreted each other's actions as being coloured by religious or political considerations; and blamed their own failures and disappointments on the perceived bigotry and bias of others.

Despite such internecine conflict, and the apparent incompatibility of the wider interests of the game's devotees, association football could also prove a unifying force. All Irishmen were united in their determination to defeat the English, and took especially great pleasure in the eventual 'long hoped and wished for victory over the Saxon'.[106] In a domestic context, support for and involvement in the game could lend a man a certain appeal and attractiveness that one at least managed to translate momentarily into success at the ballot box. Association football was capable of uniting Irishmen as well as dividing them, provided, of course, that matters of religion and the constitution could be laid aside.

6

The game 1914–24
decline and division

> No barrier would ever separate Irishmen on the field of sport. One and all they wished well to the whole country and every class of its people.
>
> *Irish News*, 1 June 1914

> There is an undercurrent to kill soccer here. Hysteria is a dreadful disease when it grips the minds of otherwise sensible people.
>
> [Dublin] *Evening Telegraph*, 14 Nov. 1919

The outbreak of war in 1914 eventually led to a scaling down of football activity in Ireland, partly in an attempt not to distract the population from the war effort. However, as this recruiting poster shows, even football had its uses in war.

Ulster Museum

GRAND INTERNATIONAL MATCH

Great Britain, Ireland and Allies

VERSUS

Germany, Austria and Allies

Where match will be played:

SOMEWHERE IN GERMANY

TEAMS—

Unlimited Number of Players on each side

Referee———**UNITED STATES**

Linesmen———**ITALY** and **HOLLAND**

Irishmen wishing to play in this—the greatest match the World has ever seen—<u>should enter their names at once</u> at the nearest Recruiting Office so that they may be thoroughly trained for the Great Day.

MEDALS WILL BE PRESENTED AFTER THE MATCH.

By the summer of 1914, association football was in a remarkably buoyant position in Ireland. The Irish Cup, still regarded as the country's blue ribbon competition, had been contested by teams from Ulster and Leinster that season; an estimated crowd of almost 20,000 saw Glentoran defeat Linfield in the final in March 1914. The cream of Irish playing talent may have migrated to clubs in England and Scotland, but the professional game in Ireland provided a good living for some men, and still managed to draw substantial crowds.

Outside the professional game, the sport also flourished. The previous year had seen the inauguration of national intervarsity championships, with teams from the University Colleges in Dublin and Galway taking on sides from the Queen's University of Belfast and Trinity College Dublin.[1] Financially too the game was enjoying some success. Football was reckoned in the summer of 1914 to 'have paid its way during the last two seasons'. The Glentoran club returned profits for the year in excess of £600, despite making a small loss on a tour of central Europe. The IFA's bank account stood in the black to the tune of almost £1,800.[2] With regard to the international side, the previous two seasons saw longed-for achievements finally realised. Two victories had been achieved over England: the first ever in Belfast in 1913, and then a decisive 3–0 victory at Middlesborough in 1914. The latter win, combined with a narrow victory over Wales in Wrexham, and a draw with Scotland in Belfast, was enough to give Ireland their first-ever outright triumph in the Home International series in three decades of competition. The IFA celebrated with a formal dinner, and by presenting gold watches to the team members.[3]

Internationally and domestically Irish association football was arguably at the peak of its achievements. A decade later, however, the game in Ireland was divided and its devotees at odds with each other. These developments were to take place in tandem with the political partition of the country, and, perhaps as a result, those who have examined the split in Irish football have generally seen it as a repercussion of partition, or at least as a sporting manifestation of the general political tensions that resulted in the creation of two Irish states. To one Irish historian, the game became 'a victim of political tensions'. To a leading football historian, politics 'inevitably affected the game', with the result being its separation into two spheres of influence co-terminus with the new political border. For another noted sports historian the times saw 'Irish soccer…disturbed by politics'. The most recent comments on the situation see it as simply the case that 'Ireland's politics…divided soccer along the lines of partition'.[4] Yet if such was the case, and Ireland's political development fundamentally and inevitably affected its sporting structures, it is perhaps strange to note that association football was almost unique as a sport in Ireland in that its administration split contemporaneously with the political division of the country. On the whole, despite the political pressures of the period, established sports of all sorts tended to retain their all-Ireland structure. Not surprisingly, given its Nationalist ethos, the GAA resisted some limited pressure to divide its administrative structures along the lines of the country's new frontier. Rugby, which in its early days had experienced rival administrations and then briefly a form of joint sovereignty, remained under a single governing body, and continued its domestic competitions on the established territorial divisions.[5] Some sports actually formed all-Ireland administrations for the first time at the same instant that Ireland, and Irish football, were undergoing partition. For example, it was not until 1923 that Irish cricket established a lasting union, and Ireland's two rival athletics bodies actually used the era of political partition as a backdrop to their final unification.[6] The underlying questions must therefore be why the pressures that caused such fundamental changes in association football could be resisted elsewhere; and to what extent football's partition was truly a result of external pressures and the changing nature of the period.

Bearing these facts in mind, the purpose of the present chapter is to chart the events that occurred in Irish football between the end of the 1913/14 season and the eventual establishment and recognition of a rival body to the IFA in Dublin. In doing so it will attempt to place these in their contemporary context, and weigh the evidence as to exactly why Irish football, unlike the vast majority of sports in Ireland, was to suffer partition along with the country itself.

Establishing a full understanding of the situation in 1914 in fact demands a longer-term appreciation of the nature, origins and development of association football in Ireland. As has already been alluded to, the game's governing authorities did not always see eye to eye over certain issues.[7] In fact, the case can be made that fundamental differences existed between football as it was played, watched and administered in Belfast, and as it existed in the capital. In turn, these created important areas of conflict of interest, and long-lasting antagonisms. One such bone of contention concerned the selection of the international team.

As early as 1893 footballers in Dublin voiced their belief that they were being excluded from international honours by an IFA dominated by the representatives of the larger northern clubs.[8] It was a call that proved exceedingly resilient and widespread. In 1894 the IFA was accused in *Sport*, a Dublin-based weekly, of 'behaving most unfairly' in 'overlooking the Dubliners'. The following year the *Irish Times* took up the call. The season after that it was noted that 'a good deal of indignation' was said to have been felt due to the continued absence of Dublin players from the Irish side. In 1897 the IFA was characterised in the Dublin press as giving 'as little encouragement...as they possibly can to football in Leinster'; and the national side was simply referred to as 'Belfast'.[9] In Belfast too the alleged vagaries of the selection procedure were noted, to such a degree that topical cartoons were twice produced detailing the complaints of the Dubliners.[10] In 1899 a Leinster delegate to the IFA annual general meeting was reported as speaking of 'sectional warfare and internecine strife between the provinces', and the perception that 'the Irish Association existed for Belfast alone'.[11] Similarly, the Dublin authorities had earlier been aggrieved by IFA decisions not to stage international matches in the capital.[12]

It had also occasionally been suggested that the IFA tended to favour Belfast clubs in its decisions regarding the running of its competitions. During the game's early years in the capital the city's leading club, Dublin Association, dissolved itself following allegations that the IFA had unfairly favoured its Belfast opponents in making a number of decisions. In 1899 it was suggested that an ongoing 'feud between Ulster and Leinster' had its origins in this incident.[13] By 1901 it was thought 'a narrow spirit of provincialism' almost invariably marked the decisions of the IFA[14] The previous year one English observer had noted the fact that as the IFA was based in Belfast, and 'the professional clubs there rule the roost', football was suffering elsewhere in Ireland.[15]

On a more general level the IFA was accused by its southern members of failing to do enough to promote the game outside Ulster. The LFA itself complained of a lack of support from the IFA within six months of its being established. Within a year the general failure of the IFA to support the newly founded LFA had been twice noted in a Belfast paper. A decade later one Dublin supporter of the game dismissed the IFA as simply 'a hard-headed business-like lot' obsessed with the minutiae of the finances of the game.[16] By 1908 the Leinster FA were £50 in debt, and approached the IFA about the possibility of a grant to cover the shortfall. The outcomes were allegedly guffaws from some IFA committee men, and the offer of a loan of £200, which was eventually refused due to the restrictive conditions attached to it.[17]

Even at this early stage, the indignation generated by the affair in Leinster was seen as potentially causing the local Association to break away from Belfast. This was seen as even more likely after the IFA's decision the following month to play the early rounds of the Irish Cup on a regional basis, thereby depriving the Dublin clubs of potentially lucrative ties with their Belfast adversaries.[18] Despite an apparent scorn for the financial aspects of the game, or perhaps because of it, the Leinster FA continued to challenge the IFA sporadically on money matters. At the 1911 IFA annual general meeting the Leinster representatives raised the point that they had been 'unfairly treated' over that year's Irish Cup final. Although both finalists had been Dublin sides, and the match had taken place in the capital, as the proprietors of the competition the IFA had taken a proportion of the gate back to Belfast, while the local Association received nothing. Additionally, they pointed out, the Leinster Association now paid annual affiliation fees of £30 to the IFA, but received nothing in return.[19]

How real the supposed anti-Dublin and pro-Belfast biases of the IFA were is debatable. Certainly it was not only Dubliners that felt themselves discriminated against. A Co. Derry player wrote to a Dublin newspaper in 1884 complaining that the international team was selected only from Belfast players; four years later an Armagh correspondent accused the IFA of being biased in favour of Belfast clubs. In 1898 another Derry writer accused the IFA committee members of being subject to 'too much clubbism', the result being a Belfast bias. Fourteen years later a correspondent from Cookstown in Co. Tyrone accused the IFA of discriminating against his club. [20]

There was also some support within Belfast for the proposition of bias. The complaints of the Dubliners regarding international selection were thought by one Belfast journalist to be 'not without justice'.[21] The 'bogus clubs affair' of 1903/04, which saw two Belfast senior clubs paying the affiliation fees of fictitious Junior sides in order to secure more votes at IFA annual general meetings, is indeed evidence of the willingness of some Belfast clubs to go to considerable lengths to gain influence and power within the game's central administration. Even then it was reckoned this could have 'disastrous consequences to sport'. [22]

At the same time, however, it is conspicuous that most criticisms of international selection tended to follow defeats of the national side. A suggestion in a Dublin newspaper on St Patrick's Day in 1906 that that they should 'drown the shamrock and the selecting five' (i.e. the international selectors) followed a defeat in Dublin by a mediocre Scottish side. In 1884 it had been pointed out that although the Dublin press had dismissed that year's defeat by the English Association team as 'a so-called international' because the Irish side was selected solely from players attached to Belfast clubs, the Irish victory over England at lacrosse had been warmly praised despite the similar make-up of team members.[23] In general, criticism of the IFA's international selectors seems to have declined somewhat from around 1903, when Ireland's results provided more uplifting reading for observers. Simultaneously it was suggested by one commentator that teams were 'built up from a gate point of view', that is Belfast players were selected for games in Belfast, while

Dubliners were picked for matches in the capital. As only six internationals were played in Dublin between 1882 and 1914, it was perhaps understandable that so few Dublin players appeared in the national side.[24]

Another consideration may have been the fact that teams were initially selected from a limited number of clubs so as to allow 'a certain amount of combination' between the players. This was certainly the suggestion as far as the selection of Ireland's international rugby teams was concerned.[25] Additionally it should be remembered that the existence of Belfast as an enclave of professionalism, and the rejection of the professional game in Dublin entirely until 1904, presented the propositions that the better Irish players would migrate to Belfast in order to profit from their skills, and that the extra training and coaching that the northern professionals were required to undertake made them better players.[26] At the same time the complaints of those involved in the game in Leinster must be seen in the contemporary administrative context, where regional Associations were composed of the members of local clubs, and as such were looked to to protect their own interests. If it was just rampant localism that critics of the IFA were railing against, their own motivation must be seen as having identical roots.

Such a view was sometimes tangible in the nature of complaints from the south. In 1894 Orlando Coote, the son of a Church of Ireland clergyman and the founder of the Athlone Town club in Westmeath, commented on an IFA ruling in favour of the Londonderry side St Columb's Court in an Irish Cup tie with Bohemians of Dublin. It was his opinion that the IFA, 'which is almost entirely composed of northern members', did 'of course, prefer Derry to Dublin'. By 1905 the focus of Dublin's criticisms had shifted slightly. That year the accusation was made that the Irish team was 'an English team, pure and simple', as the majority of the players were English-based professionals.[27] The Leinster Association was simply attending to the interests of its own members, and in doing so came into conflict with like-minded individuals from Ulster.

If there were long-standing grievances between footballers in

Ulster and Leinster, there were also fundamental sporting differences between the game of football as it was perceived and played in Belfast and in Dublin. As we have seen, the origins of the game in the two centres were strikingly different. The game in Belfast owed its origins primarily to Scottish immigrants, which resulted in football relatively quickly taking its place in the life and leisure of the working man there. In Dublin, at least initially, the sport was more closely associated with the city's educational establishments, and therefore arguably took on a less plebeian aura.[28] One of the results of this situation was a further bifurcation in the game between the predominantly amateur-oriented Dublin sport and the professionally dominated Belfast game. The division was seen contemporarily as very real. In 1906 a Leinster FA official stated proudly that he regarded his Association as the true guardians of amateurism in Ireland.[29]

Given these circumstances, it was perhaps inevitable that for almost two decades before the split a certain air of sporting and administrative jealousy seemed to have entered the relationship between the various subsidiary bodies within the sport. In 1913 for the first time the Leinster FA became the largest divisional association within the IFA, displacing the Co. Antrim FA from its leading position.[30] One Belfast correspondent had already prophetically forecast that the day when the game's headquarters would be required to shift to the capital was not far off.[31] In 1900 one northern administrator, with the same probable developments in mind, had suggested the formation of an Ulster FA to protect the future interests of the Belfast clubs.[32] At the 1904 IFA annual general meeting, despite the instigation of administrative reforms aimed at giving the provincial Associations a greater say in IFA affairs, 'an air of mutual distrust' was still said to have pervaded the proceedings.[33]

The final area of conflict between north and south in the game was provided by the issue of sabbatarianism. In 1898 a request from the LFA to the IFA to sanction Sunday play was unceremoniously rejected, and the motion that Sunday play was 'very detrimental to the interests of the game' passed unanimously. Three years later a similar request from a member of the Munster FA received the curt reply that 'while there was no specific rule to prevent matches being played on Sunday the Association had invariably prohibited same'.[34] In 1904 it was Leinster clubs that again backed the proposal for Sunday play at the IFA general meeting, when it was brought forward by the Belfast Celtic club. The situation was seen as quite ridiculous in Dublin, where 'generally games of all kinds on a Sunday are a matter of course'. This was, however, rejected by the IFA.[35] In 1906, in response to an enquiry made by the Irish League, the IFA ruled that even to play football on a pitch also used for Sunday sports meetings was unacceptable.[36]

While it can be argued that in itself sabbatarianism was in fact a specific manifestation of religious differences between Protestant observers and more liberal Catholics, the issue was not clear-cut. Although the Catholic Belfast Celtic club was in favour of Sunday play, the Catholic clergy in Derry were opposed, at least ostensibly for reasons of sabbath observance.[37] In 1884 one Dublin-based Protestant was reluctantly forced to admit that advertising for Sunday sports would 'not appear even in a Roman Catholic newspaper' in Ulster.[38]

Thus by the time of the outbreak of the Great War in August 1914, there was already a history of long-standing enmity between the football authorities in Belfast and Dublin on purely sporting grounds. There were also basic differences in the nature of the game, and men's attitudes towards it, in the sport's two main centres.

The war came as the preparations of Ireland's footballing fraternity for the new season were well under way. Yet the declaration of war placed Ireland's footballing authorities in something of a quandary. While the season initially got under way as normal, by November club delegates to the IFA were raising the question of whether the game should be suspended for the duration of hostilities. This was the decision that had been taken by the Irish rugby authorities in September, and that now had supporters in Association circles. In the event the IFA deferred any decision until it had consulted with the FA and the Scottish FA.[39]

In January 1915 a sub-committee of the FA met with representatives of the War Office, and an emergency meeting of the International Board was convened in Blackpool. While the English and Scottish associations agreed to suspend all games under their jurisdiction at the close of the present season, the IFA demurred. Its representatives agreed to suspend international matches, which in effect it could not avoid given the decisions of the FA and SFA, but contended that it would carry on with its Irish Cup competition, as the matches provided ideal venues for military recruiting.[40]

The officials of the Irish Football League followed a similar pattern of behaviour. After the completion of the competition for the 1914/15 season, when eight teams competed and Belfast Celtic emerged as winners, a British inter-League conference was held. The Irish competition was then suspended for the following year, and re-suspended in each of the following three years. However, the senior clubs that had competed in the last pre-war championship were kept in membership of the League, and permission was given 'to form district competitions'.[41] The result was that the two Dublin-based League sides, Shelbourne and Bohemians, took up places in the already established Leinster Senior League, while the remaining sides, all of which were from Belfast or the adjacent area, formed the Belfast and District Football League.[42] A practical partition of the game was already taking place.

Why exactly these decisions were taken is uncertain. It may have been the case that the game's authorities were keen to show their commitment to the war effort, and decided to scale down what could become a dangerous diversion from the task in hand. Certainly the IFA had demonstrated its support for the war in other ways. Within a month of the opening of hostilities 200 guineas had been donated to war charities, and in October 1915 the Association's secretary was 'placed at the disposal of the Recruiting Committee' in Belfast for as long as he might be required. The Irish Football League did likewise, staging a benefit game for the Prince of Wales's War Relief Fund in September 1914. [43]

At the same time, the needs of the state had to be balanced against what was best for the people. One reported reason for the initial maintenance of the game was the belief that its abandonment 'would open temptations for the masses on Saturday afternoons'.[44] The effective scaling down of the game that followed therefore answered both calls. Football was maintained at such a level that it could divert men from less savoury pastimes, but would not prove an impediment to the war effort.

In reality, however, the establishment of smaller scale competitions may have had rather less to do with aiding the war effort than with serving the self-interest of the larger clubs. As early as September 1914 it was noted that the crowds at matches in Belfast had become noticeably smaller. Of 20,000 men who were thought to have enlisted in the city, more than half were said to be 'football followers'. By the end of the month gates were said to be 35 per cent down on the previous year.[45]

The reduced income that this situation yielded was made even less by the attitudes and actions of some of those involved in the game. In September 1914 the League authorities agreed that soldiers in uniform were to be admitted free to all games under their organisation's auspices. The following month, though, it was reported that the members of the various volunteer bodies in Belfast were abusing the privilege by donning their uniforms in order to enter grounds without paying.[46]

In addition, the war had brought a surge in demand for Belfast's industrial products. Overtime in the city's mills and factories, allegedly paid at minimum rates, occupied many who would normally have been seen on the terraces on Saturday afternoons. Extra shifts in Harland and Wolff's shipyard were said to have 'spoiled the attendance' at various matches, and there were 'poor prospects of good gates' in early 1915.[47] Thus gates, and therefore club incomes from admission payments, were severely in decline in Belfast. A further factor may have been the relative decline in real incomes of workers in the city during the first two years of the war, as wages failed to keep pace with wartime inflation.[48] Football had now become an expensive luxury.

The financial pressure under which the game's authorities and the senior clubs in the north found themselves is apparent from their reactions to the situation. In November 1914 the Irish Football League management committee ruled that professional players' wages should be reduced by a quarter, and that no bonuses of any kind were to be paid. The result was a number of appeals by players to the IFA. One David Williams, an English professional with the Belfast Celtic club whose basic wages had been cut from £3 a week to £2 5s., approached the IFA seeking a release from his contract as he could no longer support his family on the money he received. The IFA, mindful of 'the peculiar circumstances surrounding football this year', urged player and club to settle on a one-eighth reduction rather than a quarter.[49]

By the beginning of the next season, even more stringent measures were adopted. Although a motion in the IFA Council to ban professionalism entirely for the duration of the war was defeated, a maximum wage of £1 per game was set. The League deferred to the IFA on all matters regarding professional players, and the Belfast and District League eventually followed suit.[50] To cap it all, summer wages, paid to retain players on a club's books, were ruled 'out of the question'.[51]

The professional game in Ulster continued in the doldrums into mid-1916. At Lurgan it had been suggested in early 1915 that 1,400 supporters of the town's Glenavon club had enlisted. Eighteen months later, with more than half of that number killed, wounded or missing, the sport in the town was 'given scant attention'.[52] The introduction of an entertainment tax in 1916, which required a levy to be placed on ticket sales, deepened the financial distress of clubs that were already struggling to meet their liabilities. At least one Belfast resident, mindful of the tax's contribution to the war effort, decided to avoid all events upon which it was levied. A letter writing campaign by the IFA seeking some exemptions elicited a limited response from the politicians targeted.[53]

The depletion of Ulster's available manpower also had serious repercussions for football at the lower levels. The Co. Antrim FA, whose area of authority included most of Belfast, was approached as early as September 1914 by clubs seeking the return of their subscriptions due to 'the War preventing clubs from being carried on'. By May 1916 the number of affiliated clubs had fallen from the pre-war total of 140 to only 63.[54] The team based at the Central Presbyterian Association was perhaps typical of many in Belfast, in that it 'vigorously carried out its programme for the season in spite of the depletion in the ranks of the players' during the 1914/15 season, but for the rest of the war was returned as 'not active'.[55]

In Dublin too the war was to affect the game. Applications for the use of the public pitches in Phoenix Park during the 1914/15 season fell by a third compared with the previous year, suggesting that far fewer junior games were being played. By December 1914 the Bohemian club was said to have lost forty playing members to the military. Membership of the Leinster FA was eventually to be halved, although all the Association's competitions continued to run.[56]

However, by the end of the 1916/17 season, football in the Belfast area at least was enjoying something of a renaissance. An estimated 19,000 crowd witnessed that year's Irish Cup final, although it was held during a snowstorm. The total income for the Belfast and District League exceeded £500, and interest in playing the game at a lower level revived enough for an unaffiliated league competition to be started by junior clubs in Belfast.[57]

The reasons for this change of fortune were probably fourfold. In the first place, recruitment in Ireland had slowed considerably by this time. The number of men enlisting in 1917 was less than a sixth of the total that had rushed to the colours during the five wartime months of 1914 and the following year.[58] The depleted number of potential spectators and junior players had at least stabilised. Also, due to the continued demands of the war, and increasing wages that were now outstripping prices, many industrial workers in the city were enjoying steady employment and regular wages that were unknown before the conflict.[59] The potential for participation in the game, as a player or a paying spectator, was growing once more.

Simultaneously, the return of some leading Irish players to their home country had allegedly led to a marked improvement in the game. Three players, including the Irish captain Val Harris, had signed for Irish clubs from English teams prior to the outbreak of the war. By early 1916 the suspension of the professional game in England, and the threat of conscription, had encouraged others to follow suit. Among these men was Elisha Scott, the Irish international goalkeeper.[60] Finally, and perhaps most importantly, football provided the escape from monotony and the drudgery of reality that it always had done. Football was the ideal antidote to the increasing demands of the workplace, and the increasingly depressing news from the front. The contribution of football to the ongoing Irish war effort was summed up by one observer in August 1917.

> Shipyards, munition works, foundries and other important industrial concerns must be kept going at full pressure if we are to come out of the struggle victoriously. Recreation also must be found for the workers engaged in the gigantic task of keeping our Army and Navy supplied with the necessaries of war, and no more innocuous, healthy, or fascinating pastime could possibly be afforded them in the open air than Soccer.

The 'benificient and soothing influence to tired work-worn toilers' that the game had generated was matched only by the tax revenue that had accrued to the Treasury, and the charitable donations made by the sport's authorities and supporters.[61] At least initially, even in Belfast, wartime circumstances had given the game a new potential for promoting the social cohesion that its early advocates had so stressed. In October 1914 Belfast's Celtic Park, which two years before had been the scene of both a massive Home Rule rally and an intense politico-sectarian riot during a football match, saw the flags of the Allied nations, including the Union flag, proudly displayed.[62]

At the front, too, football had its uses. The formidable sight of Irish soldiers going over the top dribbling a football into no-man's-land, and then on into the German trenches, was an event that quickly entered the folklore of the War. It has also been cited by later historians as an example of the recklessness and camaraderie that typified the Irish contribution to the struggle on the Western Front, and 'the power of the sporting motif' in the recruiting strategies of the day.[63] Despite its exploitation for propaganda purposes, the incident, if it happened at all, was actually perpetrated by a unit with an Irish name, but in which 'the only two real Irishmen' were the colonel of the regiment and a volunteer stretcher-bearer. The remainder were primarily Cockneys.[64] However, participation in more conventionally staged games, as players or spectators, did provide a release for the pent-up frustrations of the new Irish soldiers, and helped foster unit cohesion and morale. Prior to the battle of Passchendaele, a match between troops from Ulster and men from Dublin allegedly defused the growing political tensions that were threatening to emerge among the Irishmen.[65]

Back home, despite the continuing war, by the beginning of 1918 prospects for the domestic game in Ireland seemed once more to be good. The gate at the initial Irish Cup final tie exceeded £1,000, and two replays followed. The actions of the IFA in maintaining some competitions had ensured that Irish football was 'in a fairly flourishing and healthy condition'.[66] The same could be said of the sport's governing bodies, though perhaps not of some of the leading clubs, nor their players. Although the lack of any international fixtures for four years had greatly reduced the income of the IFA, the pre-war surplus of £2,000 remained largely untouched, as outgoings had been minimal.[67] The Irish League meeting of May 1918 heard that the organisation was 'for the first time in many years' in credit at the bank. This was in stark contrast to the situation four years before, when a deficit of £200 had to be cleared by donations from the member clubs.[68]

With regard to the clubs, though, a quite different situation existed. The Glenavon club in Lurgan had only been saved from impending bankruptcy in 1915 by a grant from the IFA of £50 and the mercy of its creditors.[69] In Dublin the landlords of the Shelbourne club were demanding an increase in the annual rent paid for the pitch to £175, and the proceeds of a fête that had been planned by the club.[70]

It was the professional players, however, that had possibly suffered most during the war. Ten days after the signing of the armistice in November 1918 the maximum wage restrictions imposed by the IFA were rescinded. The players themselves had pre-empted any reforms, though, and had set about establishing a trade union to represent them and 'secure increased remuneration'.[71] An initial meeting took place in Belfast on 18 November, when two professional trade union organisers were installed as the secretary and chairman of the organisation. Their initial objectives were twofold: they wished to end the 'retained list' system, which had been introduced just prior to the war; and they were seeking an improvement on their wages, notably a minimum payment of £3 a week.[72]

Within a month the Irish Football Players Union had 54 members. Two months after that, all but one of the Belfast-based professionals had joined.[73]

The next step was the raising of union funds. The obvious way to achieve this was through the playing of a benefit game, but this required the sanctioning of the IFA and IFL. Despite the apparent threat of a strike by the players, a meeting between a Union delegation, less its paid officials, and the IFA took place in March 1919 after a number of refusals by the Association, and the assertion by the union that it insisted 'on the right to organise'.[74] The primary outcome was a benefit match in May, though attendance was low and little profit was made. With regard to wages, on this occasion the IFA had to some extent out-manoeuvred the Union by already imposing a new maximum wage of £2. It fell well short of the hoped-for sum, but was at least an improvement on the previous official limit, and 25 per cent more than the sum the League had reckoned suitable. Overall, the press reckoned that the demands of most players were satisfied, and interest in the union began to wane.[75]

Perhaps spurred to greater efforts by these developments, in September 1919 the Union approached the IFA seeking an increase in the fee payable to players on international duty; the following month the League received a request that fees payable to players in inter-league games should also be increased. Both demands were for increases of 50 per cent, and neither was successful. In fact, the suggestion was even made that the militancy of one player in the union had led to his being passed over for international duty by the IFA. In the face of such failures and setbacks, it was perhaps no surprise that by the summer of 1920 the union was reckoned to be 'defunct'.[76]

It was against this background of potential unrest among the country's professional players that further divisive developments were taking place in the game. During the late summer of 1918 the Irish League had received contradictory messages from its two Dublin members. The amateur Bohemians club had stated its readiness for the recommencement of the League as soon as possible. The professionals at Shelbourne, however, indicated that they could not compete in any competition in the forthcoming season. In the event the decision was taken only in March 1919 to reinstate the League at the end of that year.[77] As yet no competition involving teams from outside the regional Associations had been re-established. The effective partition of the game necessitated by the war had yet to be fully breached.

Later that year the approach of the Leinster FA to the Co. Antrim FA regarding a possible inter-provincial match led to nothing, as the latter organisation could not find a suitable date.[78] In the meantime the IFA, with the intention of placing the game back at its pre-war pinnacle, established a commission 'for fostering the spread of the Association game'. The situation of the game varied greatly across the country. Within a month four of the IFA's constituent Associations had replied to the IFA's enquiries. The Mid-Ulster Association reckoned it had 'plenty of money to carry on their own Association', although more funds would be needed to allow it to attempt a further spread of the game. The Co. Antrim Association, which constituted the north-east division of the IFA, declared itself 'ready to carry on missionary work with their own funds'. The North West Association sought a grant of £100 to establish a permanent pitch in Londonderry. While no replies had yet been received from the Fermanagh and Western Association or the Munster Association, it was the Leinster Association that so far seemed to have been most badly affected. The number of clubs affiliated to it had fallen by half, and according to one club representative the game was 'at a low ebb in Dublin'. A request for a grant of £300 followed.[79] In the event the IFA granted a sum of £100 directly to the Glenavon club, £50 to the LFA and nothing at all to the Munster FA, which had eventually sought a grant of £200. This, suggested one Dublin journalist, was 'little short of an insult' to footballers outside Ulster.[80]

If financial considerations were both threatening the existence of the established professional clubs and hampering the re-establishment of the wider game, more familiar problems now recurred. Even during the war crowd troubles were not unknown, but now they returned in greater numbers.[81] While the levels of violence reached in 1912 did not recur immediately, there were other worrying developments. In October 1919 a match in Dublin between representative sides from Ulster and Leinster, played to raise funds for the LFA and to raise the profile of the game in the capital, saw members of the crowd attack one of the Ulster players. The incident was seen as serious enough for an LFA delegate to travel to Belfast to apologise personally for the assault.[82] Later the same season the replay of an Irish Cup semi-final in Belfast between the Glentoran and Belfast Celtic sides dissolved into disorder complete with rival flag-waving, anthem singing, and gunshots.[83] The result of this was the suspension, and then temporary withdrawal of Celtic from football entirely, as well as a threatened legal action.[84]

Amid the disorder on the pitches and the terraces, in the committee rooms and at the banks, the lower reaches of the game were also suffering. In May 1920 the IFA's Finance Committee successfully recommended to the IFA Council that that year's intended Junior Cup competition should be abandoned. Their grounds for this were threefold. First the finances of the IFA were seen as inadequate to subsidise the competition, and secondly there were likely to be difficulties in transporting the teams and spectators around the country by rail. Finally, 'the state of the country at the present time' was thought to be less than conducive to the playing of football.[85] The murder of two policemen at Soloheadbeg in Co. Tipperary in January 1919 had heralded the beginning of a period of armed conflict in Ireland that would drag on for four years. By the time of the IFA's decision, more than fifty policemen were dead, along with a number of soldiers and civilians. Barracks and railways had been raided and destroyed, an attempt had been made on the life of the Lord Lieutenant, and a leading Dublin magistrate had been dragged from a tram in the city in broad daylight and shot dead. On the government side, destruction of property and covert assassinations had begun as reprisals; curfews had been imposed in urban areas, and recruiting had begun in Britain to supplement the depleted ranks of the Royal Irish Constabulary.[86] The disturbed state of the country had served to sever another link in the Irish football network. With the Irish Football League competition still suspended, only the Irish Cup remained as a functioning all-Ireland tournament.

Concerns over public safety led to an event that was to be seen, both contemporarily and by later commentators, as the beginning of the end for all-Ireland football. In the 1921 Irish Cup semi-finals, one match was an all-Belfast affair, with Glentoran beating Brantwood in a close game. The other was to be between the Glenavon side, of Lurgan, and Shelbourne from Dublin. A scoreless draw played out at a neutral venue in Belfast meant that a replay was necessary.[87] Under normal circumstances this match would have been played in Dublin. However, under pressure from the Glenavon players, the replay too was fixed for Belfast by the Senior Clubs Committee acting on behalf of the IFA. The Shelbourne club protested against the decision, but without success. The LFA backed it, submitting a motion to the IFA's Emergency Committee condemning the 'unsportsmanlike action' of the Senior Clubs Committee in ordering the Dubliners back to Belfast.[88] The Nationalist press concurred. It was, said one Dublin paper, a 'cruelly unfair edict', and 'nothing other than a death dealing blow to the Dublin team, as far as their connection with the North is concerned'. Belfast's *Irish News* saw the incident as 'both unfair and unsporting'.[89] In the event Shelbourne refused to travel and the tie was awarded to Glenavon. Shelbourne's secretary condemned the decision as 'contrary to all precedents' and 'grossly unfair to our club and to football in Leinster generally'.[90]

A split did not occur immediately, however. Within a fortnight members of the IFA were reportedly attempting a reconciliation with the LFA, and opinions varied as to whether a division of Irish football would follow.[91] In the country at large the civil disorder continued, though the 'Act for the better government of Ireland', which first introduced the idea of political partition onto the statute books, had been in force since December 1920.[92] Football was apparently following in the footsteps of politics when in April 1921 the LFA organised a canvass of its member clubs on the advisability of secession from the IFA. By mid-May the LFA was effectively operating independently of the IFA in granting an extension to the season. On 8 June the LFA voted to disaffiliate from the IFA.[93] The reality of the situation was brought home a fortnight later when the IFA received a short letter from J.A. Ryder, the secretary of the LFA.

It stated simply that 'at a meeting of the representatives of our clubs it was decided to form an association independent of the IFA Ltd'. The IFA replied by warning the LFA's member clubs that they would therefore be unable to play either clubs remaining within the IFA or cross-channel teams.[94]

In Dublin, domestic reorganisation continued apace. The Football League of Ireland, formed to replace the IFL, held its first meeting on 1 June, and admitted eight clubs from the Dublin area to membership. The Football Association of Ireland (FAI) held its inaugural meeting on 2 September.[95] Six days later the new football season began in Ireland, with two rival bodies now contesting the right to control the game across the country.

With major competitions under way in the country outside its control, the IFA apparently faced a *fait accompli*. Partition in Irish football had become a reality. Three weeks before Christmas 1921 the IFA was forced to acknowledge as much when a team from the Queen's University in Belfast applied for permission to play a side from Trinity College in Dublin. Permission was refused as the latter was an LFA member, and therefore no longer affiliated to the IFA.[96] Two months later, in a development that suggests that communication between Dublin and Belfast had broken down entirely, the IFA received notification from the FA in London that the FAI had applied to the International Board for recognition. In March it was reported that the FAI had also applied to the Fédération Internationale de Football Association (FIFA) for membership.[97] FIFA was composed of most of the leading Football Associations in Europe, and acted as the ruling body in the game outside those areas, such as the actual rules of play, over which the International Board exercised authority. All four of the established UK Associations, however, had withdrawn from FIFA in early 1920 following its failure to exclude the Associations from the defeated Central Powers nations.[98] Thus the way was open for the FAI to seek international recognition without effective opposition from its rival Irish body. However, instant recognition was not forthcoming from either FIFA or the International Board, and the FAI was effectively left in international limbo, although advances were made in reorganising the sport domestically. A call for the FAI to approach the

Italian FA with regard to arranging a series of fixtures necessarily came to nothing, despite the suggestion that 'for reasons unnecessary to indicate' the Italians were likely to be sympathetic to the FAI situation.[99]

The next major development came in December 1922, when the IFA Council voted unanimously to write to the FAI seeking a conference. The Linfield club from Belfast also offered its services, by way of potentially playing a charity match in Dublin, to promote 'the reconciliation of the Dublin clubs'. Six weeks later, and after an initially curt response, the FAI agreed to a meeting, to be held in Dublin in February 1923.[100] The IFA delegation was led by the Association's chairman, Captain James Wilton, while the FAI contingent was headed by J.F. Harrison, who chaired both the FAI and the LFA.

The meeting, which lasted three hours, was held in an atmosphere described as 'frigid'.[101] It opened tentatively, with an agreement that there should be no actual chair. Wilton then opened the proceedings by enquiring as to the exact nature of the Dubliners' grievances and asking them to suggest 'a remedy to end the present dispute'. Understandably Harrison replied that he was under the impression that as the IFA had initiated the conference, Wilton's group had some new suggestions 'to put forward'. Wilton responded that he was still unaware of the Dubliners' precise grievances, and enquired whether the FAI delegation had 'Council powers'. Harrison then simply stated that although his delegation did not have Council powers, it was 'very representative and ... would have great weight with our clubs'. Wilton, apparently more sure of his ground, then made an opening offer. The 'Southern portion of Ireland' was to have 'more representation on the [IFA] Council than they had previous to the dispute'. He also promised that 'Dublin should have a fair share of all International matches' played in Ireland. Finally, a reconciliation would see all IFA Council meetings held alternately in Belfast and Dublin.

The response was not positive. J. Smurthwaite, an official of the LFA and the honorary secretary of the Football League of Ireland, said he considered that the IFA was too interested in financial matters, and did too little with regard to the 'fostering of the game throughout the country'. J.F Murphy, another FAI delegate, agreed, stressed the pressure the game was under in his area from 'another powerful body' (presumably the GAA), and then insisted that 'football being run from Belfast' was unacceptable, and suggested 'dual control'. Wilton then cited the International Board's ruling in June 1922 that there could be 'only one controlling body' in the country. Murphy again stressed the threat from the GAA and the unacceptability of football's headquarters remaining in Belfast. Wilton responded by enquiring whether the movement of the game's controlling body to the Irish capital was an indispensable condition of any settlement. Harrison stated that he thought it was so, and took up the issue of the unfair representation of the southern Associations on the old IFA Council. Two other FAI delegates than called for the IFA members to offer any further concrete proposal they had for consideration. Wilton again stated that he had 'no definite recommendation' on any matter, but noted that under any new system if the regional Associations outside Ulster had enough member clubs, they might well 'get entire control of the game'. However, he did point out that he believed that at the time of its inception in 1908, the Council structure reflected the relative position of the sport across the country.

Wilton then returned to the subject of the location of any unified body's offices, and suggested that if the delegates assembled were not to insist they be located in Dublin, other matters might be agreed. Smurthwaite noted the political connotations that the Munster clubs would put on the Association's offices remaining in Belfast. Wilton then suggested that the entire conference be postponed. A fifth FAI member, J.L. Brennan, who was also the chairman of the Football League of Ireland, rejected the possible political implications of the situation, noting instead that 'the whole question is one of control'. Wilton then repeated the outline of his initial offer of 'revised representation', and 'your fair share of internationals', and added an undertaking to make a greater effort in promoting the spread of the game.

At this stage Harrison suggested that the IFA members leave the room, to allow his delegation to formulate a new set of proposals. The IFA members agreed and retired. After some delay the meeting was reconvened and Harrison put a series of ten points to the IFA delegation. The first allowed for all football in the Irish Free State to come under the jurisdiction of the FAI; the second allowed 'any club or organisation' outside that territory to affiliate to the FAI if it so chose. Thirdly the IFA was to be reconstituted as the North of Ireland FA, 'or some similarly named body'. Fourthly and fifthly the new Association was to assume a position in relation to the FAI 'similar to the relations existing between the Football Association of England and the Army Association', though it was to have full control over clubs affiliated to it and playing in its own competitions. Sixthly, joint competitions and internationals were to be managed by a body constituted 'on a scale to be arranged'. Seventhly, each body would recognise the others disciplinary arrangements and penalties. Items eight and nine stated that each association would control its own funds, while international revenues would be shared 'on a scale to be arranged'. Finally, the new northern Association would have an undefined role in selecting the Irish international team. The IFA delegation, after some discussion, stated that it 'would not go further than clause three', and described the remaining conditions as 'absolutely impossible'. They were 'not even a basis for discussion'. The meeting then broke up, and the delegates went their separate ways.[102] Nine days later the full IFA Council considered the minutes of the meeting, and congratulated Wilton on his role. The Linfield club also withdrew its offer of playing any matches in Dublin.[103] The conflict within Irish football was no nearer to resolution.

In the summer of 1923 the FAI made another attempt to gain recognition from the International Board. Again, however, at the instigation of the IFA, this was withheld. A further application for FIFA membership had already been made in April, following the visit of the French club Gallia to Dublin. This application was to be successful in September 1923, following FIFA consultations with the British Foreign Office on the constitutional status of the Irish Free State. The FAI now became an internationally recognised sporting body as the Football Association of the Irish Free State (FAIFS).[104]

Given this development, it was perhaps inevitable that change would come within the International Board. Although in August 1923 the IFA stressed that it had not yet recognised the FAIFS, it agreed to attend a conference of the British Associations that made up the International Board, to discuss the state of football in Ireland.[105] This meeting was held in Liverpool on 18 October 1923. Two delegates attended from each of the Football Associations of England, Scotland and Wales, along with their secretaries. Four members from the IFA and five from the FAIFS were also present, and J.C. Clegg, the chairman of the FA, oversaw the meeting. The FAIFS stated that it now recognised the 'Northern Ireland Football Association as the sole governing body of football in that portion of Ireland that is outside the Irish Free State', and therefore wished to be recognised as the equivalent body within its own territory. It also sought that the IFA should change its name to one 'which will indicate precisely the extent of its control'. In addition it agreed to enforce IFA disciplinary decisions in the Free State, and looked forward to competitions which would 'facilitate intercourse' between clubs from the two jurisdictions. Crucially, the FAIFS also suggested that a joint international selection committee should be established to select an Irish team, 'with equal representation from the two Irish Associations'.

The conference could not enforce any of its decisions, but made a number of recommendations. It agreed to the FAI becoming the FAIFS, to the division of Ireland into two spheres of influence, and to the mutual recognition of the decisions of the two bodies. It also recommended the recognition of the FAIFS by the International Board as 'an Association with Dominion status' and the removal of all suspensions invoked by the IFA at the time of the initial split and since.[106] Crucially, however, the fine detail of the internal settlement was left to be negotiated between the two Associations that it now recognised in Ireland.

The initiative in these matters was now taken by the FAIFS. A month after the Liverpool conference the secretary of the FAIFS wrote to the IFA seeking compliance with the Board's recommendations, and its own demands. Another month passed before the IFA replied to arrange a meeting.[107] The IFA then received two important letters. The first arrived from the FAIFS, saying it was willing to meet to discuss international team selection. The second was from Frederick Wall, the secretary of the FA in London, stressing that there had been 'matters with which the [Liverpool] conference could not deal', and which must be settled 'by friendly conversations between the two [Irish] Associations'. The IFA Council then passed a motion to meet the FAIFS in Belfast.[108]

The meeting eventually took place in Belfast on 8 March 1924. The IFA had prepared a six-point plan for presentation to the FAIFS. It suggested that committees governing the major competitions be made up jointly of IFA and FAIFS members. A new All-Ireland Association was to be formed, with its Council membership composed similarly. The FAIFS, however, was to be internally autonomous in domestic affairs. Finally, the international team was to be selected by a committee with equal IFA and FAIFS membership, but permanently chaired by an IFA member.[109] The FAIFS delegates reserved judgement in the short term, but replied to the IFA twelve days later. Their Council rejected the IFA offer on the single issue of the chairmanship of the international selection committee, which it demanded should alternate. Negotiations were, for the time at least, at an end.[110]

Over the next three decades several attempts were made at reconciliation, and meetings between IFA members and football enthusiasts and officials from the Irish Free State and the Irish Republic were not uncommon.[111] However, a unified football administration remained unobtainable. Until 1950 the IFA continued to select its international side without reference to the Irish border, and thus 32 players were eventually to be capped by both Irish Associations. This situation was ended following an approach by the FAI to FIFA, and the last link in the all-Ireland continuity of the game was ended. Pending major political upheavals, association football in Ireland was irrevocably divided.

To summarise the apparent situation, the economic and social conditions experienced in Ireland during the Great War had created a bust and then a boom in professional football. The amateur game was also affected, though it failed to benefit from the improving economic situation from 1917. For the game's Juniors it was a period of sharp and continued decline. The civil disorder and economic slump that followed the war led to a more general downturn in the game's fortunes. The greatest sufferers this time were not the sport's authorities, who had reserves on which they could fall back, but the limited number of paid players in the game, and the clubs that employed them.

Initially the advent of war had reinstated football as a potential force for promoting social cohesion. In the longer term, though, this may have been truer for Irishmen in France than in Ireland. At home rival fans continued to promote disorder, but more worrying in the longer term was the effective partitioning of the game between Belfast and Dublin. Continued domestic strife laid further practical impediments in the way of re-establishing the game on a national basis. Specific sporting incidents then occurred, notably the decision to order the replay of Shelbourne's Irish Cup semi-final match in Belfast, which alienated some in Dublin from the game's authorities in Belfast. Despite attempted mediation and negotiation, the eventual outcome was the partitioning of the game coincident with the country's new political frontier. The immediate reasons for the division of Irish football in effect seem to have lain in the civil disorder that had occurred in the country, and then its eventual political realignment.

These events have usually been interpreted as admitting the political developments of the day into the world of Irish football, and as inevitably precipitating the division of football in Ireland along the lines of political partition. Taken at face value, there does seem to be a great deal of evidence to support this view. Politics had occasionally proved to be a divisive influence in Irish football prior to the outbreak of the Great War, and its influence after this time should not be discounted.[112] Some members of the contemporary press corps certainly portrayed the events after the Great War in this way. In September 1920 one Dublin paper noted that supporters of the game in the capital found the coincidence of sport and politics in Belfast rather distasteful. Dubliners, it suggested, 'had a better sense of the proper location of things'. In Belfast, following the founding of the rival Association to the IFA, the *Belfast Telegraph* reported the coming of the new football season, in which Irish football would effectively be partitioned, in heavily political terms. The North was to 'proceed about its football business with the motto "ourselves alone" forced upon it'. Football's partition had been instigated by 'those whose watchword in other affairs has always been "no partition"'.[113]

Those stressing the apparently political dimensions of the split received further ammunition from an incident that occurred at an amateur international match against France, in Paris, in February 1921. The exact details of what became known as 'the flag incident' are uncertain. By one account 'Sinn Fein' tricolours were waved in the crowd, by another the French authorities provided the flags for the Irish team to march behind on taking to the pitch. Whichever was correct, exception was taken by the team and officials, and the offending symbols had to be removed before the match could proceed. When questioned about the incident, the Chairman of the IFA stated that he had simply asked for all flags to be removed in an attempt to keep politics out of the game. However, the Nationalist press in Dublin took a different slant on the event. The most extreme comment came from the pages of the *Catholic Bulletin*, which alleged that the incident revealed the 'bitter anti-Irish atmosphere of Association football' and the air of 'slavery in which all important Association matches are played'.[114] The LFA reportedly 'had a desperate time' as a result of the event, and held lengthy discussions as to what it would do about it. In general, 'feeling on the matter in Dublin was high'. The outcome, however, was simply to supply football's adversaries with further ammunition at a crucial juncture.[115] Contemporary parallels were also drawn between political events and footballing ones. The ratification of the Anglo-Irish treaty by the Dáil in January 1922 led one observer to see the reunification of Irish football as now 'inevitable'.[116]

Moreover, if the press could be eager to exploit and highlight the political potential of the situation, so apparently were some football clubs. Belfast Celtic, the most important Catholic- and Nationalist-backed club in Ulster, had withdrawn from the sport in 1920, and was not to return to association football until 1924.[117] In its absence, football in Nationalist west Belfast centred on the local

Falls League competition. Previously this organisation had remained unaffiliated to any governing body. However, in the summer of 1921, as the IFA and the FAI struggled for power in Ireland, in an act of great symbolism, it opted to place itself under the auspices of the Dublin-based FAI.[118]

It should also be remembered that some of the individuals involved most intimately in the breakdown of relations between Belfast and Dublin were extremely political animals. Captain James Wilton, the Chairman of the IFA, was a case in point. Prior to the Great War he had been a prominent member of the Ulster Volunteer Force in Londonderry. Having volunteered for war service, he was badly wounded on the first day of the Battle of the Somme and again the following year, and was subsequently awarded the Military Cross for bravery.[119] Later described as 'a staunch Unionist', he was to serve two terms as the Lord Mayor of Londonderry, and was a very active member of the various loyal institutions in the city. In 1937 he received a knighthood for his services to Northern Ireland.[120] A fellow IFA member was Thomas Moles, who served on the IFA Emergency Committee that was accused in 1919 of being both too powerful and composed of men too distant from the realities of the game.[121] Moles was a journalist by trade, but had been involved in the loyalist gun-running at Larne in 1914, and was to go on to have a prominent political career as a proponent of hard-line Unionism in the Northern Ireland state. In later years he would be seen by one local GAA official as the man who not only oversaw the division of athletics in Ireland, but also engineered the 'break in Soccer football'.[122]

The simple timing of the division of the game, happening as it did in tandem with the political division of the country, seemingly suggests that politics must have played some part in events. The emergence of rival football administrations along with parallel political structures is perhaps highly suggestive of a neatly symbiotic relationship between sport and politics.

However, if some journalists saw the split as essentially fomented by politics, others did not. In Ireland's capital, *Sport* argued that politics in themselves had nothing to do with the formation of the new Dublin-based Association, though it appealed to enthusiasts' 'nationality as Irishmen' as well as 'their instincts of sportsmanship as sportsmen'.[123] It was not so sure about the apolitical nature of the IFA, but the new body had 'no relation to politics whatsoever'.[124] This may to some extent have been an example of special pleading, but nonetheless it stressed the perceived subservience of political considerations to sporting ones in the south. *Sport*'s Northern correspondent agreed that there were no political implications to the split, and that such suggestions were 'garbage of an ill-founded character'.[125]

At the same time, if some clubs used the emergent situation for political point-scoring, others at least tried to avoid the growing political divides within the sport and the country at large. Although it was the decision of the IFA concerning the replaying of their Irish Cup semi-final that had arguably catalysed the split in the first place, in May 1921 hopes were still high that Shelbourne, along with fellow Dubliners Bohemians, would rejoin the Irish League competition. Even two months after the initial meeting of the new Association, both Shelbourne and Bohemians were apparently keeping their options open with regard to rejoining the IFA.[126] By mid-1923 Saul Wigoder, the former chairman of the Shelbourne club and the president of the LFA in 1921, was organising a 'new Dublin Football Association' through which clubs in the capital could affiliate to the IFA. Representatives of the Bohemian club were also seeking to send a delegation to meet with the IFA.[127]

As for the possible intrusion of the personal political preferences of individuals within the IFA into their football decision-making, there is some evidence that this too may have been limited. James Wilton actually acted primarily as a conciliator in the period when the IFA and the rival body based in Dublin were engaged in their initial struggles. In April 1921 Wilton 'was all honey and sympathy' at the meeting between the IFA and the LFA following the dismissal of Shelbourne from the Irish Cup, and despite the fact that preparations were under way to 'sever the Belfast connection', it was reckoned by one Ulster journalist that a 'secession' was consequently unlikely. In February 1922 Wilton noted in the IFA Council that the matter of possible recognition of the FAI 'would require very careful handling', and urged the IFA not to admit former Falls

League teams to the IFA for fear of antagonising the FAI. At the initial meeting of IFA and FAI delegates in February 1923 it was Wilton, as head of the IFA delegation, who initially promoted some measure of conciliation. It was also reputedly Wilton that had 'extended the hand of friendship' the previous year, and initiated the contacts that had led to the meeting.[128] Despite his later image as a pillar of Unionism, Wilton actually entered local politics in Londonderry in 1923 as the only councillor for the city's North Ward not backed by the local Unionist party. Instead he stood, and was returned unopposed, as a 'British Legion candidate'. His first term as Lord Mayor in 1935 saw him elected to the post with the unanimous support of the city council, including the Nationalist members. It may have been something of a eulogy, but on his death in 1946 it was remembered in the city's Nationalist press that 'there was not a Nationalist or a Catholic who knew him who had other than the kindliest word for Jemmy Wilton'.[129]

With regard to the blame that can be apportioned to Moles, while he was certainly a zealous Unionist and an extremely authoritarian character, the roles of the committees on which he served during the dispute were quickly diminished by the IFA Council when they realised the seriousness of the situation. In essence Moles was denied the opportunity to become a force for division by his fellow IFA members. In fact, it might be argued that the commitment of the IFA and its member clubs to the more militant strains of Unionism was always limited. In 1913 the banning by the IFA of military teams from the Irish Junior Cup led one delegate to ask if this ban applied to 'teams from the 'Ulster Army'' [i.e. Ulster Volunteer Force]. After the laughter had subsided, the chairman of the Linfield club simply stated that '*they* are not footballers'. A year later the attempt to raise a 'Sports Battalion' as part of the Ulster Volunteer Force received an enthusiastic welcome in some quarters in Belfast, but little support from the city's Association players and administrators. The IFA did not join the Golfing Union of Ireland, the IRFU's Northern Branch, the Irish Hockey Union, the Irish Bowling Association and the Northern Cricket Union in advocating the measure, and only the gentlemen amateurs of the Cliftonville club rallied to the call.[130] Association football was neither willing nor able to act as the athletic arm of Ulster Unionism.

It is perhaps instructive to consider the extent to which developments in Irish football really mirrored the country's political development. In each case major developments within Irish football did follow on the heels of political initiatives. The first meeting of the FAI was convened in the period between the establishment of the Northern Ireland parliament and the emergence of the Irish Free State. Its final recognition was similarly to be achieved following the end of the civil war, and the consolidation of the new Irish dominion. Yet it should also be remembered that neither of the two Associations was truly partitionist. Each was in reality looking to become the sole controlling body in Ireland. The Football Association of Ireland, it was reported in August 1921, was the 'Football Association of All-Ireland [and] as its name indicates, will have jurisdiction over all Ireland, and it is expected that clubs will affiliate from all the provinces'.[131] To some extent this became true as some teams from within the new state of Northern Ireland opted to withdraw from the IFA and join the new Dublin-based Association. For the most part these were teams from predominantly Nationalist areas, such as the city of Derry and the town of Downpatrick, as well as west Belfast.[132]

By January 1923 there was real confusion in the minds of some as to the to the extent of the two Associations and their members.[133] At the major conference to seek a reconciliation in the game in 1923, the IFA initially sought an accommodation with the FAI that would see its members effectively readmitted to its own organisation. Only when then threatened with demotion to the status of a junior affiliated Association under the direction of the FAI did the IFA effectively opt for separate spheres of influence.[134] There were undoubtedly parallels in political and sporting developments, but to see one set of circumstances as directly causal of the other is in truth a massive presumption.

At the same time, if the direct relevance of political events to the partition of football can be questioned, events from 1914, and especially from 1920 onwards, do serve to demonstrate the relevance of the existing longer-term differences in the eventual partition of the game. With regard to the importance of international selection in the dispute between the two new footballing bodies, it was the single matter of the chairmanship of the proposed international selection committee that eventually ended the meaningful negotiations between the Associations in 1924.

The suggestion that the IFA was inherently biased against the interests of clubs from outside Belfast reached its apparent zenith with the decision of the Senior Clubs Committee in 1921 that Shelbourne should return to Belfast to replay its Irish Cup semi-final. The entire situation as viewed by some outside Belfast was summed up in January 1920, following the refusal of the IFA to contribute to a fund for a crippled Dublin player or to hold an international match that season in the capital. These events prompted this tirade against the Association from one Dublin journalist.

> Despite their occasional public views and an odd dole or two of a few pounds, the attitude of these northern legislators towards the rest of the country and their repeated neglect of Dublin in particular during the last twenty years are painfully consistent with a jealousy of Leinster and a desire that all districts and every person must be subservient to the game's welfare in one corner of the country only.[135]

The allegedly niggardly attitude of the IFA regarding the distribution of funds was highlighted by the derisory grant offered to the LFA in 1918, which was seen as adding insult to injury. During the 1923 conference the bugbear of the lack of financial support offered by the IFA surfaced again.

The importance of these longer-term differences was cited contemporarily, though usually in very general terms. Floating the idea of a new Association in early 1921, one journalist cited the facts that the IFA had become a 'moribund organisation' and had failed to promote the game effectively outside Ulster. Another suggested that the LFA saw the IFA as 'only a drain on the financial resources' of its own body.[136] As the split became reality in mid-1921, it was noted in Dublin that 'our point of view and theirs never coincided. There was always a rift in the lute.'[137]

On a personal level, the individuals involved in the eventual breakdown of relations between north and south may well have been divided politically and religiously, but they were also at odds over their apparent notions of the game. J.A. Ryder, who was to be responsible for drafting the letter circulated to clubs in June 1921 that effectively announced the founding of the FAI, and who acted as the Association's first secretary, had his background in Junior football in Leinster. In 1906 he was elected to the Leinster FA council with the largest vote of any candidate. The following year as the chairman of the Leinster Junior FA he advocated a boycott of the IFA-sponsored Irish Junior Cup due to what he regarded as the unfair treatment of a Junior Dublin club by the IFA.[138]

The very first rumours of a split in football's administration in 1921 had begun circulating in January of that year, due to the IFA's decision to remove both a Junior and an Intermediate Cup semi-final from Dublin to Belfast.[139] The importance of this division between amateur/Junior-dominated Dublin and professional/Senior-dominated Belfast is given more credence by the attitudes and actions of the two Senior clubs in Dublin during the period of relative uncertainty between 1921 and 1923. At the Irish Football League's annual general meeting in May 1921, the Shelbourne club, whose removal from the Irish Cup by the IFA two months earlier was seen as a turning point in wider north–south relations, let it be known that it would take part in the forthcoming programme in the new season. In the spring of 1922, as the FAI and the Football League of Ireland competitions were well under way, the Shelbourne and Bohemian clubs were said to 'hanker for the return of the pre-FAI days'.[140] In June 1923 a delegation from the Bohemian club of Dublin was received by the IFA with a view to seeing the Dubliners readmitted to the IFA; the following month the same club was mistakenly reported to have re-entered the Irish League.[141]

The influence and power of such perceptions and arguments within established sporting organisations should not be underestimated. In Britain it was the division of fledgling professionalism and die-hard amateurism, bolstering class antagonisms, that led to the establishment of the Northern Rugby Union and eventually the Rugby League, from 1894. Even the apparently monolithic association game in England was not immune. In 1907 a number of clubs broke away from the FA to form the Amateur Football Association, largely as a backlash against the perceived 'commercialisation' of the game. Eventually it was to claim a membership of more than 40,000 individuals.[142] In Ireland too at least one sport was eventually to be divided on similar lines. In 1931 the National Athletics and Cycling Association, which had been formed as an all-Ireland body in 1923 primarily from the athletics board of the GAA and the remnants of the Irish Amateur Athletic Association, split along lines coincident with the border. The dispute centred on the giving of money prizes to competitors in races, which the large Belfast clubs insisted was necessary to attract leading athletes to meetings. Allied with this was the discomfort some southern representatives in the Association felt concerning the presence of bookmakers at meetings. In the event a group of Belfast-based clubs, led by the Linfield and Belfast Celtic clubs, broke away to form the Northern Ireland Amateur Athletic Association.[143] Whatever the precise reasons for this split, its cross-community support in the north seems to suggest that they were fundamentally neither political nor religious.

Finally, even the issue of sabbatarianism found an echo in this contentious period. The relative importance of Sunday football in Leinster was recognised during the approach to the split, when the new Association was urged to 'seek accommodation' with the unaffiliated clubs playing on Sundays. Among the very first actions of the new Association was indeed a specific rule change allowing Sunday play.[144]

At the same time as reflecting on these established grievances between Belfast and Dublin, it is necessary to consider the immediate events that led to the breakdown in relations between the IFA and the LFA. The extent to which the former was completely unjustified in ordering Shelbourne back to Belfast in March 1921 is debatable. As was noted at the time, the decision certainly went against the previous precedents. However there were, to some extent, very special circumstances.

With the date for the replay set for mid-March, Dublin was a city in turmoil. A curfew had been in force in the city for more than a year, and six Republican prisoners were to be executed two days before the intended replay. An identical set of executions in Cork the previous month had led to the killing of six soldiers in the city in retaliation. If they judged the state of the capital from the reports of Belfast's Unionist press, it was little surprise that the IFA and the Glenavon players alike saw the prospects of a game there as dubious.

In government circles too there was some apprehension as to what the response to the executions in Dublin might be.[145] Some other sporting bodies certainly seem to have agreed with the fears of the Senior Clubs Committee and the Glenavon players. In June that year the Northern Cricket Union declined to play either of its two interprovincial games in Dublin, though the Leinster Cricket Union felt itself to be 'very badly treated in this matter'. The Irish Women's Hockey Union had decided not to play any interprovincial or international matches at all in 1920 and 1921.[146]

Perhaps more important, though, were the testimony and actions of the Dublin football clubs and their members. In August 1920, following a warning that any further crowd disorder might lead the government to ban future games, the secretary of the Shelbourne club had himself informed the Irish League that he considered it 'injudicious to play League football in Dublin' at that time. Over the next five months the two Senior clubs in Dublin withdrew from three further competitions 'for peace's sake'.[147]

At the same time, the anxiety of Shelbourne's team not to return to Belfast was equally understandable. Beyond the sporting considerations, the public order situation in Belfast looked no more welcoming to a Dubliner than did that in Dublin to the Ulstermen of Glenavon. In the first three months of 1921 twelve men had been killed in the city, and another two dozen seriously injured. Dublin's Nationalist press portrayed Belfast in much the same terms as the Belfast papers described the capital.[148] In January 1921 the IFA were thought by one observer to be 'living in a fool's paradise' if they thought any Dublin team would travel to play in Belfast, and the initial visit of Shelbourne to Belfast had been seen as unlikely to take place.[149] Reluctance on both sides was quite understandable. However, when the crunch came, the IFA responded more readily to the demands of its northern members than its southern.

It should be noted that once the immediate path toward partition in the game had been embarked upon, both sides made a number of conciliatory gestures. On the side of the FAI the most notable move was perhaps the appointment of Sir Henry MacLaughlin as its president in 1922, following the resignations of two earlier incumbents due to the pressure of their business interests.[150] MacLaughlin was a wealthy building contractor whose family business had branches in Dublin, Belfast and London. Born and raised in Belfast, he had played football for the Cliftonville club in the city. Rather more importantly, though, he had played a crucial role in recruiting for the British armed forces during the war, and had received his knighthood for such services in 1919. During the peace he would take a leading role in the representation of disabled servicemen.[151] Such a measure seems likely to have been undertaken with an eye to northern sensibilities.

The IFA too made some concessions, or was at least prepared to tread very softly in matters that might be seen as controversial. For example, the request by the Linfield club in March 1922, as the FAI first sought international recognition, to play a benefit match for the Southern Irish Loyalist Relief Fund was first deferred, and then refused.[152] Deliberate attempts also seem to have eventually been taken to avoid alienating clubs that had become members of the FAI. In February 1923, with an inter-association conference pending, the IFA granted the Queen's University team from Belfast permission to play university sides in the Irish Free State. Fourteen months previously it had specifically denied such permission. The IFA also sanctioned its member clubs' making their premises available to clubs in Belfast that had taken up FAI membership.[153]

It should also be recognised in dealing with Irish football in the years immediately after the Great War that the game itself was under considerable pressures. In Belfast in 1920 the levels of unemployment in the city and the imposition of martial law were reckoned to have seriously cut back gate monies for clubs.[154] In addition to falling crowds, as already stated, the economic situation in Ireland had led to potential unrest among the country's paid players. Coupled with this was the fact that a number of English clubs were allegedly hunting for talent in Ireland to replace men who had been lost in the war. The resumption of play in England also resulted in those star players who had returned to Ireland from 1916 onwards departing once more for the relative comforts of the Scottish and English games. Even players who had been contracted solely to Irish clubs could now evade the restrictions of the 'retain and transfer system' by signing for Welsh clubs. As no reciprocal agreement existed between the IFA and the Welsh FA regarding recognition of players' contracts in each other's jurisdictions, Welsh clubs emerged as 'player brokers', providing an intermediary medium through which Irish players could pass before going on to sign for leading English clubs.[155] Finally, especially in Dublin, as the FAI delegates had reported to the IFA, the sport was seen as being under sustained pressure from advocates of the games controlled by the GAA. Rumours even circulated that GAA members were deliberately exciting crowd disorders at some association games.[156] More constructively, the GAA had allegedly approached the LFA about rescinding the ban on playing foreign games in late 1920. Six months later the hope of one Nationalist periodical was that 'the Leinster soccer players ... will be completely restored to an Irish mental outlook' with the help of the GAA.[157] Association football in Ireland was apparently struggling for its very survival in some quarters. The sport's partition may, in the short term, have done much to dissipate the opposition of some to its continued existence.

In conclusion, the evidence suggests that a number of both long-term and short-term factors were important in creating the division of association football in Ireland. A number of specific sporting events, notably the recall of Shelbourne to Belfast in 1921, catalysed the actual partition of the game. However, this development was merely giving a concrete form to longer standing grievances, and differences in the very nature of the game of association football as it existed in the two main centres of the sport in Ireland. The political partition of the country did not initiate its sporting partition. Rather, in the case of association football, it provided a window of opportunity through which the various proponents of the game could leap. Long-term differences between Dublin and Belfast over the nature of the game, and where the balance of power and influence should lie, culminated in divisions that could acquire concrete form with the partition of the country politically. There was nothing inevitable about the path the future development of football in Ireland would take.

The requirements of international recognition and competition in turn led to the hardening of the division, and to the game's essential partition along the line of Ireland's new border. It was almost a happy coincidence that just as divisions on sporting grounds were reaching something of a high point, the chance arose to encapsulate these differences in the primary emergent vessel of modern sport: the nation state.

7

Conclusion

> Tell us not in mournful numbers
> Football is a foolish game:
> For beside the joys of football
> Other sports seem dull and tame.
>
> Anon., *A Psalm of Football* (Belfast, 1901).

M.F. Goodbody typified the gentleman player of the game's early heydays in Dublin. Educated in England and at Trinity College Dublin, he played for the élite Corinthians team, as well as the Irish national side. He was also a leading tennis player. He died in Egypt in 1915 while serving as an officer with the Royal Engineers.

Ulster Football and Cycling News

A FUNDAMENTAL TENET OF ASSOCIATION FOOTBALL at its introduction to Ireland was that the game would promote a greater level of social cohesion. Primarily this was to be done by encouraging interaction between men of differing classes, characters and allegiances. It was a hope that proved remarkably resilient, even in the face of considerable evidence that the contrary could be true. In the summer of 1913, while shots were being exchanged between rival supporters, and in the wake of the estrangement of the leading Irish clubs and the game's governing body, it was being suggested in Belfast that the establishment of a 'Churches League' would help 'to create a spirit of friendly intercourse between young men' of different beliefs.[1]

Despite the limits put on the game's growth and dissemination by various social, economic and cultural factors, football did eventually acquire a large following in Ireland, which was surprisingly socially, politically and religiously mixed. In fact, football did indeed succeed in partly fulfilling the hopes of some of its earliest promoters by bringing together all classes and creeds of men, on the pitch, in the committee rooms, and on the terraces. It did not, however, succeed in fully integrating or assimilating these groups. In Ulster, and especially Belfast, the segregated nature of neighbourhoods and places of employment ensured that some of the football clubs that were based in and around them remained sectarian in their memberships and followings. As a result, the game itself became occasionally troubled and divided on grounds of religion and politics. This might be in a literal sense, as young men engaged in rioting at games, or in a metaphorical sense, as officials exchanged accusations and recriminations.

The eventual political partition of Ireland was to facilitate the division of football along coincident lines. The establishment of two states in Ireland allowed football's authorities there to create two clearly defined spheres of influence. Yet it seems that politics played only a peripheral role in creating the divisions in the game that led to this sporting partition.

Long-term grievances over matters such as international team selection and supposed favouritism lay beneath the conflict in 1921 over the venues of fixtures. The preconditions for this situation had in turn been generated by wider economic and social differences between the game's two main centres. Belfast was described in 1887 by one visitor as 'the insular suburb of Liverpool and Glasgow'.[2] It not only followed the commercial pursuits of these two cities, but also their sporting preferences. Association football became the popular game here, and of the professionalised and commercialised kind that depended for its existence on a large industrial proletariat. The commercialisation of leisure in this way depended in great measure on the existence of a large potential audience, with a certain level of disposable income and regular patterns of work and rest. The shipyards and linen mills of Belfast and its hinterland provided just such a group. Football in Belfast at least took on the appearance of a business. A drive for success lay at the heart of the game.

In Dublin, meanwhile, where 'soccer football was the game talked of and played everywhere', but in which the almost complete lack of an industrial sector made young men aspire to the gentility of clerkships and civil service posts rather than industrial apprenticeships, the game assumed in large measure the gentlemanly amateur ethos that had been quickly dissipated in the north.[3] Football in Dublin was primarily a game for players and participation, not for professionals and paying spectators.

A north–south divide therefore existed in more than mere politics. Economic and resultant social bifurcation underlay the eventual division of Irish football. In turn, differing football cultures, even within the same code, were established in Belfast and Dublin. Industrialisation in the north led to the development of a mass spectator sport, and the professionalisation of the game. The embourgoisement of certain sections of the Dublin population resulted in a game dominated by the gentleman amateur, and for many more centred around playing, rather than spectating. Such basic economic and social considerations were undoubtedly also influential in the creation of Ireland's divided political allegiances. This was especially so in Ulster, where the integration of the region's economy into the wider British and imperial mercantilist system provided one underlying tenet of Unionism.[4] Quite independently, though, these economic and social considerations also acted to create a division in sport, which was in turn to be reinforced and given tangible form by political events.

Appendix
Winners of major association football competitions in Ireland 1881–1922

YEAR	IRISH CHALLENGE CUP	IRISH FOOTBALL LEAGUE
1881	Moyola Park	
1882	Queen's Island	
1883	Cliftonville	
1884	Distillery	
1885	Distillery	
1886	Distillery	
1887	Ulster	
1888	Cliftonville	
1889	Distillery	
1890	Gordon Highlanders	
1891	Linfield	Linfield
1892	Linfield	Linfield
1893	Linfield	Linfield
1894	Distillery	Glentoran
1895	Linfield	Linfield
1896	Distillery	Distillery
1897	Cliftonville	Glentoran
1898	Linfield	Linfield
1899	Linfield	Linfield
1900	Cliftonville	Belfast Celtic
1901	Cliftonville	Distillery
1902	Linfield	Linfield
1903	Distillery	Distillery
1904	Linfield	Linfield
1905	Distillery	Glentoran
1906	Shelbourne*	Cliftonville/Distillery
1907	Cliftonville	Linfield
1908	Bohemians*	Linfield

1909	Cliftonville	Linfield
1910	Distillery	Cliftonville
1911	Shelbourne*	Linfield
1912	Linfield (no final tie)	Glentoran
1913	Linfield	Glentoran
1914	Glentoran	Linfield
1915	Linfield	Belfast Celtic
1916	Linfield	No competition
1917	Glentoran	No competition
1918	Belfast Celtic	No competition
1919	Linfield	No competition
1920	Shelbourne* (no final tie)	No competition
1921	Glentoran	Glentoran
1922	Linfield	Linfield

* Dublin club

Notes

1. See, for example, J. Walvin, *The People's Game: the history of football revisited* (Edinburgh, 1994) pp. 11–12; B. Murray, *Football: a history of the world game* (Aldershot, 1994) pp. 2–3.
2. For hurling see A. Ó Maolfabhail, *Caman: Two thousand years of hurling in Ireland* (Dundalk, 1973); H. J. Lawlor, 'Calendar of the Liber Ruber of the diocese of Ossory' in *Proceedings of the Royal Irish Academy*, XXVII, Sec. C, No. 2 (July 1908) p. 165. I am extremely grateful to Dr Raymond Gillespie for this latter reference, and for other helpful comments in the writing of this work.
3. 'Statute Book of the town of Galway 1485 to 1710' in *Historical Manuscripts Commission*, 10th Report App. 1 (1885) p. 402.
4. M. Bishop, *The Life and Adventures of Matthew Bishop* (London, 1744) pp. 60–4; E. MacLysaght (ed.), *Teague Land, or a Merry Ramble to the Wild Irish* (Dublin, 1982) p. 42; 7 Wm III c. 17 (1695).
5. Anon, *A Match at FootBall* (Dublin, 1720).
6. B. Henry, *Dublin Hanged: Crime, law enforcement and punishment in late eighteenth-century Dublin* (Dublin, 1994) pp. 119–20.
7. S. Connolly, '"Ag déanamh *commanding*": elite responses to popular culture, 1660–1850' in J.S. Donnelly jnr and K. A. Miller (eds) *Irish Popular Culture, 1650–1850* (Dublin, 1998) pp. 21–2.
8. See, for example, M. de Burca, *The GAA: a history* (Dublin, 1980) p. 5.
9. A. Day and P. McWilliams (eds) *Ordnance Survey Memoirs of Ireland II: Parishes of County Antrim I, 1838–9* (Belfast, 1990) pp. 33, 113.
10. For the decline in duelling see J. Kelly, *'That Damn'd Thing Called Honour': Duelling in Ireland 1570–1860* (Cork, 1995) pp. 253–71.
11. W.R. Wilde, *Irish Popular Superstitions* (Dublin, 1852) pp. 63–4.
12. B. Griffin, *The Bulkies: Police and crime in Belfast, 1800–1865* (Dublin, 1997) p. 104.
13. See, however, M.F. Ryan, *Fenian Memories* (2nd edn, Dublin, 1946) p. 11 for a claim that 'football was generally played' in Galway in the 1860s.
14. G. Cameron, *Coleraine Football Club: a history* (Coleraine, 1984) p. 1.
15. M. Brodie, *100 Years of Irish Football* (Belfast, 1980) p. 2.
16. R.M. Peter (ed.) *Irish Football Annual* (Dublin, 1880) pp. 123–4; *Sport* 9 May 1885.
17. Murray, *Football*, pp. 13–20.
18. *Irish Sportsman* 26 Oct. 1878; *Northern Whig* 30 Oct. 1878.
19. Peter (ed.) *Football Annual*, pp. 129–31.
20. Brodie, *100 Years*, pp.2–3; IFA minute book 1880–86, entry for 18 Nov. 1880.
21. See M. Brodie (ed.) *The Irish Football League 1890–1990: Official centenary history* (Belfast, 1990) pp. 1–2.
22. IFA Cash book 1880–97.
23. *Sport* 17 Nov. 1883.
24. *Sport* 18 Oct. 1884, 21 Mar. 1885 and 20 Jan. 1894.
25. G. Briggs and J. Dodds (eds) *100 years of the* LFA: *Leinster Football Association centenary year book* (Dublin, 1993) pp. 21–2.
26. *Ulster Football and Cycling News* 19 Sept. 1890.
27. Briggs and Dodds (eds) LFA, pp. 22–6.
28. IFA minute book 1898–1903, entries for 24 Sept. and 8 Oct. 1901; IFA minute book 1903–09, entry for 26 Oct 1904.
29. For the 1911/12 dispute see Chapter 6.

30 *Sport* 21 Mar. 1914.
31 *NW* 16 Mar. 1914; *Belfast News Letter* 16 Mar. 1914; *Irish News* 16 Mar. 1914; *Freeman's Journal* 16 Mar. 1914; *Sunday Independent* 15 Mar. 1914; *Irish Times* 16 Mar. 1914.
32 *Belfast Telegraph* 16 Mar. 1914; *Ireland's Saturday Night* 14 Mar. 1914.
33 D. Fitzpatrick, 'The disappearance of the Irish agricultural labourer' in *Irish Economic and Social History* VII (1980) pp. 66–92.
34 W.E. Vaughan and A.J. Fitzpatrick (eds) *Irish Historical Statistics: Population, 1821–1971* (Dublin, 1972) p. 27.
35 W.E. Vaughan (ed.) *A New History of Ireland V: Ireland under the Union I, 1801–70* (Oxford, 1989) p. 536; Vaughan, *A New History of Ireland VI: Ireland under the Union II, 1870–1921* (Oxford, 1996) p. 332.
36 M.L. Legg, *Newspapers and Nationalism: the Irish provincial press, 1850–1892* (Dublin, 1999) pp. 30, 77, 125.
37 The *Irish Sporting Chronicle* dealt overwhelmingly with hunting and farming issues rather than athletic sports. *Ulster's Saturday Night* experienced a change in name but not format in 1896. For details of publications see J.S. North (ed.) *Waterloo Directory of Irish Newspapers and Periodicals, 1800–1900* (Waterloo, Ontario, 1986).
38 For comments on the role of the press in British sport see N. Tranter, *Sport, Economy and Society in Britain 1750–1914* (Cambridge, 1998) pp. 32–3, 76.
39 K.T. Hoppen, *Elections, Politics and Society in Ireland 1832–1885* (Oxford, 1984) p. 461.
40 P. Flanagan, *Transport in Ireland 1880–1910* (Dublin, 1969) pp. 57, 80; S. Gribbon, 'An Irish city: Belfast 1911' in D. Harkness and M. O'Dowd (eds) *The Town in Ireland: Historical Studies XIII* (Belfast, 1981) pp. 206–7.
41 22 Vic. c. 27 (1859); 32 and 33 Vic. c. 28 (1869); 35 Vic. c. 6 (1872).
42 F. Geary and T. Stark, 'Comparative output and growth in the four countries of the United Kingdom, 1861–1911' in S.J. Connolly (ed.) *Kingdoms United? Great Britain and Ireland since 1500* (Dublin, 1999) p. 159.
43 C. Ó Gráda, *Ireland: a new economic history, 1780–1939* (Oxford, 1994) pp. 272, 237–9.
44 37 and 38 Vic. c. 44 (1874); D.L. Armstrong, 'Social and economic conditions in the Belfast linen industry, 1850–1900' in *Irish Historical Studies* VII (No. 28) Sept. 1951, pp. 235–69; *Annual Report of the Belfast Chamber of Commerce, 1881* p. 4; *Report of an inquiry by the Board of Trade into the earnings and hours of labour of workpeople in the United Kingdom* (BPP 1909 LXXX [cd 4795]) pp. 88, 91.
45 J. Lynch, *A Tale of Three Cities: Comparative studies in working-class life* (London, 1998) p. 131; Sir C. Cameron, *Reminiscences* (Dublin, 1913) p. 168.
46 P. Ollerenshaw, 'Industry 1820–1914' in L. Kennedy and P. Ollerenshaw (eds) *An Economic History of Ulster 1820–1939* (Manchester, 1985) pp. 87–92.
47 M.E. Daly, *Dublin: the deposed capital, a social and economic history, 1860–1914* (Cork, 1984) pp. 39, 50.
48 Daly, *Dublin*, pp. 67, 110, 48; Lynch, *Three Cities*, pp. 130–1.
49 *ISN* 10 Dec. 1898 and 29 Dec. 1900.
50 *Annual Report of the Commissioners of Public Works in Ireland, 1901–1907* (BPP 1901 XVII [cd 724] p. 517; 1902 XXI [cd 1261] p. 631; 1903 XVIII [cd 1748] p. 289; 1904 XVII [cd 2229] p. 309; 1905 XXII [cd 2657] p. 359; 1906 XXV [cd 3109] p. 507; 1907 XIX [cd 3693] p. 425).
51 *Parliamentary Debates (4th Series)* CLII cols 1146–7 and CLXIII col. 683.
52 H.T. O'Rourke, *The Dublin Civic Survey Report* (London, 1925) pp. 19, 22.

NOTES

53 *Minutes of Evidence of the Royal Commission on Labour* II (BPP 1892 XXXVI Pt 2 [cd 6795] p. 685); M. Cronin, 'Work and workers in Cork city and county 1800–1900' in P. O'Flanagan and C. Buttimer (eds) *Cork: History and Society* (Dublin, 1993) pp. 721–54.
54 *Cork Sportsman* 22 May 1909, 29 Oct. 1910 and 6 Oct. 1911.
55 *ISN* 17 Sept. 1904.
56 *Sport* 31 Aug. 1912.
57 *NW* 9 May 1887; *Ulster Football and Cycling News* 20 Nov. 1891.
58 *ISN* 24 Dec. 1898; *NW* 23 May 1884; *Castleknock College Chronicle* (1890) p. 5.
59 *UFCN* 23 Sept. 1892.
60 *ISN* 24 Dec. 1898; *UFCN* 24 Aug. 1894. The poet was R.J. Kirkpatrick, a member of the IFA Council.
61 H. Stewart, 'The football nations' in *Blackwood's Magazine* CLXIX (Apr. 1901) p. 492; *ISN* 24 Dec. 1898.
62 *UFCN* 6 Jan. 1893; *Belfast Health Journal* March 1901; *ISN* 13 Apr. 1901.
63 *ISN* 24 Dec. 1898; *BNL* 5 Oct. 1896.
64 *Derry Journal* 31 Jan. 1898. See also *DJ* 12 May 1899 and *ISN* 13 May 1899.
65 *UFCN* 1 Nov. 1890; *ISN* 2 Feb. 1901.
66 *Londonderry Standard* 18 Dec. 1883; *Coleraine Chronicle* 15 Dec. 1883.
67 FA Cash book 1880–97, entries for 11 Aug. 1881 (Limavady), 28 Dec. 1882 (Lisburn), 8 Dec. 1883 (Dublin) and 15 Dec. 1883 (Monaghan); *Ballymoney Free Press* 16 Oct. 1890.
68 See, for example, the refusal of the request for a demonstration game in Longford in 1912 in IFA minute book 1909–25, entry for 3 Dec. 1912.
69 Brodie, *100 Years*, p. 2; Brodie, *Irish Soccer*, pp. 69–70; *Sport* 16 May 1885; R.M. Peter (ed.) *Irish Football Annual* (Dublin, 1880) p. 123.
70 *BNL* 22 Nov. 1880 and 7 Feb. 1881; *NW* 1 May 1882.
71 *ISN* 10 Feb. 1917 and 15 Oct. 1898; IFA minute book 1880–86, entry for 14 Feb. 1881; *ISN* 28 Oct. 1911.
72 See for example *BNL* 1 Nov. 1880.
73 IFA Cash book 1880–97, 'Subscriptions (private and otherwise) towards the Irish Challenge Cup', entry for 6 Apr. 1881.
74 *UFCN* 12 Apr. 1889.
75 O. St J. Gogarty, *It Isn't This Time of Year at All!* (London, 1983 edn) p. 26; E.J. O'Mahony, *Bohemian Football Club: Golden Jubilee Souvenir* (Dublin, 1940) p. 9; *UFCN* 20 Oct. 1893; *NW* 23 Mar. 1883. I am very grateful to Mr Stephen Byrne for the first reference cited here, and for directing me to other sources on the history of the Bohemian club.
76 J. Springhall, B. Fraser and M. Hoare, *Sure and Steadfast: a history of the Boys' Brigade* (London, 1983) pp. 51–3; *Irish Christian* X, No. 109 (Jan. 1892) pp. 110–11.
77 G. Briggs and J. Dodd (eds) *100 Years of the Leinster Football Association* (Dublin, 1995) pp. 60–1; *ISN* 26 Jul. 1902, 24 Jan. 1903 and 1 Jan. 1910; *UFCN* 26 Apr. 1895.
78 *Sport* 14 Jan. 1893; *UFCN* 7 Feb. 1896; J.C. Trewin, *Benson and the Bensonians* (London, 1960) p. 80; *FJ* 9 Jan. 1904.
79 See, for example, Alan Bairner, 'Ireland, sport and empire' in K. Jeffery (ed.) *An Irish Empire? Aspects of Ireland and the British Empire* (Manchester, 1996) pp. 57–76, esp. p. 61.
80 D. Hannigan, *The Garrison Game: the state of Irish football* (Edinburgh, 1998) *passim*. In fact the term 'garrison' was used contemporarily to refer to the entire Protestant

Unionist community in Ireland, rather than simply the military. In 1899 'the real English garrison in Ireland' was reportedly anyone, including Catholic clergymen, who maintained any commercial or cultural connection with Britain (*United Irishman* 8 July 1899).

81 See Chapter 3.
82 *Famous Footballers* (London, 1895) p. 106; *ISN* 3 Aug. 1907.
83 *FJ* 17 Oct. 1890; *Western Star and Ballinasloe Advertiser* 11 Feb. 1893.
84 *NW* 27 Sept. 1886; *BNL* 22 Nov. 1880; *ISN* 8 Oct. 1898.
85 *Pastime* III, No. 74 (Oct. 1884) p. 283; *UFCN* 12 Oct. 1888.
86 In 1890 the Gordon Highlanders became the only military side to win the Irish Cup. In 1892 and 1897 respectively the Black Watch and the Sherwood Foresters were runners-up in the same competition.
87 Brodie, *100 Years*, p. 6; *ISN* 13 Jan. 1900.
88 *UFCN* 15 Mar. 1889; *ISN* 5 May 1899; IFA minute book 1898–1903, entry for 6 May 1899; *Sport* 2 Jan. 1897.
89 *UFCN* 18 Apr. 1890 and 30 Oct. 1896;*Cork Sportsman* 17 Oct. 1908 and 22 May 1909; *UFCN* 28 Oct. 1892.
90 *Sport* 29 Oct. 1904; *UFCN* 11 Apr. 1890.
91 *Sport* 20 and 27 Feb. 1904.
92 See for example *Dundalk Democrat* 31 Jan. 1891; *Daily Independent* 29 Jan. 1892; *Western Star and Ballinasloe Advertiser* 18 Mar. 1899.
93 P.L. Dickinson, *The Dublin of Yesterday* (London, 1929) p. 36; A. Godley, *Life of an Irish Soldier* (London, 1939) pp. 14–29; T. de V. White, *A Fretful Midge* (London, 1957) p. 25.
94 E.A. Muenger, *The British Military Dilemma in Ireland: Occupation politics, 1886–1914* (Dublin, 1991) pp. 75, 77; S. O'Faolain, *Vive Moi! an autobiography* (London, 1965) p. 71.
95 V. Crossman, 'The army and law and order in the nineteenth century' in T. Bartlett and K. Jeffery (eds.) *A Military History of Ireland* (Cambridge, 1996) pp. 377–8. Involvement in such duties also reduced the time available to the army for events such as sports meetings and football matches. For example the Highland Light Infantry, who spent six years stationed in Ireland from 1883, were forced to abandon their regimental sports meetings in 1886 and 1887 due at least in part to their involvement in policing operations (see 71st Regiment (Highland Light Infantry) Regimental Athletic Sports Record Book 1879–1888, Royal Highland Fusiliers Regimental Museum, Glasgow).
96 T. Denman, '"The red livery of shame": the campaign against army recruitment in Ireland, 1899–1914' in *Irish Historical Studies*, XXIX (1994) pp. 208–33.
97 See for example E.B. Ewan-Muller, *Ireland: Today and tomorrow* (London, 1907) pp. 62–3.
98 W.A.H. Collison, *Dr Collison in and on Ireland* (London, 1908) p. 21.
99 *[Dublin] Evening Telegraph* 21 Mar. 1896.
100 Draft letter, W.G. Fallon to F.B. Dineen, Chairman GAA Athletics Council, 26 Apr. 1907 (Fallon papers, NLI, MS 22,577).
101 M.C. Hime, *The Efficiency of Irish Schools and Their Superiority to English Schools as Places of Education for Irish Boys, Explained and Proved* (London, 1889) pp. 1–2; F.R. Falkiner, 'The Irish schoolboy exodus and the Educational Endowments act' in *Dublin University Review* (Dec. 1885) p. 334.
102 *ISN* 19 Jan. 1901; *UFCN* 27 Feb. 1891; F.N.S. Creek, *A History of the Corinthian Football Club* (London, 1933) pp. 282, 230; W. King (ed.) *The Rossall Register 1844–1889* (London, 1889) pp. 329, 334 and 343.

103 *Sixty-seventh Report of the Commissioners for National Education in Ireland, 1900*, reprinted in T.J. Duncan, *A History of Irish Education from 1800* (Bala, 1972) App. 2, pp. 76–7; Minute book of Brown Street Sunday and Daily School Society 24 July 1899 – 4 Mar. 1927, entry for 20 May 1904 (Belfast Central Library); W.A. McKeown, *National Education in Ireland* (Belfast 1903) pp. 6, 28. See also M. Tierney 'The revised programme in National Schools' in *New Ireland Review* XV (Mar. 1901) pp. 83–4.
104 R. Briscoe, *For the Life of Me* (London, 1959) p. 20; Autobiography of Robert McElborough (PRONI, D/770/1); Autobiography of W.A. Greer (PRONI T/3249/1).
105 J.A. Mangan, *Athleticism in the Victorian and Edwardian Public School* (Cambridge, 1981) pp. 16, 88.
106 *Hillbrook School Times* No. 1, I (Apr. 1875) p. 2; Brother De Sales, 'The how and why of moral training III' in *Irish Educational Review* VII (1913–4) pp. 216–7.
107 IFA minute book 1880–86, entry for 29 Jan. 1884.
108 Co. Antrim FA minute book, 1906–9, entry for 9 Feb. 1910.
109 *Coleraine Constitution* 9 Apr. 1881; N.H. Newhouse, *A History of Friends' School Lisburn* (Lurgan, 1974) pp. 87–8.
110 *QCB* I, No. 4 (Mar. 1900) p. 15; II, No. 3 (Jan. 1901) p. 23, and IV, No. 1 (Nov. 1902) p. 11.
111 J. Jamison, *The History of the Royal Belfast Academical Institution, 1810–1960* (Belfast, 1959) p. 124; E. Van Esbeck, *One Hundred Years of Irish Rugby* (Dublin, 1974) p. 46.
112 R. Marshall, *Methodist College Belfast: the first hundred years* (Belfast, n.d.) p. 68; *Hillbrook School Times* No. 6, I (Oct. 1875) p. 2; IRFU (NB) committee minute book 1885–99, entry for 19 Oct. 1887 (PRONI, D/3876/A/1). Scylla and Charybdis are the twin obstacles posed by a sea-monster and a whirlpool that threatened Odysseus and Jason in classical mythology (see M. Grant, *Myths of the Greeks and Romans* (London, 1962) pp. 75, 296).
113 L. Fleming, *Head or Harp* (London, 1965) pp. 45–6; S. Bullock, *After Sixty Years* (London, 1936) p. 79.
114 J.A. Murphy, *The College: a history of Queens/University College Cork* (Cork, 1995) p. 172; *UCC Gazette* III, No. 8 (Mar. 1913) pp. 63–4 and III, No. 9 (July 1913) p. 75; O'Faolain, *Vive moi!*, p. 139.
115 W. Mc Donald, *Reminiscences of a Maynooth Professor* (London, 1925) pp. 48–9 and 66–7; P. J. Corish, *Maynooth College 1795–1995* (Dublin, 1995) pp. 280–1.
116 *QCG* I No. 2 (Feb. 1903) p. 52; IV No. 1 (Nov. 1905) p. 31 and VI No. 1 (Mar. 1908) p. 32.
117 *Sport* 24 Nov. 1883; T. West, *The Bold Collegians: the development of sport in Trinity College, Dublin* (Dublin, 1991) p. 55; K.C. Bailey, *A History of Trinity College, Dublin 1892–1945* (Dublin, 1947) pp. 120–1.
118 *UFCN* 19 Sept. 1890.
119 *Castleknock College Chronicle*, I (1886) p. 9; III (1888) p. 15 and IV (1889) p. 7.
120 *Castleknock College Chronicle* XIV (1899) p. 25; XV (1900) p. 34; XVII (1902) pp. 12–3; XIX (1903) p. 49; XX (1904) pp. 16, 44–5; XXII (1906) p. 19; XXV (1909) p. 78; *Sport* 7 Nov. 1908.
121 *Irish Field* 7 Feb. 1907.
122 *The Clongownian* No. 1, I (Dec. 1895) pp. 41–3.
123 *The Clongownian* No. 4, I (June 1897) p. 43 and No. 5, I (Dec. 1897) p. 60; *Irish Times* 19 Mar. 1895.
124 *Sport* 2 and 16 Nov. 1895, and 13 Feb. 1897.

125 P.N. Meenan, *St Patrick's Blue and Saffron: a miscellany of UCD sport since 1895* (Dublin, 1997) pp. 59–61.
126 *FJ* 21 Feb. and 16 Mar. 1896; *Irish Times* 8 Mar. 1901; *FJ* 7 Mar. 1902; *ISN* 29 Dec. 1900.
127 *UFCN* 27 Sept. 1889; *Sport* 20 Jan. 1894 and 21 Mar. 1885.
128 See, for example, *Leader* 10 Nov. 1900. I am very grateful to Dr Senia Paseta for this reference.
129 Van Esbeck, *One Hundred Years*, pp. 14–41; Peter (ed.) *Football Annual*, pp. 32–66.
130 *Pastime* I, No. 21 (Oct. 1883) p. 327.
131 *Pastime* I, No. 20 (Oct. 1883) pp. 311–2; *NW* 23 May 1884.
132 *Pastime* I, No. 26 (Nov. 1883) p. 420; *Sport* 19 Apr. 1884.
133 J.J. MacCarthy, 'International football: Ireland' in F. Marshall (ed.) *Football: the rugby union game* (London, 1892) p. 222.
134 *UFCN* 29 Mar. 1895.
135 On the history of the GAA and its sports see P. Puirséal, *The GAA in Its Time* (Dublin, 1982), W.F. Mandle, *The Gaelic Athletic Association and Irish Nationalist Politics 1884–1924* (Dublin, 1987) and M. de Burca, *The GAA, a history* (Dublin, 1980).
136 B. MacLua, *The Steadfast Rule: a history of the GAA ban* (Dublin, 1967) pp. 23–47; Paul Rouse, 'The politics of culture and sport in Ireland: a history of the GAA ban on foreign games 1884–1971. Part One: 1884–1921' in *International Journal of the History of Sport*, X, No. 3 (Dec. 1993) pp. 333–60.
137 *Sport* 13 July 1912; J.M. Judge, 'The Irish Movement – a talk with a man in the street' in *New Ireland Review* XXIX (1908–9) p. 177; 'Autobiography and memoirs of John [Sean] McKeown' (LHL) p. 13.
138 Mandle, *Gaelic Athletic Association*, pp. 159, 187; S.P. O'Ceallaigh (ed.) *Gaelic Athletic Memories* (Dublin, 1945) p. 23; *Cork Sportsman* 26 Sept. 1908.
139 Mandle, *Gaelic Athletic Association*, p. 150; IFA minute book, 1903–9, entry for 11 May 1907. It should of course be remembered that GAA clubs were not only involved in Gaelic football, but also hurling and athletics.
140 IFA minute book 1903–9, entry for 7 Aug. 1906; *Fermanagh Herald* 31 Mar. 1906. The Association received a £50 grant from the IFA and was subsequently reconstituted as the Fermanagh and Western FA.
141 'Autobiography and memoirs of John [Sean] McKeown' (LHL) pp. 27–8; Mandle, *Gaelic Athletic Association*, p. 145; *IN* 26 May 1913.
142 *Sport* 21 Oct. 1916.
143 See for example *[Dublin] Evening Telegraph* 20 and 23 Mar. 1896.
144 IFA minute book 1903–9, entry for 5 June 1906.
145 *ISN* 8 Apr. 1899; *Fermanagh Herald* 18 June 1904.
146 W.F. Mandle, 'Parnell and sport' in *Studia Hibernica* XXVIII (1994) pp. 103–116; Mandle, *Gaelic Athletic Association*, p. 92; *UFCN* 9 Sept. 1892, 20 Jan. and 18 Aug. 1893; *ISN* 9 Jul. 1898; D. Gallogly, *Cavan's Football Story* (Cavan, 1979) p. 45.
147 See for example *Sport* 22 Jan. and 8 Apr. 1916.
148 However, see Chapter 4 for conflicts over fixture clashes, and Chapter 5 for a revealing exchange in the press between sporting officials.
149 IFA minute book 1909–25, entries for 8 Nov. 1910 and 20 May 1913.
150 IFA minute book 1880–86, entry for 30 Nov. 1880.
151 Murray, *Football*, pp. 21–2.
152 T. Mason, *Association Football and English Society, 1863–1915* (Brighton, 1980) pp. 211, 233; *UFCN* 22 Nov. 1889 and 29 May 1891. For McCracken see Chapter 3.
153 M.A. Shearman, *Athletics and Football* (London, 1888) p. 335.

NOTES

154 Mason, *Association Football*, pp. 207–10.
155 *ISN* 19 Apr. 1902.
156 *Sport* 7 Dec. 1895 and 17 Sept. 1904.
157 *Sport* 18 Nov. 1905; *ISN* 24 Aug. 1901.
158 IFA minute book 1880–1886, entries for 16 Mar. 1881 and 13 Mar. 1882.
159 *UFCN* 18 Mar. 1892; *Sport* 9 Dec. 1893.
160 IFA minute book 1903–9, entry for 5 June 1906 and loose insertion J.W. Gordon to J. Ferguson, 2 June 1906.
161 *Belfast Evening Telegraph* 2 and 3 Mar. 1894. (Newton Heath won the case, but was awarded only one farthing in damages. Peden returned the following season to Belfast, and went on to win another nine Irish caps. However, in 1898 Peden was forced to leave the Distillery club and return to Linfield after proving too physical a player for the former club (see *ISN*, 6 Aug. 1898). The Newton Heath club eventually succumbed to financial pressures, but is looked upon as the ancestor of the current Manchester United club.
162 *UFCN* 15 Feb. 1889; *Pastime* XII, No. 299, 13 Feb. 1889 and VII, No. 185, 8 Dec. 1886; *UFCN* 24 Jan. 1890.
163 *Sport* 1 Dec. 1894; *ISN* 9 Apr. 1904; *Cork Sportsman* 8 May 1909.
164 F.N.S. Creek, *A History of the Corinthian Football Club* (London, 1933) pp. 181–3; *UFCN* 2 Jan. 1891.
165 *Pastime* XVI, No. 398, 7 Jan. 1891 and XXII, No. 555, 10 Jan. 1894.
166 These figures are extracted from M. Brodie (ed.) *Northern Ireland Soccer Year Book* (annual publication).
167 *Sport* 27 Feb. 1897.
168 *ISN* 17 Mar. 1900; A. Gibson and M. Pickford, *Association Football and the Men who Made It* (London, 1906) IV, p. 114.
169 Stewart, 'The football nations', p. 495; *ISN* 29 Aug. 1903.
170 *ISN* 17 Sept. 1910; *Nomad's Weekly and Belfast Critic* 21 Mar. 1908.
171 *Pastime* VIII, No. 205, 27 Apr. 1887, p. 272.
172 See for example *ISN* 26 Nov. 1898 and 21 May 1904; *Sport* 3 Mar. 1894 and 11 Feb. 1905. For a further discussion of this issue, see Chapter 6.
173 *ISN* 16 Feb. 1895.
174 *ISN* 2 Apr. and 19 Mar. 1904.
175 *UFCN* 1 Mar. 1895; *ISN* 4 Mar. 1899.
176 *ISN* 26 July 1902; *Sport* 20 Aug. 1904.
177 IFA minute book 1909–25, entry for 8 May 1909.
178 Autobiography of William Greer of Belfast (PRONI, T/3249/1) p. 23; Briscoe, *For the life of me*, p. 20; Autobiography of William Topping of Belfast and Ballymena (PRONI, D/3134/1) pp. 43–4.
179 *ISN* 18 Mar. 1899; *Newtownards Chronicle* 17 May 1913.
180 See plates in R.C. Bannister and R.V. Hamilton, *Sport in Lisburn, Past and Present: Its history and development* (Belfast, 1910) pp. 85, 94.
181 F. Weir, 'Flour bags and the domestic economy' in *Ulster Folklife* XLII (1996) pp. 109–12.
182 *BNL* 20 Sept. 1879; *NW* 30 Oct. 1878.
183 IRFU (NB) committee book 1885–99, entry for 7 Nov. 1887; E. McKee, *A Century of Bessbrook Football 1893–1993* (Bessbrook, 1993). I am very grateful to Mr Eddie McKee for bringing this event to my notice.
184 *Belfast Morning News* 25 Oct. 1878.
185 *Sport* 26 Jan. 1895.

186 *Fermanagh Herald* 31 and 17 Mar. 1906.
187 For the issue of Sunday play, see Chapter 6.
188 The original rules were published in *United Ireland* 7 Feb. 1885. The size of a Gaelic football pitch was in fact further enlarged ten years later to more than three times the size of an association or rugby pitch.

CHAPTER 2 NOTES

1 T. West, *The Bold Collegians: the development of sport in Trinity College, Dublin* (Dublin, 1991) p. 32; P. Hone, *Cricket in Ireland* (Tralee, 1955) p. 8.
2 Co. Antrim FA minute book 1898–1910, entries for 17 and 31 Dec. 1902; *ISN* 3, 10, 17 and 24 Jan., 21 Feb. and 16 May 1903; IFA minute book 1898–1903, entry for 3 Feb. 1903; IFA minute book 1903–9, entry for 9 May 1903.
3 IFA minute book 1903–9, entry for 8 Jan. 1907.
4 *UFCN* 30 Oct. 1891; *Cork Sportsman* 25 Dec. 1909 and 15 Jan. 1910.
5 IFA minute book 1909–25, entry for 7 Dec. 1909; IFA minute book 1903–9, entry for 2 June 1908.
6 Mandle, *GAA and Nationalist Politics*, p. 116; IFA minute book 1909–25, entry for 14 May 1910.
7 R.M. Peter, *The Irish Football Annual* (Dublin, 1880) pp. 129, 124; R.C. Bannister and R.V. Hamilton, *Sport in Lisburn, Past and Present: Its history and development* (Belfast, 1910) p. 92; S. Burke, *Bohemians Football Club: a history* (Dublin, forthcoming). I am extremely grateful to Mr Stephen Burke for his allowing me to see parts of a draft of his forthcoming book, and for his help in several other ways.
8 G.H. Basset, *The Book of County Armagh* (Dublin, 1888) p. 107; *UFCN* 30 Aug. 1889.
9 Mountpottinger YMCA minute book 1895–1906 (PRONI D/3788/4/1/1) entries for 3 Sept. 1900 and 3 June 1901.
10 IFA minute book 1898–1903, entry for 30 Sept. 1902; E.B. Barrett, 'Working Boys' Clubs for Irish cities' in *Studies* III (1914) p. 492; M.J. Wigoder, *My Life* (Leeds, 1935) p. 167; L. Hyman, *The Jews of Ireland from Earliest Times to 1910* (Shannon, 1972) p. 199.
11 E. Malcolm, 'The rise of the pub: a study in the disciplining of popular culture' in J.S. Donnelly and Kerby A. Miller (eds) *Irish Popular Culture, 1650–1850* (Dublin, 1998) p. 71; M. Brodie (ed.) *Irish Football League 1890–1990: Official Centenary History* (Belfast, 1990) p. 117; C.V. Herbert, *Shelbourne Football Club Golden Jubilee Souvenir* (Dublin, 1945) p. 11; *ISN* 24 Sept. 1898; *A History of Belfast Celtic Football Club: a wonderful record* (Belfast, 1939) pp. 7–34; *UFCN* 14 Aug. 1891.
12 R.J. Patterson, *Catch-My-Pal: a story of good samaritanship* (London, 1912) pp. 15–18, 159; list of clubs affiliated to the IFA 1911/12 season, loose insertion in IFA Emergency committee book, 1909–43.
13 See Chapter 1.
14 Peter (ed.) *Football Annual*, p. 129; *NW* 4 Jan. 1882; IFA minute book 1880–86, entry for 18 Nov. 1880.
15 F. Lynch, *A History of Athlone Town F.C.: the first 101 years* (Athlone, 1991) pp. 3–9.
16 Sean Connolly, '"Ag déanamh *commanding*: elite responses to popular culture, 1660–1850' in Donnelly and Miller (eds) *Irish Popular Culture*, pp. 1–29.
17 Ballymena Cricket Club minute book, 1878–86 (PRONI, D/1638/1); Ranfurly estate rentals and accounts, 1861–2 (PRONI, D/1932/2/5).
18 L.T. and N. Robinson, *Three Homes* (London, 1938) p. 194.

19 *ISN* 12 Sept. 1898; *BNL* 22 Nov. 1880; *ISN* 10 Sept. 1898.
20 M. Brodie, *Linfield: 100 years* (Belfast, 1985) pp. 3–5; *ISN* 5 Nov. 1898 and 1 Dec. 1900; *UFCN* 17 Apr. 1896.
21 *ISN* 23 Apr. 1910 and 6 Aug. 1898; G.A. Birmingham (J.O. Hannay), *The Red Hand of Ulster* (London, 1912) p. 73.
22 Bannister and Hamilton, *Sport in Lisburn*, p. 87; *ISN* 12 June 1897 and 22 June 1901. For the Barbour family firm see E.R.R. Green, 'Thomas Barbour and the American linen-thread industry' in J.M. Goldstrom and L.A. Clarkson (eds) *Irish Population, Economy and Society* (Oxford, 1981) pp. 213–30.
23 S.R. Dennison and O. MacDonagh, *Guinness 1886–1939: from incorporation to the Second World War* (Cork, 1998) p. 125. For rather idealised contemporary views of Jacobs' factory see A. Wright, *Disturbed Dublin: the story of the great strike of 1913–14* (London, 1914) pp. 64–8 and B. Meakin, *Model Factories and Villages* (London, 1905) pp. 276, 284.
24 J. Gray, *City in Revolt: James Larkin and the Belfast Dock Strike of 1907* (Belfast, 1985) pp. 21–2; J.W Boyle, *The Irish Labor Movement in the Nineteenth Century* (Washington, DC, 1988) pp. 145–50.
25 P. Joyce, *Work, Society and Politics: the culture of the factory in later Victorian England* (Brighton, 1980) pp. 134–57, 152.
26 *Pastime* III, No. 73, 15 Oct. 1884; *FJ* 18 Oct. 1890; *Newry Telegraph* 26 Feb. 1889; *[Dublin] Evening Telegraph* 23 Mar. 1896.
27 IFA minute book 1898–1903, entry for 3 Oct. 1899. For street games, see Chapter 1.
28 Mason, *Association Football*, pp. 21–31; D. Russell, *Football and the English: a social history of association football in England, 1863–1995* (Preston, 1998) pp. 14–16.
29 *ISN* 22 Apr. 1899. See, for example, *Belfast Telegraph* 1 Mar. 1902; *Derry Journal* 1 May 1899; *ISN* 5 Jan. 1901; E.J. O'Mahony, *Bohemians Football Club, Golden Jubilee Souvenir* (Dublin, 1940) p. 33.
30 IFA minute book 1898–1903, entries for 28 Apr. 1903, 9 Feb. 1904, 23 July 1902 and 29 Sep. 1903; IFA minute book 1903–9, entry for 29 Sept. 1909; *FJ* 6 May 1907.
31 Rules of St Columb's Court Cricket and Football Club [*c.*1904] in Borough of Londonderry, Town Clerk's Dept Files (Derry City Archives, file 832); *Sport* 28 Apr. 1906; 'The choice of a representative' in *New Ireland Review* XXXIV (1910–11) p. 345.
32 Bassett, *Armagh*, p. 183; Rules of St Columb's Court Cricket and Football Club; J. Gray (ed.) *Thomas Carnduff: Life and writings* (Belfast, 1994) p. 139; *ISN* 29 June and 17 Aug. 1901; *CPA Annual Report, 1907* p. 6.
33 *UFCN* 19 Apr. 1889.
34 *UFCN* 26 Oct. 1888.
35 IFA minute book 1880–86, entry for 1 Nov. 1885.
36 *UFCN* 31 July 1896.
37 *UFCN* 16 Nov. 1888, 4 Oct. and 27 Sept. 1889.
38 *NW* 28 Mar. 1887.
39 Accounts of CIYMS Athletic Club 1886–8, loose insertion in CIYMS minute book 1884–91 (PRONI, D/3936/A/1/1); *ISN* 12 June 1897;*Ulster Echo* 11 Jan. 1908; S.J. McGuiness to Londonderry Corporation, 25 Feb. 1904 and Sir F.H. Miller to Alderman P. Maxwell, 8 Nov. 1904 in County Borough of Londonderry, Town Clerk's Dept (Derry City Archives, file no. 832).
40 For coaches and professional players see Chapter 3.
41 For continued patronage and paternalism see, for example, IFA Protest and Appeals

minute book 1909–14, entries for 15 Feb. 1912 and 30 Jan. 1913; also G. Black, *The Rovers 80 Years: a history of Tandragee Rovers Football Club 1909–1989* (Portadown, 1989?) pp. 1–4.
42 *UFCN* 28 Dec. 1888, 29 Nov. 1889, 15 Aug. and 17 Oct. 1890.
43 *UFCN* 17 Aug. 1894.
44 Belfast Celtic Football and Athletic Company Ltd, minute book 1924–40, general meeting 8 July 1924.
45 *IN* 2 Sept. 1901; *Belfast Telegraph* 3 Mar. 1902; *Sport* 12 Oct. 1912; J. Kennedy, *Belfast Celtic* (Belfast, 1979) pp. 1–10; M. Brodie, *The Story of Glentoran* (Belfast, 1981) pp. 3–5; Herbert, *Shelbourne*, pp. 12–20. The Derry Celtic Park Company was in existence in Londonderry by 1913, and associated with the Derry Celtic club. Unfortunately I have been unable to locate any details about this flotation.
46 Mason, *Association Football*, pp. 37–8; *ISN* 29 Jan. 1898.
47 W. Vamplew, *Pay Up and Play the Game: Professional sport in Britain 1875–1914* (Cambridge, 1988) p. 155.
48 *ISN* 27 Aug. 1898; Returns of Distillery Football and Athletic Club Ltd (Registry of Companies (N.I.) file R.187); IFA minute book, 1909–25, entry for 5 Oct. 1909. The other internationals were T.E. Alexander and W.K. Gibson, both solicitors, whose domestic playing careers were at the Cliftonville club. James Reid, who held five shares, was probably the former international who played for the Ulster club in the 1880s.
49 *UFCN* 14 June 1889; M. Brodie, *History of Irish Soccer* (Glasgow, 1964), p. 72; Cliftonville Football and Athletic Club Ltd (Registry of Companies, N.I. file R.145); Brodie (ed.) *Irish Football League*, p. 108.
50 *Belfast Celtic FC: Souvenir and History 1891–1939* (Belfast, 1939) p. 9.
51 Shelbourne Sports Co. Ltd (NAI, Dissolved Company Records, file 6191); Distillery Football and Athletic Club Ltd (Registry of Companies, N.I. (file R187); Glentoran Recreation Company Ltd (Registry of Companies N.I. file R.263).
52 Though outside our period, perhaps not untypical was the Ballymena Football and Athletic Club Ltd, which was floated in May 1928 and wound-up eight years later, when a 'first and only dividend' of 2s. 1d. per share was paid on each of the 2,775 10s. shares. Income included at least £1,300 from transfer fees. (See PRONI COM/40/2/2/478.)
53 *Belfast Telegraph* 3 Mar. 1902; Glentoran Recreation Company Ltd (R.263); Gibson and Pickford, *Association Football*, p. 100.
54 For odds being offered on matches see *UFCN* 4 Oct. 1889. For opposition to gambling, see Chapter 4.
55 For the importance of other sports to the Celtic club see M. Tuohy, *Belfast Celtic* (Belfast, 1978) pp. 23–8.
56 For crowd sizes see Chapter 4; *Western Star and Ballinasloe Advertiser* 26 Sept. 1896; G.A. Birmingham [J.O. Hannay], *The Lighter Side of Irish Life* (London, 1912) pp. 54–5.
57 The relevance of this argument is admittedly more applicable to the nine publicans who were shareholders than the single boat merchant.
58 *IN* 2 Sep 1901.
59 For the issue of footballing involvement leading to local prominence see Chapter 3.
60 *UFCN* 27 Oct. 1893; Gibson and Pickford (eds) *Association football*, p. 102; *IN* 4 Jan. 1909; *ISN* 17 Sept. 1910.
61 *UFCN* 5 June 1896; *ISN* 26 May 1900; *ISN* 31 May 1902; *IN* 24 Aug. 1914.
62 *ISN* 11 May 1901; *Belfast Telegraph* 3 Apr. 1902.

63 *UFCN* 14 June 1889; *ISN* 11 May 1901; *Belfast Telegraph* 2 Apr. 1902; Distillery Football and Athletic Club Ltd, Articles of Association (Registry of Companies (N.I.), file R.187).

64 *Sport* 12 Oct. 1912; Glenavon Football and Athletic Club Ltd, Articles of Association (Registry of Companies (N.I.), file R.261). Informal arrangements also existed for purchasers of Belfast Celtic shares to pay in very small instalments over a long period. I am very grateful to Mr Michael McGuigan for this information.

65 See *Belfast and Province of Ulster Directory 1912* and *1921/2* (Belfast 1912 and 1922) pp. 1269 and 1252. It should be noted that the nature of shareholders lists in English clubs also exhibited little change over time. (Mason, *Association Football*, p. 38).

66 Shareholders lists that are potentially comparable to the original subscribers exist only for the three clubs detailed in Tables 2.2–2.4. The occupational categories employed are in many ways arbitrary. There is no means of confirming a given occupation, or of distinguishing between artisans and proprietors in cases where occupations such as 'tailor' or 'baker' are given. Given these caveats, all conclusions drawn must be seen as impressionistic, and any attempt to present definitive facts has been avoided.

67 The possession of shares by those not resident in the direct vicinity can probably be accounted for by migration of shareholders after they had acquired their shares. This is probably most evident from the two Glentoran shareholders resident in Canada.

68 A.C. Hepburn, *A Past Apart: Studies in the history of Catholic Belfast 1850–1950* (Belfast, 1996) pp. 120–1.

69 Hepburn, *A Past Apart*, pp. 76, 149, 137.

70 *NW* 13 Mar. 1899; J. Lynch, *A Tale of Three Cities: Comparative studies in working-class life* (London, 1998) pp. 132–3.

CHAPTER 3 NOTES

1 IFA minute book, 1880–86, entries for 29 Jan. 1884 and 5 May 1886.
2 See Chapter 1.
3 D. Murphy, *Derry, Donegal and Modern Ulster 1790–1921* (Londonderry, 1981) pp. 170–2.
4 See Chapter 2; *Fermanagh Herald* 29 Oct. 1904.
5 IFA minute book 1880–86, entries for 18 Nov. 1880; *Belfast and Province of Ulster Directory* (Belfast, 1884) p. 198; Peters, *Irish Football Annual*, p. 30; *UFCN* 3 Apr. 1891.
6 C.W. Alcock (ed.) *The Football Annual 1883* (London, 1883) pp. 170–1.
7 I. Hawe, *A Brief Chronicle of Moyola Park Football Club* (Cookstown, 1982) pp. 3–4; *ISN* 30 Apr. 1910; *Pastime* II, No. 46, 9 Apr. 1884; see Chapter 1.
8 *The Clongownian* V, No. 1 (1908) pp. 43–5; *Castleknock College Chronicle* XXV (1910) pp. 57–9, 72–4.
9 R. Marshall, *Methodist College Belfast: the first hundred years* (Belfast, n.d.) p. 68.
10 T. West, *The Bold Collegians: the development of sport in Trinity College, Dublin* (Dublin, 1991) pp. 55, 91; W.S. Armour, *Armour of Ballymoney* (London, 1934) p. 15; T.W. Moody and J.C. Beckett, *Queen's Belfast 1845–1949: the history of a university* (London, 1959) I, p. 370.
11 Michael Taaffe, *These Days Are Gone Away* (London, 1959) pp. 30, 143.
12 *Sport* 3 Dec. 1904; Memoirs of John [Sean] Francis McKeown (Linen Hall Library, Belfast) p. 23.
13 *Freeman's Journal* 11 Jan. 1904; *Northern Whig* 17 Mar. 1913; Earl of Suffolk and

14   Berkshire, *The Encyclopaedia of Sports and Games* (London, 1911) III, p. 166.
     J. Lawrence, *Handbook of Cricket in Ireland (15th number), 1879–80* (Dublin, 1879) p. 176.
15   IFA minute book 1880–1886, entries for 9 Feb. 1882 and 16 Mar. 1881.
16   Walvin, *People's Game Revisited*, p. 81; Russel, *Football and the English*, pp. 23–4.
17   Russell, *Football and the English*, pp. 22–9; J. Arlott (ed.) *The Oxford Companion to Sports and Games* (Oxford, 1975) p. 335.
18   IFA minute book 1880–86, entry for 15 May 1883; *Pastime* I, Nos 21, 22 (1883) pp. 327, 382.
19   *Report of the Commissioners appointed to take the census of Ireland, 1841* [cd 504] XXIV, p. 440, Table VI; *Census of Ireland, 1881 Part II, General report* (BPP 1882 LXXVI [cd 3365], p. 535, Table XVIII). The initial reference to 'sportsmen' may refer to those involved in hunting or blood sports.
20   F. D'Arcy, *Horses, Lords and Racing Men: the Turf Club 1790–1990* (Curragh, 1991) p. 66; P. Myler, *Regency Rogue: Dan Donnelly, His life and legends* (Dublin, 1976) p. 52.
21   A. Steven, 'The Game of Rackets in Ulster' in *Ulster Folklife* XLII (1996) p. 106; N.D. McMillan, *One Hundred and Fifty Years of Cricket and Sport in County Carlow* (Dublin, 1984) pp. 6–7.
22   Walvin, *People's Game Revisited*, p. 83.
23   S.J.S. Ickringill, 'Amateur and professional: sport in Britain and America at the turn of the twentieth century', in J.C. Binfield and J. Stevenson (eds) *Sport, Culture and Politics* (Sheffield, 1993) pp. 30–48.
24   *UFCN* 17 Apr. 1891.
25   *UFCN* 25 Apr. and 9 May 1890; Co. Antrim FA minute book 1888–1897, entry for 2 Apr. 1890.
26   *NW* 4 May 1891.
27   *UFCN* 29 May 1891.
28   *NW* 2 Oct. 1890; *UFCN* 31 Oct. 1890.
29   *Belfast Evening Telegraph* 14 Aug. 1890; *UFCN* 22 Aug. 1890.
30   *Pastime* XV, No 397 (31 Dec. 1890) p462–3; *UFCN* 2 Jan. 1891.
31   *UFCN* 27 Feb. 1891.
32   *UFCN* 4, 18 Mar. and 1, 8 Apr. 1892.
33   *UFCN* 11 Mar. 1892.
34   *BNL* 10 May 1892.
35   *BNL* 9 May 1893
36   *UFCN* 3 Nov. 1893, 29 Nov. 1889 and 26 Sept. 1890. See also *Sport* 30 Sept. 1893.
37   *UFCN* 11 May 1894; *BNL* 1 May 1894.
38   *Sport* 9 Sept. 1893; J.J. MacCarthy, 'International Football: Ireland' in F. Marshall (ed.) *Football: the Rugby Union Game* (London, 1892) p. 222.
39   *UFCN* 4 May 1894; Brodie, *100 Years*, p. 3.
40   *ISN* 20 Aug. 1898, 14 Jun 1902; *Sport* 13 May 1905; see, for example, *Freeman's Journal* 11 Jan. 1904.
41   *Scottish Referee* 13 Aug. 1894.
42   *Sport* 8, 29 Sept. 1894; *UFCN* 6 Sept. 1895.
43   *NW* 6 May 1895; *BNL* 15 Jan. 1895.
44   See Chapter 2.
45   *UFCN* 22 Mar. 1889; *IN* 13 Mar. 1905; *ISN* 3 Sept. 1898.
46   *UFCN* 20 Nov. 1896.
47   IFA minute book 1898–1903, entry for 21 Mar. 1899; *Sport* 9 Sept. 1893.

NOTES

48 *ISN* 27 Aug. 1898, 29 June, 19 Oct. 1901.
49 *ISN* 1 Mar. 1902.
50 IFA minute book 1898–1903, entry for 30 Apr. 1901; *ISN* 28 June 1902; IFA register of professionals 1889–1903; *ISN* 23 Apr. 1904.
51 *Sport* 6 May 1905; *IN* 4 May 1914.
52 *Sport* 3 Oct. 1914; *IN* 10 Nov. 1913; *ISN* 1 Mar. 1913; *IN* 20 Apr. 1913.
53 *UFCN* 7 Sept. 1894; IFA Emergency committee book 1909–43, entry for 4 Dec. 1911.
54 *UFCN* 4 Jan. 1895; IFA International sub-committee minute book 1902–8, entries for 28 Feb. 1903 and 20 Feb. 1904.
55 Irish League Committee minute book 1909–13, entries for 5 Oct. 1910 and 27 Aug. 1913.
56 *ISN* 11 Mar. 1899, 7 May 1910 and 5 June 1909.
57 *UFCN* 13 Nov. 1896; Mason, *Association Football*, pp. 96–7; Vamplew, *Pay Up*, p. 243.
58 Mason, *Association Football*, p. 97.
59 *ISN* 10 May 1902, 11 June and 13 Aug. 1904; *Sport* 20 Aug. 1904.
60 D'Arcy, *Horses, Lords and Racing Men*, p. 185; Sir William Orpen, *Tales of Old Ireland and Myself* (London, 1924) p. 26; C. Smith and B. Shaw (eds) *Whigs on the Green* (Dublin, 1996) p. 111.
61 For comparative wage rates see *Board of Trade Reports, Standard Time rates of wages, 1900, 1906 and 1914* (BPP 1900 LXXXII [cd 317], 1906 CXII [cd 3245] and 1914 LXXX [cd 7194]); *Statistical tables: earnings of agricultural labourers 1898 and 1905* (BPP 1905 XCVII [cd 2376]); *Commission on the Royal Irish and Dublin Metropolitan Police* (BPP 1914 XLIV [cd 7421]); *Board of Trade Reports, Standard time wages 1914* (BPP 1914 LXXX [cd 7194]); Autobiography of John [Sean] Francis McKeown (LHL) pp. 107–8.
62 *UFCN* 9 Nov. 1894; *ISN* 18 Feb. 1899.
63 *ISN* 27 Aug. 1898 and 9 Aug. 1902; *Nomad's Weekly* 10 Oct. 1908 and 17 Apr. 1909; *Ideas* 25 Oct. 1913.
64 B. Dabscheck, 'Defensive Manchester: a history of the Professional Footballers' Association' in R. Cashman and M. McKernan (eds) *Sport in History* (Brisbane, 1980) pp. 230–2.
65 *Nomad's Weekly* 17 Apr. 1909.
66 IFL management committee minute book 1913–23, entries for 3 Sept. 1913 and 29 May 1914.
67 See, for example, Autobiography of William Greer of Belfast (PRONI, T/3249/1) p. 33.
68 *ISN* 8 Dec. 1900; John Gray (ed.) *Thomas Carnduff: Life and Writings* (Belfast, 1994) p. 136.
69 *[Dublin] Evening Telegraph* Apr. 1906 and 4 Feb. 1907.
70 See Chapter 1.
71 Dick Fitzgerald, *How to Play Gaelic Football* (Dublin, 1914) pp. 14–15.
72 C.M. Ruxton, Sec. IRFU, to [Sec. Northern Branch, IRFU], 8 Dec. 1913, in IRFU (Northern Branch) minute book 1913–22 (PRONI, D/3867/A/5).
73 IFA minute book, 1898–1903, entry for 22 Nov. 1898.
74 *ISN* 31 Aug. 1901; J.J. Bentley, 'Professionalism in sport' in *Athletic News Football Annual 1896* (London, 1895) p. 13.
75 *ISN* 18 Jan, 11 Jan., 29 Nov. 1902.
76 *FJ* 11 and 13 Jan. 1904.

77 *IN* 2 Jan. 1905.
78 *ISN* 9 Apr. 1910.
79 *ISN* 17 Sept. 1910.
80 *Report of Improvement Commission adopted by the council, 1909* (Belfast, 1909) p. 7 (copy in Co. Antrim FA Council and Senior Council Minute book 1906–1912).
81 IFA Register of professionals 1899–1903; *ISN* 24 Jan., 29 Aug. 1903.
82 *Sport* 30 Jan., 19 Mar., 26 Mar., 2 Apr. 1904.
83 *ISN* 16 Apr. 1904.
84 IFA minute book 1903–9, entry for 6 Dec. 1898; *ISN* 30 Apr. 1904; *Sport* 17 Sept. 1904.
85 *Sport* 17 Feb. 1906.
86 *Ulster Echo* 17 Feb. 1908; *Sport* 22 Feb. 1908.
87 *Nomad's Weekly and Belfast Critic* 22 Feb. 1908.
88 IFA minute book 1903–1909, AGM report 9 May 1908 and loose insert headed 'Minutes of the International FA Board meeting 19–20 June 1908'.
89 IFA minute book 1909–25, entry for 4 Jan. 1910; *ISN* 8 Jan. 1910.
90 *ISN* 12 Nov., 8 Jan. 1910; *Sport* 13 Jan. 1912, 10 Jan. 1914.
91 IFA Emergency Committee book 1909–43, entry for 11 Dec. 1917; IFA Rules Revision Committee minute book 1909–47, entries for 27 Aug. and 13 Sept. 1918.
92 Russel, *Football and the English*, p. 85; *Sunday News* 21 Jan. 1979.
93 U. O'Connor, *Oliver St John Gogarty: a Biography* (London, 1969 edn) pp. 14–15.
94 J. Kennedy, *Belfast Celtic* (Belfast, 1979) p. 18. See also obituary in *Irish Press* 16 Dec. 1963.
95 IFA register of professionals, 1899–1903.
96 *Sport* 5 Sept. 1896; S. McGarrigle, *Green Gunners: Arsenal's Irish* (Edinburgh, 1991) pp. 43–4; *ISN* 2 July 1898.
97 *Sport* 21 Nov. 1896; *ISN* 12 Nov. 1898.
98 *ISN* 30 Jan. 1909.
99 *ISN* 13 Feb. 1909; *Nomad's Weekly* 18 Feb. 1911.
100 For the number of clubs affiliated to the IFA see Chapter 2.
101 *ISN* 29 June, 7 Sept. 1901.
102 The clubs were: Distillery, Distillery Seconds, Linfield, Linfield Sandsvale, Belfast Celtic, Belfast Amateurs, Glentoran, Glentoran Nettlefield, Ulster, Bloomfield, Glenbank, Knockbreda, Castlereagh, Ormeau, and Belfast Hibernians, all of Belfast. The Lisburn and Lagan Valley clubs were Wesley, Hilden, Dunmurray, Dunmurray Sandsvale, Balmoral, Primrose, Suffolk, and Lambeg Rangers. The Cookstown club was situated in Tyrone; Holywood, Holywood Swifts and Dromore in Down, and Lurgan in Armagh. Definite locations for the Stanley and Templeton clubs were not found.
103 Vamplew, *Pay Up*, pp. 281–3; but see also M. Mullan, 'The devolution of the Irish economy in the nineteenth century and the bifurcation of Irish sport' in *International Journal of the History of Sport* III, Pt 2 (1996) pp. 42–60.
104 A. Synan, 'What to do with our police' in *New Ireland Review* XXVIII (1907–8), p. 196.
105 Memoirs of John [Sean] Francis McKeown (LHL) p. 110. Derry Celtic engaged in professionalism for a short period, but did not sustain the practice.
106 M. Brodie (ed.) *The Irish Football League: Official centenary history* (Belfast, 1990) p. 203.

107 *Census of Ireland, 1901 (Pt I, Vol. III) No. 1a, City of Belfast*, BPP 1902 [cd 1123] p. 221, table XXIV.
108 *ISN* 3 Dec. 1898.
109 *Sport* 17 Oct. 1885; *ISN* 5 Jul. 1902.
110 See Chapter 1.
111 *ISN* 24 Sept. 1898; *Famous Footballers* (London, 1895) p. 10; *Athletic News Football Annual* (London, 1893 edn) p. 35; M. Tuohy, *Belfast Celtic* (Belfast, 1978) p. 20; A.P. Hatton, 'Regimental cricket' in *Badminton Magazine* XXXI, (July–Dec. 1910) p. 79.
112 *Sport* 8 Sept. 1894; *UFCN* 20 July 1894.
113 *ISN* 13, 27 June 1903; *IN* 2 Sept. 1901.
114 *ISN* 5 July 1902; *Sport* 3 Feb. 1906 and 2 May 1914.
115 *ISN* 15 Feb. 1902, 2 May 1903, 11 Feb. 1899.
116 The census returns are available on the PRONI Mic 354 series.
117 All the individuals identified had addresses within the city of Belfast.
118 *IN* 17 July 1901.
119 C.J.N. Fleming, 'Rugby football' in *Badminton Magazine* III (July–Dec. 1896) pp. 565–6; *ISN* 1 Feb. 1902; *Athletic News Football Annual* 1902–3, p. 6.
120 *ISN* 13 Aug. and 6 Aug. 1898; *Sport* 17 Sept. 1904 and 5 May 1906; *Castleknock College Chronicle* XXIV (1909) p. 78.
121 I am very grateful to the Rev. Jack McCandless for discussing his father's career and circumstances with me.
122 *IN* 7 Aug. 1927; *ISN* 31 Mar. 1917.
123 *Sport* 5 Dec. 1914; *ISN* 7 July 1917.
124 *ISN* 24 Mar. and 2 June 1917.
125 *A History of Belfast Celtic Football Club: a wonderful record* (Belfast, 1929) p. 25.
126 IFA Finance committee minute book, 1909–35; entry for 25 Aug. 1924.
127 *Barnsley Independent* 2 Sept. 1899; *Birmingham Daily Mail* 13 Sept. 1899; *ISN* 17 Mar. 1917.
128 The census instructions required the word 'Irish ' to be entered in the appropriate column for only those who were monolingual Irish speakers, while bilingual subjects were to be marked 'Irish and English'. For monolingual English speakers no entry was to be made at all. In this case it seems likely that these four subjects were in fact bilingual.
129 *ISN* 24 Sept. 1898, 30 Sept. 1899, 4 June 1904.
130 Mason, *Association Football*, pp. 90–3.
131 I have taken this latter concept from a paper presented by Dr John Lynch to the 1997 annual conference of the Economic and Social History Society of Ireland.
132 A.C. Hepburn, *A Past Apart*, pp. 125ff.
133 Springhall *et al.*, *Sure and Steadfast*, p. 51; *UFCN* 30 Aug. 1889; *CPA Monthly Magazine* VII No. 99, Sept. 1907) p. 115 and VII, No. 12 (Dec. 1907) p. 153; Minute book of the General Committee of the CIYMS 1884–1891 (PRONI D/3936/A/1/1).
134 *Census of Ireland, 1901, III, BPP (1902) CXXVI*, Table XXXIII, pp. 232–3. The wards were Falls, Shankill and Pottinger.
135 Four Catholic players were registered for more than one club. Patrick Barry and Bernard Dorrian played for Belfast Amateurs and Belfast Hibernians prior to being transferred to Belfast Celtic. William Brown moved from Celtic to Distillery, and William McAreavy from Celtic to Glentoran.
136 See for example *The Times*, 16 Sept. 1912.

137 For competition winners see the appendix.
138 P. Byrne, *The Football Association of Ireland – 75 years* (Dublin, 1996) pp. 20–1.

CHAPTER 4 NOTES

1   IFA minute book 1880–86, entry for 23 May 1884.
2   *IN* 17 Mar. 1913; *Irish Times* 17 Mar. 1913.
3   See for example *ISN* 12 Mar. 1904 for estimates of 14,000 and 19,000 at the same match.
4   No final tie was played in 1912 due to a dispute between the senior clubs and the IFA. Sources used in addition to the records of the IFA were *Coleraine Constitution and Northern Advertiser* 16 Apr. 1881, *NW* 7 May 1883, 29 Mar. 1886, 10 Mar. 1890, 19 Mar. 1894, 20 Mar. 1899, 26 Mar. 1900 and 15 Apr. 1901; *Sport* 26 Apr. 1884 and 28 Mar. 1885; *BNL* 14 Feb. 1887, 19 Mar. 1888 and 26 Mar. 1895; *UFCN* 22 Mar. 1889, 14 Mar. 1890, 20 Mar. 1891, 18 Mar. 1892 and 20 Mar. 1896; *IN* 22 Mar. 1897, 17 Mar. 1902, 16 Mar. 1903, 21 Mar. 1904, 13 Mar. 1905, 30 Apr. 1906, 25 Mar. 1907, 30 Mar. 1908, 12 Apr. 1909, 28 Mar. 1910, 27 Mar. 1911, 31 Mar. 1913 and 30 Mar. 1914; *ISN* 19 Mar. 1898, 24 Mar. 1900, 13 Apr. 1901, 15 Mar. 1902 and 10 Apr. 1909; *[Dublin] Evening Telegraph* 25 Mar. 1907; *FJ* 23 Mar. 1908. It should also be noted that these figures may represent minimum estimates rather than definitive figures. Club and IFA members and officials were admitted without charge, while by 1914 a number of tricks, varying from leaping turnstiles to paying with counterfeit coins, were being employed by 'dead heads' to gain free admission to games (*ISN* 31 Jan. 1914).
5   *UFCN* 25 Nov. 1892. The two clubs were Linfield and Cliftonville.
6   *ISN* 19 Mar. 1898.
7   *UFCN* 25 Aug. 1893; *Nomad* 22 Feb. 1908.
8   These trends are also reflected in reported attendances at international games and in domestic League matches.
9   *ISN* 4 Sept. 1897; *IN* 27 Oct. 1913.
10 *NW* 4 Jan. 1886.
11 IFA Emergency committee book 1909–43, entry for 18 Oct. 1914; *Sport* 21 Mar. 1914.
12 See, for example, *NW* 20 Dec. 1886 and *Sport* 24 Nov. 1906.
13 See Chapter 2.
14 IFA minute book 1880–86, entry for 16 Mar. 1881; Co. Antrim FA minute book 1906–12, entry for 19 Dec. 1910.
15 *NW* 18 Feb. 1882; *UFCN* 7 Mar. 1890.
16 *Sport* 30 Nov. 1895; *ISN* 3 Dec. 1895, 12 Oct. 1896 and 12 Nov. 1910.
17 *UFCN* 15 Nov. 1889; *[Dublin] Evening Telegraph* 28 Jan. 1907; *Sport* 1 Feb. 1908 and 12 Oct. 1912.
18 W.F. Mandle, *The Gaelic Athletic Association and Irish Nationalist politics 1884–1924* (Dublin, 1987) pp. 105, 150.
19 W.F. Mandle, 'Sport as politics: the Gaelic Athletic Association 1884–1916' in R. Cashman and M. McKernan (eds) *Sport in History* (Brisbane, 1980) pp. 99–123.
20 See for example *United Irishman* 29 July 1905.
21 E. Malcolm, *Ireland Sober, Ireland Free: Drink and temperance in nineteenth-century Ireland* (Dublin, 1986) pp. 238–49, 273–4. The distance was extended to five miles in 1906.

NOTES

22 Bulmer Hobson, *Ireland Yesterday and Tomorrow* (Tralee, 1968) p. 34; *Newry Reporter* 30 Oct. 1886; D. Gallogly, *Cavan's Football Story* (Cavan, 1979) pp. 23–4.
23 Suffolk and Berkshire, Earl of, *The Encyclopaedia of Sports and Games* (London, 1911) III, p. 166.
24 See Chapter 5.
25 IFA International committee book 1909–49, entry for 19 Feb. 1923; IFA minute book 1903–9, entry for 5 Feb. 1907. The latter motion was passed only by 11 votes to 8.
26 *UFCN* 21 Oct. 1892; IFL minute book 1909–13, entry for 5 Oct. 1910.
27 *UFCN* 9 Oct. 1896; IFA minute book 1903–9, entry for 5 Jan. 1909.
28 *Sport* 14 Sept. 1912.
29 IRFU (NB) minute book 1885–89 (PRONI D/3867/A/1), entry for 16 Jan. 1891; *UFCN* 13 Feb. 1891; IRFU (NB) minute book 1902–7 (PRONI D/3867/A/3), entry for 1 Oct. 1907; *ISN* 17 Feb. 1906. The latter figure was seen by some as disappointing (see *IN* 19 Feb. 1906.)
30 IRFU (NB) minute book 1902–7, entry for 17 Dec. 1903. Letters from the secretaries of the two bodies were eventually published in the Belfast press (see *ISN* 16 Jan. and 23 Jan. 1904).
31 *IN* 14 Mar. 1904; *Irish Times* 14 Mar. 1904.
32 [Douglas Goldring] *A Stranger in Ireland* (Dublin, 1918) p. 42.
33 See Chapter 1.
34 *Sport* 23 Apr. 1904.
35 *ISN* 17 Mar. 1900; *IN* 5 Mar. 1900; *ISN* 3 Mar. 1900.
36 *IN* 30 Apr. 1906 and 25 Mar. 1907.
37 *Sport* 27 Jan. 1906, 2 Apr. 1904; *ISN* 12 Mar. 1904; *IN* 14 Mar. 1904.
38 *Sport* 3 Mar. 1906; *FJ* 26 Feb. 1906
39 *IN* 12 Jan. 1914.
40 *Sport* 22 Sept. 1906; *Dublin Evening Telegraph* 17 Sept. 1906; IFA International sub-committee minute book 1902–8, entry for 3 Mar. 1906.
41 J. Gray (ed) *Thomas Carnduff: Life and Writings* (Belfast, 1994) p. 135; *UFCN* 28 Dec. 1888, 17 May 1895 and 10 Jan. 1896; Londonderry Borough Council Parks, Libraries and Museums Committee minute book 1908–17, p. 43 (Derry City Archives, file no 255).
42 *UFCN* 30 Aug. 1889, 4 Oct. 1889 and 28 Aug. 1891.
43 *UFCN* 26 Sept. 1890. See also *Nomad* 21 Sept. 1912.
44 *UFCN* 23 Sept. and 20 May 1892.
45 *Sport* 16 Sept. 1893, 21 and 28 Dec. 1895; *BNL* 5 Nov. 1895.
46 *UFCN* 25 Dec. 1891; *Minutes of evidence of the Royal commission on Labour* II (BPP 1892 XXXVI Pt 2 [cd 6795]) pp. 520–4; *UFCN* 18 Dec. 1891.
47 IFA minute book 1903–9, entries for 3 Sept. 1907 and 5 Jan. 1909.
48 *Sport* 23 Apr. 1904 and 24 Mar. 1906; *IN* 13 Oct. 1913.
49 *UFCN* 14 Mar. 1890.
50 *NW* 3 May 1886; *UFCN* 7 Oct. 1892.
51 David Smyth to Chairman IFA, 4 June 1906 (loose insert in IFA minute book 1903–9).
52 *IN* 20 and 27 1913.
53 *UFCN* 2 May 1890; *NW* 4 Jan. 1886 and 29 Dec. 1887; *UFCN* 23 Nov. 1888.
54 *Sport* 10 Mar. 1894.
55 IFA international sub-committee minute book 1902–8, entry for 25 Mar. 1905.
56 *NW* 2 May 1891; *Nomad* 11 Mar. 1911.

57 IRFU (NB) minute book 1902–7 (PRONI, D/3867/A/3), entry for 28 Mar. 1905; *NW* 17 Apr. 1905.
58 See M. Neill, 'Women at work in Ulster, 1845–1911' (unpublished Ph.D. thesis, QUB, 1996) pp. 47–8, 307–8, 312.
59 *ISN* 18 Oct. 1902.
60 The honorary treasurer of the IRFU created something of a sensation in 1904 by stating that association crowds, though larger and generally more interested in the games they watched, were inferior to those at rugby matches, as they were not of 'the same class and didn't pay so much' (IRFU (NB) minute book 1902–7, entry for 29 Sept. 1904). See also *NW* 14 Mar. 1904 for the attendance of 'the classes' at rugby matches, and 'the masses' at association games.
61 Autobiography and reminiscences of James L. Nevin, III, p. 18 (Ballymoney Branch Library, Co Antrim); Autobiography of William Greer, 1896–1914 (PRONI T/3249/1) p. 33; Gray (ed.) *Thomas Carnduff*, pp. 162–4; C.S. Andrews, *Dublin Made Me: an autobiography* (Dublin, 1979) p. 39.
62 *NW* 16 Sept. 1912.
63 *The Times* 17 Sept. 1912; *BNL* 18 Mar. 1920.
64 For a consideration of the relationship between occupations and social class see W.A. Armstrong, 'The use of information about occupation', in E.A. Wrigley (ed.) *Nineteenth-Century Society* (Cambridge, 1972) pp. 191–210. It should also be noted that in this case the Directory from which the occupations of individuals are derived lists only heads of households and therefore probably only the older men among the injured.
65 All the injured gave addresses in Belfast, and all but three were resident in the western half of the city.
66 *UFCN* 28 Mar. 1890; *ISN* 14 Mar. 1903; *IN* 30 Apr. 1906; *[Dublin] Evening Telegraph* 18 Mar. 1907; *ISN* 23 Mar. 1907.
67 *BNL* 17 Apr. 1882; *UFCN* 19 Oct. 1888; *NW* 6 May 1895.
68 *Sport* 29 Nov. 1884; *UFCN* 14 Dec. 1888; *ISN* 17 Sept. 1898; *UFCN* 1 Nov. 1889; *BNL* 2 Nov. 1896; Co. Antrim FA minute book 1898–1906, entry for 20 Dec. 1905.
69 *Amusements* I, No. 4 24 Sept. 1900; *UFCN* 11 Jan. 1889; *Sport* 18 and 25 Apr. 1885; IFA Protest and Appeals minute book 1909–14, entry for 5 Oct. 1911. Henderson, the goalkeeper in question in 1885, played three games for Ireland, conceding a total of 20 goals.
70 See for example Co. Antrim FA minute book 1898–1906, entry for 27 Jan. 1904.
71 *UFCN* 2 Nov. 1888; Co. Antrim FA minute book 1888–97, entry for 7 Nov. 1888.
72 *UFCN* 1 Mar. 1889 and 28 Mar. 1890.
73 *Sport* 9 Oct. 1895.
74 *UFCN* 20 Sept. and 13 Dec. 1895.
75 *FJ* 13 Mar. 1899; *Fermanagh Herald* 2 Jan. 1902; *Portadown News* 19 Nov. 1904; *Cork Sportsman* 5 Mar. 1910.
76 *NW* 14 Sept. 1896; *UFCN* 18 Sept. 1896; *Fermanagh Herald* 13 Aug. and 29 Oct. 1904.
77 This fact may well be related to growing opposition to association football in rural areas from the GAA, and consequently more regular reporting of trouble in the Nationalist press, rather than any real increase in incidents.
78 IFA minute book 1903–9, entry for 28 Mar. 1907.
79 *UFCN* 13 Nov. 1896; *Belfast Telegraph* 7 Apr. 1902. It was later suggested that at least one stand in Belfast was demolished after the Ibrox incident (*Ulster Echo* 11 Jan. 1908).

80 *FJ* 13 Mar. 1899; IFA Protest and appeals minute book 1909–14, entry for 24 Feb. 1910.
81 *Sport* 9 Dec. 1905; *ISN* 15 Oct. 1898.
82 *UFCN* 28 Mar. 1890.
83 *UFCN* 1 Nov. 1889.
84 *NW* 13 Mar. 1899. For less damning reports see *BNL* 13 Mar. 1899 and *ISN* 11 Mar. 1899. IFA minute book 1898–1903, entry for 14 Mar. 1899.
85 *BNL* 7 Sept. 1899.
86 *ISN* 11 Jan. 1902.
87 *UFCN* 1 Nov. 1889 and 19 Sept. 1890; *ISN* 30 Sept. 1899 and 17 Sept. 1898.
88 *NW* 16 Mar. 1891; *UFCN* 17 Mar. 1893; *NW* 13 Mar. 1893; *BNL* 14 Mar. 1893.
89 *UFCN* 12 May 1893; *ISN* 30 Sept. 1899.
90 *Parliamentary Debates* (Series 4) CLXXXVIII (7 May 1908) Col. 406.
91 IFA minute book 1898–1903, entries for 29 Aug. 1899 and 25 Oct. 1898.
92 *ISN* 23 Oct. 1897; *UFCN* 25 Nov. 1892.
93 IFA minute book 1898–1903, entries for 10 Oct. 1899 and 3 Dec. 1901.
94 *ISN* 2 Mar. 1901.
95 *Report of the Improvement Commission* (Belfast, 1909) p. 7 (copy in Co. Antrim FA minute book 1906–12); *ISN* 11 Dec. 1909.
96 *Nomad* 18 Feb. 1911; IFA minute book 1903–9, entry for 7 Apr. 1908; *IN* 7 Mar. 1910.
97 *ISN* 14 Sept. 1912; *BNL*, *NW* and *IN* 16 Sept. 1912.
98 *Sport* 21 Sept. 1912; *The Times* 25 Sept. 1912.
99 J.H. Holmes, Stockport to [Sec. IFA], 16 Sept. 1912, loose insertion in Senior League clubs protest and appeals committee minute book 1912–22; RIC Commissioner for Belfast monthly report 1 Oct. 1912 (PRO CO 904/88/39).
100 *BNL* 15 Sept. 1912.
101 S. Connolly, *Religion and Society in Nineteenth-century Ireland* (Dundalk, 1994) pp. 22–3; A. Boyd, *Holy War in Belfast* (Belfast 1987) pp. 1–173.
102 C. Hirst, 'Religious and political conflict in nineteenth century Belfast: a case study of the Pound and Sandy Row 1820–1886' (unpublished Ph.D. thesis, QUB, 1997) pp. 14–110 (see pp. 178–9 for bowling competitions between the two areas). For a fictionalised autobiographical account of sporting conflicts escalating to violence in the same area see M. McLaverty, *Call My Brother Back* (Dublin, 1970 edn) p. 109.
103 *BNL* 2 Apr. 1895; *ISN* 27 Apr. 1907. For Linfield FC see also Chapter 2.
104 E.M. Forster to Jessica Darling, 6 Feb. 1912 and same to Alice Forster, 9 Feb. 1912, in M. Lago and P. N. Furbank (eds) *Selected Letters of E. M. Forster, I, 1879–1920* (London, 1983) pp. 128–9; Gray (ed.) *Thomas Carnduff*, pp. 98, 144; A. Morgan, *Labour and Partition: the Belfast working class*, (London, 1991) p. 215.
105 Copy of handbill dated 20 Sept. 1912 in IFL minute book 1909–13; *NW* 28 Sept. 1912; IFL minute book 1909–13, entries for 2 Oct., 22 Nov. and 6 Dec. 1912.
106 RIC Commissioner for Belfast, Monthly report, 1 Oct. 1912 (PRO CO 904/88/39); *Sport* 28 Sept. 1912.
107 *The Times* 17 Sept. 1912; *IN* 18 Sept. 1912.
108 *BNL* 14 Dec. 1912
109 *Sport* 23 Nov. 1912; *IN* 19 May 1913; Sir F. Wall, *Fifty Years of Football* (London, 1935) p. 210; *IN* 8 and 15 Sept. 1913.
110 Copy of handbill in IFL minute book 1909–13; IFL minute book 1913–23, entry for 4 Feb. 1914; Co. Antrim FA minute book 1912–20, entry for 11 Feb. 1914. See also *IN* 10 and 16 Feb. 1914 for suggestions that the Co. Antrim Association did not press hard enough for a stiffer sentence.

111 *Sport* 21 Mar. 1914; Mandle, GAA *and Nationalist Politics*, pp. 150–1.
112 The 1911 census suggests a population of 36 million for England and Wales, and 4.4 million for Ireland.
113 Russell, *Football*, pp. 56–7.
114 E. Dunning, P. Murphy and J. Williams, *The Roots of Football Hooliganism: an historical and sociological study* (London, 1988) pp. 74, 49, 48.
115 W. Vamplew, 'Ungentlemanly conduct: the control of soccer-crowd behaviour in England, 1881–1914', in T.C. Smout (ed.) *The Search for Wealth and Stability: Essays in economic and social history presented to M.W. Flinn* (London, 1979) p. 140.
116 W. Murray, *The Old Firm: Sectarianism, sport and society in Scotland* (Edinburgh, 1984) pp. 165–6, 168–9. For sectarianism elsewhere in Scottish football see also N. Tranter, 'The Cappielow riot and the composition and behaviour of soccer crowds in late Victorian Scotland' in *International Journal of the History of Sport* XII (1995) pp. 125–40.
117 See above; also *IN* 27 Oct. 1913.
118 *Fermanagh Herald* 29 Oct. 1904; *Gaelic Athlete* 13 Jan. 1912.
119 IFA minute book 1909–25, entry for 7 Apr. 1913; *IN* 24 Mar. 1913; IFA international sub-committee minute book 1902–8, entry for 18 Apr. 1904.
120 *Sport* 24 Sept. 1914 and 21 Sept. 1912; J.W. Good, *Ulster and Ireland* (Dublin, 1919) p. 268.

CHAPTER 5 NOTES

1 R.P. Davis, *Arthur Griffith and Non-violent Sinn Fein* (Tralee, 1974) pp. 3–36; L. O'Broin, *Revolutionary Underground: the story of the Irish Republican Brotherhood 1858–1924* (Dublin, 1976) pp. 34–62.
2 J.E. and G.W. Dunleavy, *Douglas Hyde: a maker of modern Ireland* (Oxford, 1991) pp. 169–287.
3 L.P. Curtis, *Coercion and Conciliation in Ireland, 1880–92: a study in Conservative Unionism* (Princeton, 1963) pp. 331–92; A. Gailey, *Ireland and the Death of Kindness: the experience of constructive unionism 1890–1905* (Cork, 1987) pp. 161–210.
4 E. O'Connor, *A Labour History of Ireland 1824–1960* (Dublin, 1992) pp. 46–66; A. Morgan, *Labour and Partition: the Belfast working class 1905–23* (London, 1991) pp. 43–144.
5 R.F. Foster, 'Thinking from hand to mouth: Anglo-Irish literature, Gaelic Nationalism and Irish politics in the 1890s' in id., *Paddy and Mr Punch: Connections in Irish and English history* (London, 1995) pp. 262–280.
6 W.F. Mandle, 'Sport as politics: the Gaelic Athletic Association 1884–1916' in R. Cashman and M. McKernan (eds) *Sport in History: the making of modern sporting history* (Brisbane, 1979) pp. 99–123; P. F. McDevitt, 'Muscular Catholicism: Nationalism, masculinity and Gaelic team sports, 1884–1916' in *Gender and History* IX, No. 2 (August 1997) pp. 262–84.
7 W.F. Mandle, 'The Irish Republican Brotherhood and the beginnings of the Gaelic Athletic Association' in *Irish Historical Studies* XX (1977) pp. 418–38.
8 *Western People* 12 Apr. 1890; *Fermanagh Herald* 18 June 1904; Mandle, *GAA and Nationalist politics*, pp. 129–30; M. Cronin, 'Enshrined in blood: the naming of Gaelic Athletic Association grounds and clubs' in *The Sports Historian* No. 18 (1), May 1998, pp. 90–104.
9 R. Holt, *Sport and the British: a modern history* (Oxford, 1992) p. 240.

NOTES

10 Mandle, GAA *and Nationalist politics*, p. 161.
11 *[Dublin] Evening Telegraph* 21 Mar. 1896; *Shan Van Vocht* 3 Oct. 1898; *United Irishman* 30 Dec. 1899. See also Chapter 1.
12 See Chapters 2, 3 and 4.
13 IFA minute book 1880–86, entries for 18 Nov. 1881, 10 Aug. 1881 and 28 Apr. 1881.
14 *UFCN* 11 May 1894.
15 Unfortunately the IFA records for this period have not survived, and the contemporary press generally contains few details of the administrative structure of the Association.
16 IFA cash book 1880–1897, entries for 1887–90.
17 IFA minute book 1898–1903, entry for 26 Mar. 1901.
18 IFA minute book 1903–9, entries for 27 Sept. 1904, 10 Apr., 12 May and 2 June 1906. At that year's AGM the Leinster FA returned 79 affiliated clubs, while the Co. Antrim FA returned 92 and the Mid-Ulster FA 53.
19 IFA minute book 1903–1909, entry for 23 Mar. 1907. Opposition came exclusively from representatives of Dublin clubs. The six constituent 'districts' within the IFA became the North-eastern (effectively Antrim and Belfast); the Leinster; the Munster; the North-western (effectively Counties Londonderry and Donegal); the Mid-Ulster (actually County Armagh and adjacent areas of Counties Tyrone and Down); and the Fermanagh and Western (which covered all the remaining areas of the country).
20 Biggs and Dodd (eds), *Leinster Football Association*, p. 15; O'Mahony, *Bohemian Football Club*, pp. 29–33.
21 *ISN* 11 Nov. 1911. For Moles see M. Brodie, *The Tele: A history of the Belfast Telegraph* (Belfast, 1995) pp. 43–7.
22 See Chapter 2.
23 The surviving personal papers of all the individuals known to have held honorary offices within the IFA have been examined, but in not one case has any mention of IFA business been found.
24 IFA minute book 1880–86, entry for 18 Nov. 1880; *Coleraine Constitution and Northern Advertiser* 9 Mar. and 16 Mar. 1901; I. Hawe, *Moyola Park Football Club* (Cookstown, 1982) pp. 2–5. I am very grateful to Mr Samuel Heuston of Castledawson for information on the early years of the Moyola club.
25 *Pastime* VII, No. 185, 8 Dec. 1886 pp. 396, 391; *UFCN* 13 May 1892.
26 R.M. Young, *Belfast and the Province of Ulster in the Twentieth Century* (Brighton, 1909) p. 14; H. Montgomery Hyde, *The Londonderrys: a family portrait* (London, 1979) pp.72–94; J. Vincent (ed.) *The Crawford Papers: the journals of David Lindsey, twenty-seventh Earl of Crawford and tenth Earl of Balcarres 1871–1940, in the years 1892 to 1940* (Manchester, 1984) p. 277; *Vanity Fair* 7 June 1879.
27 T. MacKnight, *Ulster as It Is or Twenty-Eight Years' Experience as an Irish Editor* (London, 1896) II, pp. 243, 313–4; A. Jackson, *The Ulster Party* (Oxford, 1989) pp. 194–5. It is also worth noting, however, that Londonderry was already prominent in the patronage of football in areas of north-east England contiguous to his estates there. For example, in 1898 he opened the Sunderland club's new ground at Roker Park, and in 1892 he had presented the Northern League's trophies at Middlesbrough. The latter occasion saw Londonderry offer glowing praise for the 'great benefit' that was derived from the game (see *Sunderland Daily Echo* 12 Sept. 1898 and *North Eastern Daily Gazette* 30 Sept. 1892).
28 R.F. Foster, *Modern Ireland, 1600–1972* (Oxford, 1988) pp. 433, 444; S. Paseta, *Before the Revolution: Nationalism, social change and Ireland's Catholic elite,*

1879–1922 (Cork, 1999) p. 65; D.P. McCracken, 'The impact of developments in South Africa on Irish politics, 1877–1902' (unpublished DPhil thesis, UUC, 1980) p. 383.
29 McCracken, 'Developments in South Africa'.
30 J. A. Gaughan, *The Memoirs of Senator Joseph Connolly* (Dublin, 1998) pp. 38–9; A. Synan, 'Our Protestant brother' in *New Ireland Review* XXX (1908–9) p. 234.
31 Tuohy, *Belfast Celtic*, pp. 8–9; *ISN* 23 Sept. 1899. In fact the Kaffirs went on to play several more games in England and Scotland after their match in Belfast (see *The Times* 6 Sept. 1899; *Barnsley Independent* 21 Oct. 1899).
32 IFA minute book 1898–1903, entries for 2 Jan. and 12 May 1900.
33 *Belfast and Province of Ulster Directory for 1897* (Belfast, 1897) pp. 46, 54 and 59.
34 Of the main Belfast Unionist newspapers the *Northern Whig* did not report the AGM at all, while the *Belfast News Letter* and *Evening Telegraph* reported the meeting but not Londonderry's appointment. The Nationalist *Irish News* followed suit. Neither the Dublin-based Unionist *Irish Times* nor the Nationalist *Freeman's Journal* reported the AGM at all.
35 For both White and Roberts see *DNB*.
36 M. Barthorp, *The Anglo-Boer Wars* (Poole, 1987) pp. 113–120.
37 IFA minute book 1880–86, entries for 13 Dec. 1880 and 5 Dec. 1881; *The Gael* May 1903, p. 140. See also P. Alter, 'Symbols of Irish Nationalism' in *Studia Hibernica* XIV (1974) pp. 106–9.
38 IFA minute book 1909–25, entry for 12 Sept. 1911; *ISN* 17 Mar. 1913.
39 Co. Antrim FA book 1898–1906, entry for 15 May 1900; *ISN* 16 May 1903. The motion failed as it did not find a seconder.
40 *Fermanagh Herald* 21 Jan. 1911 and *ISN* 21 Jan. 1911.
41 For such an interpretation see Brodie, *Irish Soccer*, p. 10.
42 IFA minute book 1909–25, entry for 2 May 1911; *Belfast Telegraph* 15 May 1911.
43 IFL book 1909–13, entry for 17 May 1911; IFA minute book 1909–25, entry for 12 Sept. 1911; *IN* 4 Jan. 1912.
44 IFA Emergency Committee book, 1909–43, entries for 17 Jan. and 27 Jan. 1912.
45 The IFA also received subscription fees from its affiliated clubs, but these were comparatively insignificant.
46 *IN* 10 Jan. 1912; IFA minute book 1909–25, entry for 12 Jan. 1912; IFA Emergency Committee book 1909–43, entry for 29 Jan. 1912. The increase demanded was from 10% to 20% of the gross gate.
47 *IN* 15 Jan. 1912; IFA Emergency committee book 1909–43, entries for 27 Jan, 9 Feb. and 22 Feb. 1912.
48 *IN* 25 Jan. and 15 Feb. 1912. The clubs making up the 'New FA' were Shelbourne, Derry Celtic, Belfast Celtic, Distillery, Glenavon, Glentoran and Cliftonville.
49 *IN* 22 Jan. 1912; *BNL* 27 Feb. 1912; IFL book 1909–13, entry for 31 May 1912; Co. Antrim FA book 1906–12, entry for 15 May 1912.
50 *IN* 22 Jan. 1912; Co. Antrim FA book 1906–12, entry for 25 June 1912; IFA minute book 1909–25, entry for 25 June 1912.
51 M. Brodie, *Northern Ireland Soccer Yearbook* (annual publication).
52 *Northern Whig* 24 Feb. 1913; *Ulster Echo* 16 Mar. 1912; IFA minute book 1909–25, entries for 6 Mar. and 7 Mar. 1912.
53 IFA minute book 1909–25, entries for 25 June and 9 July 1912. The IFA also agreed to meet all the financial liabilities of the new FA, which was duly dissolved.
54 IFA minute book 1909–25, entry for 3 Dec. 1912.
55 *Londonderry Sentinel* 21 and 23 May 1912; *Derry Journal* 22 May 1912.

NOTES

56 *Londonderry Sentinel* 30 May and 11 June 1912.
57 *Derry Journal* 24 and 27 May 1912.
58 *Londonderry Sentinel* 25 June 1912.
59 *Derry Journal* 6 Sept., 14 Oct. and 11 Nov. 1912.
60 *Derry Journal* 9 Dec. 1912. Notes on a conference held at the City Hotel, Londonderry, 31 Dec. 1912 (loose insertion in IFA Rules revision committee minute book 1909–47).
61 *ISN* 14 May 1910; IN 17 May 1910.
62 IFA Emergency committee book 1909–43, entries for 18 and 25 June 1910. McAnerny's writings for the *Irish News* under the pseudonym 'Celt' give an invaluable, if occasionally jaundiced, view into the inner workings of the IFA.
63 *UFCN* 6 Sept. 1895.
64 IFA minute book 1898–1903, entries for 25 Oct. and 1 Nov. 1898, 14 Mar. 1899 and 3 Dec. 1901.
65 IFA minute book 1898–1903, entry for 10 Oct. 1899.
66 IFA minute book 1898–1903, entries for 8 and 15 Nov. 1898; IFA minute book 1903–9, entries for 26 Apr. and 14 May 1904; *ISN* 14 May 1904. For further details on Sunday play see Chapter 1.
67 IFA Protests and Appeals minute book 1909–14, entries for 24 Feb. and 10 Mar. 1910; *Sport* 5 Dec. 1908.
68 *ISN* 26 Feb. and 5 Mar. 1910; *A History of Belfast Celtic Football Club: a wonderful record* (Belfast, 1929] p. 22; Kennedy, *Belfast Celtic*, p. 14.
69 *Parliamentary debates (Fourth series)* CLII, cols 1146–7 (28 Feb. 1906); CLXV cols 985–6 (22 Nov. 1906); CLXXXVIII, cols 405–6 (7 May 1908).
70 *BNL* 21 May 1912; B. MacGiolla Choille (ed) *Intelligence Notes 1913–16* (Dublin, 1966) pp. 18, 74, 276; J. Gray (ed.) *Thomas Carnduff: Life and writings* (Belfast, 1984) pp. 98, 144. E. M. Forster to Jessica Darling, 6 Feb. 1912 in M. Lago and P.N. Furbank (eds) *Selected Letters of E. M. Forster 1879–1920*, I (London, 1983) pp. 127–9.
71 *Irish Worker* 30 Aug. 1913; *IN* 1 Sept. 1913; *Irish Times* 1 Sept. 1913; A. Wright, *Disturbed Dublin: the story of the great strike of 1913–14* (London, 1914) pp. 132–5.
72 *NW* 17 Mar. 1913; *FJ* 17 Mar. 1913. For the interpretation of the national anthem as a 'party tune' by Nationalists see S. Gwynn, *Ulster* (London, 1911) pp. 35–6.
73 *UFCN* 25 Mar. 1892. For various Irish political figures appearing at Glasgow Celtic games see Murray, *Old Firm*, pp. 70–4.
74 *FJ* 9 Sept. 1902 and *Irish Times* 9 Sept. 1901.
75 L.M. Geary, *The Plan of Campaign* (Cork, 1986) pp. 23–5. For Harrington's career in general see the obituary at *FJ* 14 Mar. 1910 and *DNB*, second supplement, II. See also T. Harrington, *A Diary of Coercion: Being a list of the cases tried under the criminal laws* (Dublin, 1888).
76 *Derry Journal* 19 Jan. 1910. Unfortunately the game was disrupted by the weather, and the Institute players left the field after only ten minutes' play. However, Hamilton subsequently won the seat by 57 votes.
77 *IN* 7 Mar. 1910; Typescript biography of Joseph Devlin [c.1919] (PRONI T/2420/5).
78 I. Budge and C. O'Leary, *Belfast: Approach to crisis. A study of Belfast politics 1613–1970* (London, 1973) pp. 116–121; B.M. Walker, *Ulster Politics: the formative years, 1868–86* (Belfast, 1989) pp. 215–6, 252; B.M. Walker (ed.) *Parliamentary Election Results in Ireland, 1801–1922* (Dublin, 1978) pp. 330–1; H. Patterson, 'Independent Orangeism and class conflict in Edwardian Belfast: a reinterpretation' in

Proceedings of the Royal Irish Academy LXXX, series C, May (1980) pp. 1–27; A. Jackson, *The Ulster Party: Irish Unionists in the House of Commons* (Oxford, 1989) pp. 222–5.

79 H. Patterson, *Class Conflict and Sectarianism: the Protestant working class and the Belfast Labour Movement 1868–1920* (Belfast, 1980) pp. 38–41.
80 *ISN* 9 Jan. 1909.
81 For an assessment of the role and influence of the United Irish League see P. Bew, *Conflict and Conciliation in Ireland, 1890–1910* (Oxford, 1987).
82 *IN* 8 Nov. 1923; E. Phoenix (ed). *A Century of Northern Life: the Irish News and 100 years of Ulster history* (Belfast, 1995) p. 20.
83 J. Kennedy, *Belfast Celtic* (Belfast, 1986) pp. 8–9, E. Phoenix, *Northern Nationalist Politics, Partition and the Catholic Minority in Northern Ireland* (Belfast, 1994) p. 202.
84 *BT* 4 Feb. 1902; *IN* 16 Jan. 1902; *BNL* 16 Jan. 1902.
85 Glentoran Recreation Co. Ltd (Companies registry NI, file R.263); *Amusements* 24 Sept. 1900.
86 *IN* 16 Jan. 1909. McIlroy's political career ended when he did not stand for re-election in 1912.
87 W.T. Pike (ed.), *Ulster: Contemporary biographies* (Brighton, 1910) p. 92; J. Killen, *A History of the Linen Hall Library: 1788–1988* (Belfast, 1990) pp. 79–81, 189–90.
88 *BNL* 2 and 10 May 1892.
89 *BNL* 5 Mar. 1894.
90 *BNL* 21 Feb., 28 Mar. 1898; *Belfast Telegraph* 3, 24 Mar. 1902; Sir F. Wall, *Fifty Years of Football* (London, 1935) p. 213.
91 *BNL* 14 Mar. 1898. Club and national records have been taken from M. Brodie (ed.), *Northern Ireland Soccer Yearbook* (annual publication).
92 IFA minute book 1903–9, entry for 11 May 1907; A. Gibson and M. Pickford, *Association Football and the Men Who Made It* (London, 1906) IV, pp. 98–9. For a summary of Gibson's careers to 1909 see *ISN* 9 Jan. 1909.
93 *IN* 4 Jan. 1909.
94 A.C. Hepburn, *A Past Apart: Studies in the history of Catholic Belfast 1850–1950* (Belfast, 1996) pp. 49–53, 120.
95 *IN* 7 Jan. 1909; *BNL* 7, 11, 14 and 22 Jan. 1909.
96 J. Gray, *City in Revolt: James Larkin and the Belfast Dock Strike of 1907* (Belfast, 1985) p. 35; Budge and O'Leary, *Approach to Crisis*, pp. 122–3.
97 *BNL* 11 Jan. 1909.
98 *BNL* 9 and 13 Jan. 1909; *Ulster Echo* 7 Jan. 1909.
99 *IN* 11 Jan. 1909; *Ulster Echo* 12 Jan. 1909.
100 *IN* 13 and 14 Jan. 1909.
101 *IN* 13 Jan. 1909; *BNL* 13 Jan. 1909.
102 *ISN* 9 Jan. 1909.
103 *IN* 16 and 18 Jan. 1909; *BNL* 16 Jan. 1909.
104 *IN* 14 Jan. 1920; IFA minute book 1909–25, entry for 2 Feb. 1909.
105 For Gibson's later political career see N. Garnham, 'Association football and politics in Belfast: the careers of William Kennedy Gibson' in *International Journal of the History of Sport* XVI, No. 1 (March 1999) pp. 128–36.
106 IFA minute book 1903–9, entry for 14 May 1904; *IN* 16 Feb. 1914; *BNL* 16 Feb. 1914.

CHAPTER 6 NOTES

1. *IN* 30 Mar. 1914; *Sport* 7 Feb. 1914.
2. *IN* 24 Aug. 1914; *Sport* 25 Apr. 1914.
3. Brodie, *100 Years*, pp. 10–12; *Coleraine Chronicle* 2 June 1914.
4. D. Keogh, *Twentieth-century Ireland: Nation and state* (Dublin, 1994) p. 35; B. Murray, *Football*, p. 20; Derek Birley, *Playing the Game: Sport and British society, 1910–45* (Manchester, 1995) p. 179; M. Cronin, *Sport and Nationalism in Ireland: Gaelic games, soccer and Irish identity since 1884* (Dublin, 1999) p. 121. See also Brodie, *History of Irish Soccer* (Glasgow, 1964) p. 11; P. Byrne, *The Football Association of Ireland – 75 years* (Dublin, 1996) pp. 19–20.
5. Mandle, *GAA and Nationalist Politics*, pp. 202–18; E. Van Esbeck, *The Story of Irish Rugby* (London, 1986) pp. 1–95.
6. J. Sugden and A. Bairner, *Sport, Sectarianism and Society in a Divided Ireland* (Leicester, 1993) p. 50; P. Griffin, *The Politics of Irish Athletics* (Ballinamore, 1990) pp. 57–66.
7. See Chapter 1.
8. *UFCN* 27 Jan. 1893.
9. *Sport* 3 Mar. 1894; *Irish Times* 12 Mar. 1895; *Sport* 22 Feb. 1896; *Sport* 13 Feb. and 27 Mar. 1897.
10. *ISN* 5 Feb. and 15 Oct. 1898.
11. *ISN* 5 May 1899.
12. *ISN* 18 Mar. 1899.
13. Byrne, *Football Association of Ireland*, pp. 15–16; *ISN* 18 Mar. 1899.
14. *ISN* 2 Mar. 1901.
15. N.L. Jackson, *Association Football* (London, 1900) p. 249.
16. *UFCN* 10 Feb. 1893; *UFCN* 27 Jan. and 10 Feb. 1893; *Sport* 9 Jan. 1904.
17. IFA minute book 1903–9, entries for 4 Feb. and 3 Mar. 1908; *Ulster Echo* 10 Feb. 1908; *Sport* 9 May and 10 Oct. 1908.
18. *Sport* 17 Oct. and 7 Nov. 1908.
19. *IN* 15 May 1911.
20. *Sport* 13 Dec. 1884; *UFCN* 16 Nov. 1888; *ISN* 26 Nov. 1898; *ISN* 25 May 1912.
21. *ISN* 2 Mar. 1901.
22. See Chapter 2; *ISN* 21 Feb. 1903. Perhaps with an eye to potential legal proceedings, few specifics were either reported or recorded in the IFA records concerning the events of 1903–4. However, on the death of Alex Thompson, the then Chairman of the IFA, it was reported that the clubs involved were Linfield and Cliftonville of Belfast (*BT* 3 May 1926).
23. *Dublin Evening Mail* 17 Mar. 1906; *Pastime* 9 Apr. 1884.
24. *ISN* 2 Apr. 1904.
25. P.C.W. Trevor, 'Football during the season' in *Badminton Magazine* VI (Jan.–June 1898) p. 433; id., 'The season's football' in *Badminton Magazine* VIII (Jan.–June 1899) p. 429.
26. For professionalism see Chapter 3.
27. *Pastime* 10 Jan. 1894; *Sport* 11 Feb. 1905. For similar complaints emanating from Belfast see *Nomad's Weekly* 4 Feb. 1911. This article followed a surprise Irish defeat by Wales in Belfast.
28. See Chapter 1.
29. *Sport* 22 Dec. 1906.
30. *Belfast Telegraph* 12 May 1913.

31 *IN* 2 Jan. 1905.
32 *ISN* 19 May 1900.
33 *ISN* 14 May 1904.
34 *ISN* 20 Aug. 1898; IFA minute book 1898–1903, entries for 8 Nov. 1898 and 5 Nov. 1901.
35 *ISN* 14 May 1904; *Sport* 21 May 1904.
36 IFA minute book 1903–9, entry for 5 June 1906. Strictly speaking, Sunday football was still actually illegal under the Irish Sunday Observance Act (7 Wm III c. 17 (1695)).
37 Murphy, *Derry, Donegal and Modern Ulster,* pp. 170–2.
38 *Irish Christian* II, No. 17 (May 1884) p. 99.
39 IRFU (NB) minute book 1913–22, entries for 15 Sept. and 25 Sept. 1914; IFA minute book 1909–47, entry for 17 Nov. 1914.
40 IFA minute book 1909–43, entry 12 Jan. 1915. For the position taken in England see C. Veitch, '"Play up! Play up! and win the war!" Football, the nation and the First World War 1914–15' in *Journal of Contemporary History* XX (July 1985) pp. 363–78.
41 IFL Management committee minute book 1913–23, entries for 14 July 1915, 27 May 1916, 25 May 1917 and 31 May 1918.
42 The six northern sides were Distillery, Linfield, Glentoran, Cliftonville, and Belfast Celtic from Belfast and Glenavon from Lurgan. In the event Celtic withdrew from the competition, and Glenavon was required to play all its fixtures away from home. Belfast United was elected to Celtic's place to make the League a viable competition. (See Belfast and District Football League minute book 1915–17, entries for 11 Aug., 25 Aug. and 15 Sept. 1915.)
43 IFA minute book 1909–25, entry for 8 Sept. 1914; IFA Emergency Committee Book 1909–43, entry for 14 Oct. 1915; IFL book 1913–23, entry for 19 Aug. 1914.
44 *Sport* 5 Dec. 1914.
45 *Sport* 26 Sept. and 3 Oct. 1914.
46 IFL Management committee book 1913–23, entry for 9 Sept. 1914; *Sport* 31 Oct. 1914.
47 J.A. Gaughan (ed.) *Thomas Johnson 1872–1963* (Dublin, 1980) pp. 23–4; *Sport* 21 Nov. 1914 and 23 Jan. 1915.
48 D.S. Johnson, 'The Northern Ireland economy, 1914–39' in L. Kennedy and P. Ollerenshaw (eds) *Economic history of Ulster, 1820–1939* (Manchester, 1985) pp. 184–8.
49 IFL management committee book 1913–23, entry for 25 Nov. 1914; *Sport* 9 Jan. 1915; David Williams, Belfast to IFA Secretary, 30 Dec. 1914 in Senior clubs protests and appeals committee minute book 1912–22, with entry for 2 Jan. 1915.
50 IFA minute book 1909–25, entries for 10 Aug. 1915 and 30 May 1916; IFL book 1913–23, entry for 14 July 1915; Belfast and District League book 1915–17, entry for 27 May 1916.
51 *Sport* 13 Feb. and 15 May 1915.
52 *Sport* 17 Apr. 1915 and 9 Dec. 1916.
53 *The Irishman* I, No. 6 (15 Apr. 1916) p. 12; IFA minute book 1909–25, entries for 8 Aug. 1916, 22 May and 4 Sept. 1917. Only four Irish MPs responded to the IFA, although all were written to. Interestingly these consisted of three Unionist members for Ulster constituencies and John Redmond, the leader of the Nationalist Irish Parliamentary Party. For the effects of the tax in England see N. Fishwick, *English Football and Society, 1910–50* (Manchester, 1989) p. 40.
54 Co. Antrim FA book 1912–20, entries for 30 Sept. 1914 and 12 May 1916.

NOTES

55 *Thirty-third CPA Annual Report* (1914/15) pp. 6, 15; *Thirty-sixth CPA Annual Report* (1918) p. 3.
56 Annual Reports of the Commissioners of Public Works (Ireland) 1914 and 1915 (BPP 1914 XLVII [cd 7563] and 1914–16 XXXIV [cd 8119]); *Sport* 19 Dec. 1914; Briggs and Dodd, *Leinster Football Association*, pp. 40–2.
57 *ISN* 31 Mar. 1917; Belfast and District League book 1915–17, entry for 25 May 1917; Co. Antrim FA book 1912–20, entry for 22 Sept. 1917.
58 D. Fitzpatrick, 'Militarism in Ireland, 1900–22' in T. Bartlett and K. Jeffery (eds) *A Military History of Ireland* (Cambridge, 1996) p. 388.
59 See above, note 12.
60 *ISN* 31 Mar. 1917; *Sport* 23 May 1914 and 22 Jan. 1916; IFA Emergency Committee book 1909–43, entry for 24 Feb. 1916.
61 *ISN* 18 Aug. 1917.
62 [Nora Connolly] to James Connolly, 25 Oct. 1914 in N. C. O'Brien, *Portrait of a Rebel Father* (Dublin, 1935) pp. 201–2. For continued disorders, however, see *Sport* 14 Nov. 1914 and Senior clubs protest and appeals minute book 1912–22, entry for 12 Apr. 1915.
63 M. MacDonagh, *The Irish at the Front* (London, 1916) pp. 119–27; S. Parnell Kerr, *What the Irish Regiments Have Done* (London, 1916) pp. 127–8; P. MacGill, *The Great Push: an episode of the Great War* (London, 1917) pp. 67, 73 and 81; H. Harris, *The Irish Regiments in the First World War* (Cork, 1968) p. 41; M. Dungan, *They Shall Not Grow Old: Irish soldiers and the Great War* (Dublin, 1997) pp. 131–2; D. Fitzpatrick, 'The logic of collective sacrifice: Ireland and the British army, 1914–1918' in *Historical Journal* XXXVII (1995) pp. 1029–30; Fitzpatrick, 'Militarism in Ireland' p. 390.
64 The unit in question was the London Irish, a battalion within the County of London Regiment, who were subsequently to be known as the 'Loos footballers'. On its constitution see P. MacGill, *The Amateur Army* (London, 1915) p. 15.
65 *Coleraine Chronicle* 25 Nov. 1915; G.A. Birmingham [J.O. Hannay], *A Padre in France* (London, 1918) pp. 78–81; D. Reitz, *Trekking on* (London, 1933) p. 182.
66 *ISN* 30 Mar., 13 Apr. and 19 Jan. 1918.
67 *Sport* 10 May 1919.
68 IFL minute book 1913–23, entries for 31 May 1918 and 29 May 1914.
69 *Sport* 6 Mar., 17 Apr. and 1 May 1915.
70 *[Dublin] Evening Telegraph* 12 Aug. 1919.
71 IFA minute book 1909–25, entry for 19 Nov. 1918; *ISN* 16 Nov. 1918.
72 *IN* 19 Nov. 1918. Such aims were largely comparable to those of the Professional Footballers Association in England, which was formed in 1908. See Mason, *Association Football*, pp. 110–7; Dabscheck, 'Defensive Manchester' in Cashman and Mandle (eds) *Sport in History* pp. 227–57.
73 *IN* 10 Dec. 1918; *Sport* 1 Feb. 1919.
74 *Sport* 11 Jan. 1919; IFA Emergency committee book 1909–43, entries for 22 Jan., 5 Feb. and 25 Feb. 1919; *Sport* 22 Feb. 1919; *Sport* 1 Mar. 1919.
75 *Sport* 17 May 1919; IFA Emergency committee book 1909–43, entry for 25 Feb. 1919; *ISN* 23 Nov. 1918; *Sport* 24 May 1919.
76 IFA International sub-committee minute book 1909–49, entry for 13 Sept. 1919; IFL minute book 1913–23, entry for 15 Oct. 1919; *Sport* 7 Aug. 1920.
77 IFL minute book 1913–23, entries for 28 June 1918 and 12 Mar. 1919.
78 Co. Antrim FA book 1912–20, entry for 17 Sept. 1919.
79 IFA minute book, entries for 20 May and 24 June 1919; IFA Rules revision

committee minute book 1909–47, entry for 2 June 1919; IFA Emergency committee book 1909–43, entry for 5 Feb. 1919.
80 *Sport* 17 May and 30 Aug. 1919.
81 For wartime disorders see *IN* 26 Oct. 1914; *Sport* 6 Feb. 1915; *ISN* 15 Sept. 1917 and 1 June 1918.
82 *[Dublin] Evening Telegraph* 27 Oct. 1919; Co. Antrim FA minute book 1912–20, entry for 8 Dec. 1919.
83 *NW* 18 Mar. 1920; *IN* 18 Mar. 1920.
84 Senior League clubs Protest, appeals and reinstatements Committee minute book 1912–22, entry for 19 Mar., 1 Apr., 8 Oct., 28 Oct. 1920; IFA minute book 1909–25, entry for 30 Mar. 1920.
85 IFA Finance Committee minute book 1909–35, entry for 13 May 1920.
86 For a summary of the situation see C. Townshend, *The British Campaign in Ireland 1919–21* (Oxford, 1975).
87 *BNL* 7 Mar. 1921.
88 IFA Emergency Committee book 1909–43, entry for 17 Mar. 1921. Reportedly the Glenavon club's directors voted in favour of travelling to Dublin, but the players refused to travel (see *Sport* 19 Mar. 1921).
89 *Sport* 12 Mar. 1921; *IN* 14 Mar. 1921.
90 Senior Clubs Protests and Appeals Committee minute book 1912–22, entry for 17 Mar. 1921. Glenavon lost the final tie to Glentoran.
91 *Sport* 2 Apr. 1921; *IN* 21 Mar. 1921.
92 M. Laffan, *The Partition of Ireland 1911–25* (Dundalk 1983) pp. 8–27.
93 *Sport* 16 Apr., 21 May and 11 June 1921.
94 IFA Emergency Committee book 1909–43, entry for 24 June 1921.
95 Byrne, *Football Association of Ireland*, pp. 22–3; Briggs and Dodd, *Leinster Football Association*, p. 72.
96 IFA minute book 1909–25, entry for 6 Dec. 1921.
97 IFA minute book 1909–25, entry for 7 Feb. 1921; *Sport* 25 Feb. 1921.
98 P.J. Beck, *Scoring for Britain: International football and international politics 1900–1939* (London, 1999) pp. 81–3.
99 *Sport* 13 May 1922. The reasons mentioned, or rather unmentioned, were presumably religious ones.
100 IFA minute book 1909–25, entries for 12 Dec. 1922, 9 Jan. 1923 and 22 Jan. 1923.
101 *Sport* 10 Feb. 1923.
102 A complete transcript of this meeting is included in IFA Rules revision committee minute book 1909–47. This is perhaps evidence of the importance the IFA attached to the meeting. This transcript, or perhaps an alternative one, in an abbreviated form and with some confusion over dates and personalities, is cited in Brodie, *Irish Football*, pp. 14–16; Byrne, *Football Association of Ireland*, p. 22; Briggs and Dodd, *Leinster Football Association*, p. 72.
103 IFA minute book, entry for 12 Feb. 1923.
104 IFA Rules revision committee minute book 1909–47, entry for 1 May 1923; *Sport* 7 and 28 Apr. 1923; S. Ryan, *The Boys in Green: the* FAI *international story* (Edinburgh, 1997) p. 13.
105 IFA minute book 1909–25, entry for 21 Aug. 1923.
106 Printed minutes of this meeting are in IFA Rules revision committee minute book 1909–47, entry for 13 Nov. 1923.
107 IFA minute book 1909–25, entries for 27 Nov. and 10 Dec. 1923.
108 Copies of these letters are at IFA minute book 1909–25, entry for 8 Jan. 1924.

NOTES

109 IFA minute book 1909–25, entries for 12 Feb. and 11 Mar. 1924.
110 IFA minute book 1909–25, entries for 11 Mar. and 1 Apr. 1924. The fact that the IFA paid four guineas for a typescript copy of the 'verbatim report' of this meeting is perhaps an indication of the importance that it attached to it. (See IFA Finance committee minute book 1909–35, entry for 3 Apr. 1924.)
111 For official encounters see IFA Rules revision committee minute book 1909–47.
112 See Chapter 5.
113 *Sport* 4 Sept. 1920; *BT* 5 Sept. 1921.
114 IFA minute book 1909–25, entry for 22 Mar. 1921; *Irish Times* 24 Mar. 1921;*Catholic Bulletin* XI (1921) p. 246. On the *Catholic Bulletin* see M. O'Callaghan, 'Language, nationality and cultural identity in the Irish Free State, 1922–7: the *Irish Statesman* and the *Catholic Bulletin* reappraised' in *Irish Historical Studies* XXIV (Nov. 1984) p. 235. On the repercussions of the incident itself in Irish sport, see also the letter from a fictitious correspondent in *FJ* 24 Feb. 1921.
115 *IN* 7 Mar. and 28 Mar. 1921; *NW* 23 Mar. 1921. 'Many years later' it was alleged that the flags displayed in Paris were carried by South African medical students who had travelled from Dublin to Paris for the match. (See Byrne, *Football Association of Ireland,* p. 21.)
116 *Sport* 28 Jan. 1922.
117 For the return see Belfast Celtic Football and Athletic Co. Ltd minute book 1924–40, entry for 8 July 1924.
118 *Sport* 30 July 1921.
119 G. Mitchell, *Three Cheers for the Derrys!* (Derry, 1991) pp. 67, 101, 104. See also obituaries in *NW* 9 Feb. 1946 and *BT* 8 Feb. 1946.
120 *BT* 13 and 29 July 1937; *NW* 29 1937.
121 *Sport* 5 Apr. 1919.
122 Brodie, *The Tele*, pp. 43–7; Garnham, 'Football and politics', pp. 132–3; McKeown memoirs, pp. 58–63.
123 *Sport* 20 Aug. and 5 Nov. 1921.
124 *Sport* 4 Feb. and 6 May 1922.
125 *Sport* 10 Feb. 1923.
126 IFL minute book 1913–23, entry for 27 May 1921; IFA Emergency Committee book 1909–43, entries for 22 July and 19 Aug. 1921.
127 IFA Emergency committee book 1909–43, entries for 6 and 21 June 1923. For Wigoder, who was generally known as 'Harry' or 'Barney', see Anon, *Saul Harris Wigoder* (Dublin, 1932) and M.J. Wigoder, *My Life* (Leeds, 1935) pp. 167–72.
128 *Sport* 2 Apr. 1921; IFA minute book 1909–25, entry for 7 Feb. 1922; IFA Rules revision committee minute book 1909–47, entry for 3 Feb. 1923. This latter entry is a verbatim typescript of the conference between the Associations. *Sport* 19 Aug. 1922.
129 *NW* 6 Jan. 1923; *Londonderry Sentinel* 9 Feb. 1946; *Derry Journal* 11 Feb. 1946. The last of these attributed his understanding of his Catholic neighbours to the fact that although he was a Presbyterian, Wilton had been raised in the predominantly Catholic area of the Bogside.
130 *IN* 21 May 1913; S. Lee to G. MacCrea 12 Sept. and 20 Sept. 1914 in IRFU (NB) minute book 1913–22 (PRONI D/3867/A/5).
131 *Irish Weekly Mail and Sports Mail* 27 Aug. 1921.
132 *Sport* 4 Feb. 1922 and 31 Mar. 1923.
133 *Sport* 27 Jan. 1923.
134 Transcript of the conference between delegates of the IFA and FAI, Dublin 3 Feb. 1923 in IFA Rules revision committee minute book 1909–47.

135 *Sport* 24 Jan. 1920.
136 *Sport* 12 Mar. 1921; *Irish Weekly Mail and Sports Mail* 9 Mar. 1921.
137 *Sport* 28 May 1921.
138 *Sport* 5 and 12 May 1906; *FJ* 6 May 1907. Ryder's letter is reproduced in Byrne, *Football Association of Ireland*, p. 21. An original copy is at IFA Emergency Committee book 1909–43, entry for 24 June 1921.
139 *BT* 17 Jan. 1921; *Sport* 8 Jan. 1921.
140 *Sport* 2 June 1921 and 11 Mar. 1922. Bohemians were of course an amateur side, but their Senior status gave them as a club responsibilities more akin to their professional rivals than their amateur Junior compatriots.
141 IFA Emergency committee book 1909–47, entry for 21 June 1923; *Sport* 7 July 1923.
142 For rugby see T. Collins, *Rugby's Great Split: Class, culture and the origins of rugby league football* (London, 1998). For football see Mason, *Association Football*, p. 249; Fishwick, *English Football*, p. 143; W. Greenland, *The History of the Amateur Football Alliance* (Harwich, 1966). Interestingly, both of these splits were essentially also along north–south divisions.
143 Griffin, *Politics of Irish Athletics*, pp. 72–80.
144 *Sport* 28 May 1921; *Irish Weekly Mail and Sports Mail* 27 Aug. 1921.
145 *BNL* 9, 14, 15 and 16 Mar. 1921; M. Hopkinson (ed.) *The Last Days of Dublin Castle: the diaries of Mark Sturgis* (Dublin, 1999) pp. 140–3.
146 NCU of Ireland minute book 1919–28, entries for 22 June and 9 Sept. 1921 (PRONI D/4213/A/1); Ulster Women's Hockey Union minute book 1919–21, entry for 23 Jan. 1920 (PRONI D/3982/A/2/1).
147 IFL minute book 1913–23, entries for 16 Aug., 20 Aug., 28 Oct. 1920 and 13 Jan. 1921.
148 Boyd, *Holy War*, p. 195.
149 *Sport* 8 Jan. and 5 Mar. 1921.
150 T.P. Walsh, *Twenty Years of Irish soccer (under the auspices of the Football Association of Ireland) 1921–41* (Dublin, 1941) pp. 13–16, 24, 31; *Sport* 19 Nov. 1921 and 28 Jan. 1922.
151 P. Callan, 'Voluntary recruiting for the British army in Ireland during the First World War' (unpublished Ph.D. thesis, TCD, 1984) pp. 106–110, 328, 349, 339 and 343. See also obituary in *Irish Times* 22 Nov. 1927.
152 IFA minute book 1909–25, entry for 7 Mar. 1922; IFA Emergency Committee book 1909–43, 24 Apr. 1922. Ultimately no donations seem to have been made to the fund from any football-related source. See summary of accounts of the Southern Irish Loyalist Relief Fund 1922–51 (PRONI D/989/B/5/1).
153 IFA minute book 1909–25, entries for 12 Feb. 1923 and 6 Dec. 1921; *Sport* 3 Feb. 1923.
154 *Sport* 11 Sept. 1920.
155 *Sport* 6 Dec. 1919, 30 July 1921; *IN* 21 Nov. 1921.
156 *Sport* 22 Nov. 1919 and 12 Feb. 1921.
157 *Sport* 27 Nov. 1920; *Catholic Bulletin* XI (1921) p. 309.

CHAPTER 7 NOTES

1 *ISN* 30 Aug. 1913.
2 P. Grousset, *Ireland's Disease* (London, 1887) p. 287.
3 C.S. Andrews, *Dublin Made Me: an autobiography* (Dublin, 1979) p. 45;

4   G.A. Birmingham [J.O. Hannay], *An Irishman looks at his world* (London, 1919) pp. 242–7.
P. Gibbon, *The Origins of Ulster Unionism* (Manchester, 1975) pp.138–40; H. Patterson, *Class Conflict and Sectarianism: the Protestant working class and the Belfast labour movement 1868–1920* (Belfast, 1980) pp. 22–3; T. Hennessey, 'Ulster Unionist territorial and national identities 1886–1893: Province, Island, Kingdom and Empire' in *Irish Political Studies* VIII (1993) pp. 22–3. However, see also F. Wright, *Two Lands on One Soil: Ulster politics before Home Rule* (Dublin, 1996) pp. 518–9.

Bibliography

1
MANUSCRIPT SOURCES

Belfast Celtic Football and Athletic Co. Ltd
Belfast Celtic Football and Athletic Company Ltd committee minute book, 20 June 1924 – 24 June 1940.

Belfast Central Library
Brown Street School papers 1826–1927.

Companies Registry for Northern Ireland
Shareholders' returns and financial statements for the following companies:
- Belfast Celtic Football and Athletic Company Ltd (R.77)
- Cliftonville Football and Athletic Company Ltd (R.145)
- Distillery Football and Athletic Company Ltd (R.187)
- Glenavon Football and Athletic Club Ltd (R.261)
- Glentoran Recreation Company Ltd (R.263)
- Irish Football Association Ltd (R.327).

Co. Antrim Football Association
Co. Antrim Football Association committee minute book, 9 Apr. 1888 – 6 Oct. 1897.
Co. Antrim Football Association committee minute book, 2 Nov. 1898 – 11 May 1906.
Co. Antrim Football Association council and senior committee minute book, 3 Oct. 1906 – 21 Aug. 1912.
Co. Antrim Football Association council minute book, 25 Sept. 1912 – 20 Apr. 1920.
Co. Antrim Football Association committee minute book, 14 May 1920 – 13 May 1938.

Derry City Archives
Town Clerk's Dept. files.

Irish Football Association (IFA)
IFA Committee minute book, 18 Nov. 1880 – 22 May 1886.
IFA Committee minute book, 25 Oct. 1898 – 3 Feb. 1903.
IFA Council minute book, 31 Mar. 1903 – 2 Feb. 1909.
IFA Ltd Council minute book, 2 Feb. 1909 – 10 Aug. 1925.
(No committee book has survived for the period June 1886–Sept. 1898.)

IFA International sub-committee minute book,
  17 July 1902 – 29 Feb. 1908.
IFA Ltd International committee minute book,
  27 Feb. 1909 – 25 Jan. 1949.
IFA Ltd Emergency Committee minute book,
  6 Mar. 1909 – 27 May 1943.
IFA Ltd Rules revision committee minute book,
  25 Oct. 1909 – 17 Jan. 1947.
IFA cash book, 1880–1897.
IFA Ltd Finance committee minute book,
  9 Feb. 1909 – 15 Oct. 1935.
IFA Ltd Protests, appeals and reinstatement committee minute book,
  16 Feb. 1909 – 7 May 1914.
Senior League clubs protests, appeals and reinstatement committee minute book, 11 Dec. 1912 – 7 Sept. 1922.
Register of professional players 21 Apr. 1899 – 27 Dec. 1903.

Irish Football League
Irish Football League minute book, 20 Oct. 1909 – 18 Oct. 1913.
Irish Football League Management Committee minute book,
  22 Oct. 1913 – 12 Apr. 1923.
Belfast and District Football League minute book,
  11 Aug. 1915 – 16 Nov. 1917.

Linen Hall Library, Belfast
Autobiography and memoirs of John [Sean] McKeown.

National Library of Ireland
Fallon papers (MS 22,577).

National Archives, Dublin
Shelbourne Sports Co. Ltd (Dissolved company file 6191).

North-Eastern Education and Library Board, Ballymoney Branch Library
Autobiography, diary and memoirs of Dr James L. Nevin (IR 920 NEV).

Public Record Office of Northern Ireland
Autobiography of W.A. Greer (T/3249/1).
Autobiography of Robert McElborough (D/770/1).
Ballymena Cricket Club minute book 1878–86 (D/1638/1).
Minute book of general Committee of Church of Ireland's Young Men's Society 1884–91 (D/3936/A/1/1).
Irish Rugby Football Union (Northern branch) committee minute book, 1885–99 (D/3867/A/1).

Irish Rugby Football Union (Northern branch) committee minute book, 1902–7 (D/3867/A/3).
Irish Rugby Football Union (Northern branch) committee minute book, 1913–22 (D/3867/A/5).
Irish Provincial Towns Rugby Football Union minute book, 2 Nov. 1897–18 Jan. 1902 (D/3867/B/1).
Mountpottinger YMCA minute book 1895–1906 (D/3788/4/1/1).
Northern Cricket Union of Ireland minute book 14 Apr. 1919 – 13 Feb. 1928 (D/4213/A/1).
Ranfurly estate papers (D/1932/2/5).
Records of Ballymena Football and Athletic Club Ltd (COM/40/2/2/478).
Summary of accounts of Southern Irish Relief Fund 1922–51 (D/989/B/5/1).
Typescript biography of Joseph Devlin [c.1919] (T/2420/1).
Ulster Women's Hockey Union minute book, 28 Oct. 1919 – 19 Mar. 1921 (D/3982/A/2/1).

Public Record Office, Kew
Royal Irish Constabulary reports (CO 904).

Royal Highland Fusiliers Regimental Museum, Glasgow
71st (Highland Light Infantry) Regimental Athletic Sports Record Book 1879–88.

2
PUBLISHED PRIMARY SOURCES

Historical Manuscripts Commission, Tenth Report (1885).
Day, A. and McWilliams, P. (eds) *Ordnance Survey Memoirs of Ireland II: Parishes of Co. Antrim* I, 1838–9 (Belfast, 1990).
Gaughan, J.A., *The Memoirs of Senator Joseph Connolly* (Dublin, 1998).
Gaughan, J.A., *Thomas Johnson 1872–1963* (Dublin, 1980).
Gogarty, O. St J., *It Isn't This Time of Year at All* (London, 1983 edn).
Gray, J. (ed.) *Thomas Carnduff: Life and writings* (Belfast, 1994).
Hopkinson, M. (ed.) *The Last Days of Dublin Castle: the diaries of Mark Sturgis* (Dublin, 1999).
Lago, M. and Furbank, P.N., (eds) *Selected Letters of E.M. Forster* (3 vols, London, 1983).
Lawlor, J., 'Calendar of the Liber Ruber of the diocese of Ossory' in *Proceedings of the Royal Irish Academy* XXVII, Sec. C, No. 2 (July 1908) .
MacGiolla Choille, B. (ed.) *Intelligence Notes 1913–16* (Dublin, 1966).

MacLysaght, E. (ed.) *Teague Land, or a Merry Ramble to the Wild Irish* (Dublin, 1982).
O'Brien, N. C., *Portrait of a Rebel Father* (Dublin, 1935).
Vincent, J. (ed.) *The Crawford Papers: the journals of David Lindsey twenty-seventh Earl of Crawford and tenth Earl of Balcarres 1871–1940, in the years 1892–1940* (Manchester, 1984).

3
GOVERNMENT PUBLICATIONS

Annual reports of the Commissioners of Public Works in Ireland, 1901–7, 1914–15 (BPP 1901 XVII [cd 724]; 1902 XXI [cd 1261]; 1903 XVIII [cd 1748]; 1904 XVII [cd 2229]; 1905 XXII [cd 2657]; 1906 XXV [cd 3109]; 1907 XIX [cd 3693]; 1914 XLVII [cd 7563]; 1914–16 XXXIV [cd 8119]).

Report of an inquiry by the Board of Trade into the earnings and hours of labour of workpeople in the United Kingdom (BPP 1909 LXXX [cd 4795]).

Reports of the Commissioners appointed to take the census of Ireland, 1841 (BPP 1842 XXIV [cd 504]).

Census of Ireland, 1881, Part II, General Report (BPP 1882 LXXVI [cd 3365]).

Census of Ireland, 1901 (Pt I, Vol III) No. 1a, City of Belfast (BPP 1902 [cd 1123]).

Minutes of evidence of the Royal Commission on Labour, Part II (BPP 1892 XXXVI pt 2 [cd 6795]).

Board of Trade report on standard time rates of wages 1900 (BPP 1900 LXXXII [cd 317]).

Board of Trade report on standard time rates of wages 1906 (BPP 1906 CXII [cd 3245]).

Board of Trade report on standard time rates of wages 1914 (BPP 1914 LXXX [cd 7194]).

Statistical tables: earnings of agricultural labourers 1898 and 1905 (BPP 1905 XCVII [cd 2376]).

Commission of the Royal Irish and Dublin Metropolitan Police (BPP 1914 XLIV [cd 7521]).

4
NEWSPAPERS, PERIODICALS AND ANNUAL PUBLICATIONS

[Dublin] Evening Telegraph
Amusements

Annual Reports of the Belfast Chamber of Commerce
Badminton Magazine
Ballymoney Free Press
Barnsley Independent
Belfast [Evening] Telegraph
Belfast and Province of Ulster Directory
Belfast Health Journal
Belfast Morning News
Belfast Newsletter
Birmingham Daily Mail
Castleknock College Chronicle
Catholic Bulletin
Central Presbyterian Association Annual Reports
Central Presbyterian Association Monthly Magazine
Clongownian
Coleraine Chronicle
Coleraine Constitution [and Northern Advertiser]
Cork Sportsman
Daily Independent
Derry Journal
Dublin Evening Mail
Dundalk Democrat
Fermanagh Herald
Freeman's Journal
The Gael
Gaelic Athlete
Hillbrook School Times
Ideas
Ireland's Saturday Night
Irish Christian
Irish Educational Review
Irish Field
Irish News
Irish Press
Irish Sportsman
Irish Times
Irish Weekly Mail and Sports Mail
Irish Worker
Irishman
Leader
Londonderry Sentinel
Londonderry Standard

New Ireland Review
Newry Reporter
Newry Telegraph
Newtownards Chronicle
Nomad's Weekly and Belfast Critic
Northern Whig
Pastime
Portadown News
Punch
QCB
QCG
Scottish Referee
Shan Van Vocht
Sport
Studies
Sunday Independent
Sunday News
Times
UCC Gazette
Ulster's Saturday Night
Ulster Echo
Ulster Football and Cycling News
United Ireland
Vanity Fair
Western People
Western Star and Ballinasloe Advertiser

5
CONTEMPORARY BOOKS, PAMPHLETS AND ARTICLES
(PRIOR TO 1924)

Anon, *A match at FootBall* (Dublin, 1720).
Anon, *Famous Footballers* (London, 1895).
Anon, 'The choice of a representative' in *New Ireland Review* XXXIV (1910–11) pp. 345–53.
Alcock, C.W. (ed.), *The Football Annual 1883* (London, 1883).
Bannister, R.C. and Hamilton, R.V., *Sport in Lisburn, Past and Present: Its history and development* (Belfast, 1910).
Barrett, E.B., 'Working Boys' Clubs for Irish cities' in *Studies* III (1914) pp. 487–93.
Bassett, G.H., *The book of Co. Armagh* (Dublin, 1888).
Bentley, J.J., 'Professionalism in sport' in *Athletic News Annual 1896* (London, 1895).

BIBLIOGRAPHY

Birmingham, G. [Hannay, J.O.], *The Red Hand of Ulster* (London, 1912).
Birmingham, G. [Hannay, J.O.], *The Lighter Side of Irish Life* (London, 1912).
Birmingham, G. [Hannay, J.O.], *A Padre in France* (London, 1918).
Birmingham, G. [Hannay, J.O.], *An Irishman Looks at His World* (London, 1919).
Bishop, M., *The Life and Adventures of Matthew Bishop* (London, 1744).
Cameron, Sir C., *Reminiscences* (Dublin, 1913).
Collison, W.A.H., *Dr Collison in and on Ireland* (London, 1908).
de Sales, Brother, 'The how and why of moral training III' in *Irish Educational Review* VII (1913–14) pp. 206–18.
Ewan-Muller, E.B., *Ireland: Today and Tomorrow* (London, 1907).
Falkiner, F.R., 'The Irish schoolboy exodus and the Educational Endowments act' in *Dublin University Review* (Dec. 1885), pp. 328–38.
Fitzgerald, D., *How to Play Gaelic Football* (Dublin, 1914).
Fleming, C.J.N., 'Rugby football' in *Badminton Magazine* III (July–Dec. 1896) pp. 554–68.
Gibson, A. and Pickford, M., *Association Football and the Men Who Made It* (4 vols, London, 1906).
[Goldring, D.,] *A Stranger in Ireland* (Dublin, 1918).
Good, J.W., *Ulster and Ireland* (Dublin, 1919).
Grousset, P., *Ireland's Disease* (London, 1887).
Gwynn, S., *Ulster* (London, 1911).
Harrington, T., *A Diary of Coercion: Being a List of the Cases Tried under the Criminal Laws* (Dublin, 1888).
Hatton, A.P., 'Regimental cricket' in *Badminton Magazine* XXXI (July–Dec. 1910) pp. 72–80.
Hime, M.C., *The Efficiency of Irish Schools and Their Superiority to English Schools as Places of Education for Irish Boys, Explained and Proved* (London, 1889).
Jackson, N.L., *Association Football* (London, 1900).
Judge, J.M., 'The Irish Movement – a talk with a man in the street' in *New Ireland Review* XXIX (1908–9) pp. 169–78.
King, W. (ed.) *The Rossall Register 1844–1889* (London, 1889).
Lawrence, J., *Handbook of Cricket in Ireland (15th number), 1879–80* (Dublin, 1879).
MacCarthy, J.J., 'International football: Ireland' in Rev. F. Marshall (ed.) *Football: the Rugby Union Game* (London, 1892) pp. 222–48.
MacDonagh, M., *The Irish at the Front* (London, 1916).
MacGill, P., *The Amateur Army* (London, 1915).
MacGill, P., *The Great Push: an episode of the Great War* (London, 1917).

McKeown, W.A., *National Education in Ireland* (Belfast, 1903).
McKnight, T., *Ulster as It Is, or Twenty-eight Years' Experience as an Irish Editor* (2 vols, London, 1896).
Meakin, B., *Model Factories and Villages* (London, 1905).
Parnell Kerr, S., *What the Irish Regiments Have Done* (London, 1916).
Patterson, R.J., *Catch-My-Pal: a Story of Good Samaritanship* (London, 1912).
Peter, R.M. (ed.), *Irish Football Annual* (Dublin, 1880).
Pike, W.T. (ed.) *Ulster: Contemporary Biographies* (Brighton, 1910).
Shearman, M.A., *Athletics and Football* (London, 1888).
Stewart, H., 'The Football nations' in *Blackwood's Magazine* CLXIX (Apr. 1901) pp. 489–504.
Suffolk and Berkshire, Earl of, *The Encyclopaedia of Sports and Games* (5 vols, London, 1911).
Synan, A., 'What to do with our police' in *New Ireland Review* XXVIII (1907–8) pp. 193–8.
Synan, A., 'Our Protestant brother' in *New Ireland Review* XXX (1908–9) pp. 234–8.
Tierney, M., 'The revised programme in National Schools' in *New Ireland Review* XV (Mar. 1901) pp. 83–92.
Trevor, P.C.W., 'Football during the season' in *Badminton Magazine* VI (Jan.–June 1898) pp. 428–36.
Trevor, P.C.W., 'The season's football' in *Badminton Magazine* VIII (Jan.–June 1899) pp. 423–9.
Wright, A., *Disturbed Dublin: the story of the great strike of 1913–14* (London, 1914).
Young. R.M., *Belfast and the Province of Ulster in the Twentieth Century* (Brighton, 1909).

6
PUBLISHED MEMOIRS AND BIOGRAPHIES

Anon, *Saul Harris Wigoder* (Dublin, 1932).
Andrews, C.S., *Dublin Made Me: an autobiography* (Dublin, 1979).
Briscoe, R., *For the Life of Me* (London, 1959).
Bullock, S., *After Sixty Years* (London, 1936).
Dickinson, P.L., *The Dublin of Yesterday* (London, 1929).
Fleming, L., *Head or Harp* (London, 1965).
Godley, A., *Life of an Irish Soldier* (London, 1939).
Hobson, B., *Ireland Yesterday and Today* (Kerry, 1968).
McDonald, W., *Reminiscences of a Maynooth Professor* (London, 1925).
O'Ceallaigh, S. (ed.) *Gaelic Athletic Memories* (Dublin, 1945).

O'Faolain, S., *Vive Moi! An autobiography* (London, 1965).
Orpen, Sir W., *Tales of Old Ireland and Myself* (London, 1924).
Reitz, D., *Trekking On* (London, 1933).
Robinson, L.T. and N., *Three Homes* (London, 1938).
Ryan, M.F., *Fenian Memories* (2nd edn, Dublin, 1946).
Taafe, M., *These Days are Gone Away* (London, 1959).
Wall, Sir F., *Fifty Years of Football* (London, 1935).
White, T. de V., *A Fretful Midge* (London, 1957).
Wigoder, M.J., *My Life* (Leeds, 1935).

7
SECONDARY SOURCES: BOOKS

Anon, *A History of Belfast Celtic Football Club: a wonderful record* (Belfast, 1929).
Anon, *Belfast Celtic FC: Souvenir and history 1891–1939* (Belfast, 1939).
Arlott, J., *The Oxford Companion to Sports and Games* (Oxford, 1975).
Armour, W.S., *Armour of Ballymoney* (London, 1934).
Bailey, K.C., *A History of Trinity College, Dublin 1892–1945* (Dublin, 1947).
Barthorp, M., *The Anglo-Boer Wars* (Poole, 1987).
Beck, P.J., *Scoring for Britain: International football and international politics 1900–1939* (London, 1999).
Bew, P., *Conflict and Conciliation in Ireland, 1890–1910* (Oxford, 1987).
Black, G., *The Rovers 80 Years: a history of Tandragee Rovers Football Club 1909–1989* (Portadown, 1989?).
Birley, D., *Playing the Game: Sport and British society, 1910–45* (Manchester, 1995).
Boyd, A., *Holy War in Belfast* (Belfast, 1987).
Boyle, W., *The Irish Labor Movement in the Nineteenth Century* (Washington, 1988).
Briggs, G. and Dodds, J. (eds) *100 Years of the LFA: Leinster Football Association centenary year book* (Dublin, 1993).
Brodie, M., *History of Irish Soccer* (Glasgow, 1964).
Brodie, M., *100 Years of Irish Football* (Belfast, 1980).
Brodie, M., *The Story of Glentoran* (Belfast, 1981).
Brodie, M., *Linfield: 100 years* (Belfast, 1985).
Brodie, M. (ed.) *The Irish Football league 1890–1990: Official centenary history* (Belfast, 1990).
Brodie, M., *The Tele: a history of the Belfast Telegraph* (Belfast, 1995).
Bugde, I. and O'Leary, C., *Belfast: Approach to crisis. A study of Belfast politics 1613–1970* (London, 1973).

Byrne, P., *The Football Association of Ireland – 75 years* (Dublin, 1996).
Cameron, G., *Coleraine Football Club: a history* (Coleraine, 1984).
Collins, T., *Rugby's Great Split: Class, culture and the origins of rugby league football* (London, 1998).
Connolly, S., *Religion and Society in Nineteenth-century Ireland* (Dundalk, 1994).
Corish, P.J., *Maynooth College 1795–1995* (Dublin, 1995).
Creek, F.N.S., *A History of the Corinthian Football Club* (London, 1933).
Cronin, M., *Sport and Nationalism in Ireland: Gaelic games, soccer and Irish identity since 1884* (Dublin, 1999).
Curtis, L.P., *Coercion and Conciliation in Ireland, 1880–92: a study in conservative unionism* (Princeton, 1963).
Daly, M.E., *Dublin: the deposed capital, a social and economic history, 1860–1914* (Cork, 1984).
D'arcy, F., *Horses, Lords and Racing Men: the Turf Club 1790–1990* (Curragh, 1991).
Davis, R.P., *Arthur Griffith and Non-violent Sinn Fein* (Tralee, 1974).
De Burca, M., *The GAA: a history* (Dublin, 1980).
Dennison, S.R. and MacDonagh, O., *Guinness 1886–1939: from incorporation to the Second World War* (Cork, 1998).
Diffley, S., *The Men in Green Shirts: the story of Irish rugby* (London, 1975).
Duncan, T.J., *A History of Irish Education from 1800* (Bala, 1972).
Dungan, M., *They Shall Not Grow Old: Irish soldiers and the Great War* (Dublin, 1997).
Dunleavy, J.E. and G.W., *Douglas Hyde: a maker of modern Ireland* (Oxford, 1991).
Dunning, E., Murphy, P. and Williams, J., *The Roots Of Football Hooliganism: an historical and sociological study* (London, 1988).
Fishwick, N., *English Football and Society, 1910–50* (Manchester, 1989).
Flanagan, P., *Transport in Ireland 1880–1910* (Dublin, 1969).
Foster, R.F., *Modern Ireland, 1600–1972* (London, 1988).
Gailey, A., *Ireland and the Death of Kindness: the experience of constructive unionism 1890–1905* (Cork, 1987).
Gallogly, D., *Cavan's Football Story* (Cavan, 1979).
Geary, L., *The Plan of Campaign* (Cork, 1986).
Gibbon, P., *The Origins of Ulster Unionism* (Manchester, 1975).
Gray, J., *City in Revolt: James Larkin and the Belfast dock strike of 1907* (Belfast, 1985).
Greenland, W., *The History of the Amateur Football Alliance* (Harwich, 1966).

Griffin, P., *The Politics of Irish Athletics* (Ballinamore, 1990).
Hannigan, D., *The Garrison Game: the state of Irish football* (Edinburgh, 1998).
Harris, H., *The Irish Regiments in the First World War* (Cork, 1968).
Hawe, I., *A Brief Chronicle of Moyola Park Football Club* (Cookstown, 1982).
Henry, B., *Dublin Hanged: Crime, law enforcement and punishment in late eighteenth-century Dublin* (Dublin, 1994).
Hepburn, A.C., *A Past Apart: studies in the history of Catholic Belfast 1850–1950* (Belfast, 1996).
Herbert, C.V., *Shelbourne Football Club Golden Jubilee Souvenir* (Dublin, 1945).
Holt, R., *Sport and the British: a modern history* (Oxford, 1992).
Hone, P., *Cricket in Ireland* (Tralee, 1955).
Hoppen, K.T., *Elections, Politics and Society in Ireland 1832–1885* (Oxford, 1984).
Hyman, L., *The Jews of Ireland from Earliest Times to 1910* (Shannon, 1972).
Jackson, A., *The Ulster Party: Irish Unionists in the House of Commons* (Oxford, 1989).
Jamison, J., *The History of the Royal Belfast Academical Institution, 1810–1960* (Belfast, 1959).
Joyce, P., *Work, Society and Politics: the culture of the factory in later Victorian England* (Brighton, 1980).
Kelly, J. *'That Damn'd Thing Called Honour': Duelling in Ireland 1570–1860* (Cork, 1995).
Keogh, D., *Twentieth-century Ireland: Nation and state* (Dublin, 1994)
Legg, M.L., *Newspapers and Nationalism: the Irish provincial press, 1850–1892* (Dublin, 1999).
Lynch, F., *A History of Athlone Town FC: the first 101 years* (Athlone, 1991).
Lynch, J., *A Tale of Three Cities: Comparative studies in working-class life* (London, 1998).
Kennedy, J., *Belfast Celtic* (Belfast, 1979).
Killen, J., *A History of the Linen Hall Library: 1788–1988* (Belfast, 1990).
Laffan, M., *The Partition of Ireland 1911–25* (Dundalk, 1983).
MacLua, B., *The Steadfast Rule: a history of the GAA ban* (Dublin, 1967).
Malcolm, E., *Ireland Sober, Ireland Free: Drink and temperance in nineteenth-century Ireland* (Dublin, 1986).
Mandle, W.F., *The Gaelic Athletic Association and Irish nationalist politics 1884–1924* (Dublin, 1987).

Mangan, J.A., *Athleticism in the Victorian and Edwardian Public School* (Cambridge, 1981).
Marshall, R., *Methodist College Belfast: the first hundred years* (Belfast, n.d.).
Mason, T., *Association Football and English Society 1863–1915* (Brighton, 1980).
McGarrigle, S., *Green Gunners: Arsenal's Irish* (Edinburgh, 1991).
McKee, E., *A Century of Bessbrook Football 1893–1993* (Bessbrook, 1993).
McLaverty, M., *Call My Brother Back* (Dublin, 1970 edn).
McMillan, N.D., *One Hundred and Fifty Years of Cricket and Sport in Co. Carlow* (Dublin, 1984).
Meenan, P.N., *St Patrick's Blue and Saffron: a miscellany of UCD sport since 1895* (Dublin, 1997).
Mitchell, G., *Three Cheers for the Derrys!* (Derry, 1991).
Montgomery Hyde, H., *The Londonderrys: a family portrait* (London, 1979).
Moody, T.W. and Beckett, J.C., *Queens Belfast 1845–1949: the history of a university* (2 vols, London, 1959).
Morgan, A., *Labour and Partition: the Belfast working class 1905–23* (London, 1991).
Muenger, E.A., *The British Military Dilemma in Ireland: Occupation politics, 1886–1914* (Dublin, 1991).
Murphy, D., *Derry, Donegal and Modern Ulster 1790–1921* (Derry, 1981).
Murphy, J.A., *The College: a history of Queen's/University College Cork* (Cork, 1995).
Murray, B., *Football: a history of the world game* (Aldershot, 1994).
Murray, W., *The Old Firm: Sectarianism, sport and society in Scotland* (Edinburgh, 1984).
Myler, P., *Regency Rogue: Dan Donnelly, his life and legends* (Dublin, 1976).
Newhouse, N.H., *A History of Friends' School Lisburn* (Lurgan, 1974).
North, J.S. (ed.) *Waterloo Directory of Irish Newspapers and Periodicals, 1800–1900* (Waterloo, Ontario, 1986).
O'Broin, L., *Revolutionary Underground: the story of the Irish Republican Brotherhood 1858–1924* (Dublin, 1976).
O'Connor, E., *A Labour History of Ireland 1824–1960* (Dublin, 1992).
O'Connor, U., *Oliver St John Gogarty: a biography* (London, 1969 edn).
Ó Gráda, C., *Ireland: a new economic history, 1780–1939* (Oxford, 1994).
O'Mahony, E.J., *Bohemian Football Club: Golden Jubilee Souvenir* (Dublin, 1940).

O'Maolfabhail, A., *Caman: Two thousand years of hurling in Ireland* (Dundalk, 1973).
O'Rourke, H.T., *The Dublin Civic Survey Report* (London, 1925).
Paseta, S., *Before the Revolution: Nationalism, social change and Ireland's Catholic elite, 1879–1922* (Cork, 1999).
Patterson, H., *Class Conflict and Sectarianism: the Protestant working class and the Belfast labour movement* (Belfast, 1980).
Phoenix, E., *Northern Nationalism: Nationalist Politics, Partition and the Catholic Minority in Northern Ireland* (Belfast, 1994).
Phoenix, E., *A Century of Northern Life: the Irish News and 100 years of Ulster history* (Belfast, 1995).
Puirseal, P., *The GAA in Its Time* (Dublin, 1982).
Russell, D., *Football and the English: a social history of association football in England, 1863–1995* (Preston, 1997).
Ryan, S., *The Boys in Green: the FAI international story* (Edinburgh, 1997).
Smith, C. and Shaw, B., *Whigs on the Green* (Dublin, 1996).
Springhall, J., Fraser, B. and Hoare M., *Sure and Steadfast: a history of the Boy's Brigade* (London, 1983).
Sugden, J. and Bairner, A., *Sport, Sectarianism and Society in a Divided Ireland* (Leicester, 1993).
Townshend, C., *The British Campaign in Ireland 1919–21* (Oxford, 1975).
Tranter, N., *Sport, Economy and Society in Britain 1750–1914* (Cambridge, 1998).
Trewin, J.C., *Benson and the Bensonians* (London, 1960).
Tuohy, M., *Belfast Celtic* (Belfast, 1978).
Vamplew, W., *Pay Up and Play the Game: Professional sport in Britain 1875–1914* (Cambridge, 1988).
Van Esbeck, E., *One Hundred Years of Irish Rugby* (Dublin, 1974).
Van Esbeck, E., *The Story of Irish Rugby* (London, 1986).
Vaughan, W.E. (ed.) *A New History of Ireland V: Ireland under the Union, I, 1801–70* (Oxford, 1989).
Vaughan, W.E. (ed.) *A New History of Ireland VI: Ireland under the Union II, 1870–1921* (Oxford, 1996).
Vaughan, W.E. and Fitzpatrick, A.J. (eds) *Irish Historical Statistics: Population, 1821–1971* (Dublin, 1978).
Walker, B., (ed.) *Parliamentary Election Results in Ireland, 1801–1922* (Oxford, 1978).
Walker, B., *Ulster Politics: the formative years, 1868–86* (Belfast, 1989).
Walsh, T.P., *Twenty Years of Irish Soccer (under the auspices of the Football Association of Ireland)* (Dublin, 1941).

Walvin, J., *The People's Game: the history of football revisited* (Edinburgh, 1994).
West, T., *The Bold Collegians: the development of sport in Trinity College, Dublin* (Dublin, 1991).
Wilde, W.R., *Irish Popular Superstitions* (Dublin, 1852).
Wright, F., *Two Lands on One Soil: Ulster politics before Home Rule* (Dublin, 1996).

8
SECONDARY SOURCES: ARTICLES

Alter, P., 'Symbols of Irish nationalism' in *Studia Hibernica* XIV (1974) pp. 106–9.
Armstrong, D.L., 'Social and economic conditions in the Belfast linen industry, 1850–1900' in *Irish Historical Studies* VII (No. 28) Sept. 1951, pp. 235–69.
Bairner, A., 'Ireland, sport and empire' in K. Jeffery (ed.) *An Irish Empire? Aspects of Ireland and the British Empire* (Manchester, 1996) pp. 57–76.
Connolly, S., '"Ag déanamh commanding": elite responses to popular culture, 1660–1850' in J.S. Donnelly Jr and K.A. Miller (eds) *Irish Popular Culture, 1650–1850* (Dublin, 1998), pp. 1–29.
Cronin, M., 'Work and workers in Cork city and co. 1800–1900' in P. O'Flanagan and C. Buttimer (eds) *Cork: History and society* (Dublin, 1993) pp. 721–54.
Cronin, M., 'Enshrined in blood: the naming of Gaelic Athletic Association grounds and clubs' in *The Sports Historian* No. 18 (1) May 1998, pp. 90–104.
Crossman, V., 'The army and law and order in the nineteenth century' in T. Bartlett and K. Jeffery (eds) *A Military History of Ireland* (Cambridge, 1996) pp. 358–79.
Dabscheck, B., 'Defensive Manchester: a history of the Professional Footballers' Association' in R. Cashman and M. McKernan (eds) *Sport in History* (Brisbane, 1980) pp. 227–57.
Denman, T., '"The red livery of shame;" the campaign against army recruitment in Ireland, 1899–1914' in *Irish Historical Studies* XXIX (1994) pp. 208–33.
Fitzpatrick, D., 'The disappearance of the Irish agricultural labourer' in *Irish Economic and Social History* VII (1980) pp. 66–92.
Fitzpatrick, D., 'The logic of collective sacrifice: Ireland and the British army, 1914–18' in *Historical Journal* XXXVII (1995) pp. 1017–30.
Fitzpatrick, D., 'Militarism in Ireland, 1900–22' in T. Bartlett and

K. Jeffery (eds) *A Military History of Ireland* (Cambridge, 1996) pp. 379–406.

Foster, R.F., 'Thinking from hand to mouth: Anglo-Irish literature, Gaelic nationalism and Irish politics in the 1890s' in id., *Paddy and Mr. Punch: Connections in Irish and English history* (London, 1995) pp. 262–80.

Garnham, N., 'Association football and politics in Belfast: the careers of William Kennedy Gibson' in *International Journal of the History of Sport* XVI, No. 1 (March 1999) pp. 128–36.

Geary, F. and Stark, T. (eds) 'Comparative output and growth in the four countries of the United Kingdom, 1861–1911' in S.J. Connolly (ed.) *Kingdoms United? Great Britain and Ireland since 1500: Integration and diversity* (Dublin, 1999) pp. 153–68.

Green, E.R.R., 'Thomas Barbour and the American linen-thread industry' in J.M. Goldstrom and L.A. Clarkson (eds) *Irish Population, Economy and Society* (Oxford, 1981) pp. 213–30.

Gribbon, S., 'An Irish city: Belfast 1911' in D. Harkness and M. O'Dowd (eds) *The Town in Ireland: Historical Studies XIII* (Belfast, 1981), pp. 203–20.

Hennessey, T., 'Ulster Unionist territorial and national identities 1886–1893: province, island, kingdom and empire' in *Irish Political Studies* VIII (1993) pp. 21–36.

Ickringill, S.J.S., 'Amateur and professional; sport in Britain and America at the turn of the twentieth century' in J.C. Binfield and J. Stevenson (eds) *Sport, Culture and Politics* (Sheffield, 1993) pp. 30–48.

Johnson, D., 'The Northern Ireland economy, 1914–39' in L. Kennedy and P. Ollerenshaw (eds) *Economic History of Ulster*, pp. 184–223.

Malcolm, E., 'The rise of the pub: a study in the disciplining of popular culture' in J.S. Donnelly Jr and K.A. Miller (eds.) *Irish Popular Culture, 1650–1850* (Dublin, 1998) pp. 50–77.

Mandle, W.F., 'The Irish Republican Brotherhood and the beginnings of the Gaelic Athletic Association' in *Irish Historical Studies* XX (1977) pp. 418–38.

Mandle, W.F., 'Sport as politics: the Gaelic Athletic Association 1884–1916' in R. Cashman and M. McKernan (eds) *Sport in History* (Brisbane, 1980) pp. 99–123.

Mandle, W.F., 'Parnell and sport' in *Studia Hibernica* XXVIII (1994) pp. 103–116.

McDevitt, P.F., 'Muscular Catholicism: nationalism, masculinity and Gaelic team sports, 1884–1916' in *Gender and History* IX, No. 2 (August 1997) pp. 262–84.

Mullan, M., 'The devolution of the Irish economy in the nineteenth century and the bifurcation of Irish sport' in *International Journal of the History of Sport* III, Pt 2 (1996) pp. 42–60.

O'Callaghan, M., 'Language, nationality and cultural identity in the Irish Free State, 1922–27: the "Irish Statesman" and the "Catholic Bulletin" reappraised' in *Irish Historical Studies* XXIV (1984) pp. 226–45.

Ollerenshaw, P., 'Industry 1820–1914' in L. Kennedy and P. Ollerenshaw (eds) *An Economic History of Ulster, 1820–1939* (Manchester, 1985), pp. 87–92.

Patterson, H., 'Independent Orangeism and class conflict in Edwardian Belfast: a reinterpretation' in *Proceedings of the Royal Irish Academy* LXXX, Series C (May 1980) pp. 1–27.

Rouse, P., 'The politics of culture and sport in Ireland: a history of the GAA ban on foreign games 1884–1971. Part one: 1884–1921' in *International Journal of the History of Sport* X, No. 3 (Dec. 1993) pp. 333–360.

Steven, A., 'The game of rackets in Ulster' in *Ulster Folklife* XLII (1996) pp. 109–12.

Tranter, N., 'The Cappielow riot and the composition and behaviour of soccer crowds in late Victorian Scotland' in *International Journal of the History of Sport* XII (1995) pp. 125–40.

Vamplew, W., 'Ungentlemanly conduct: the control of soccer-crowd behaviour in England, 1881–1914' in T.C. Smout (ed.) *The Search for Wealth and Stability: Essays in economic and social history presented to M. W. Flinn* (London, 1979) pp. 139–54.

Veitch, C., '"Play up! Play up! and win the war!' Football, the nation and the First World War 1914–15' in *Journal of Contemporary History* XX (July 1985) pp. 363–78.

Weir, F., 'Flour bags and the domestic economy' in *Ulster Folklife* XLII (1996) pp. 109–12.

9
UNPUBLISHED THESES

Callan, P., 'Voluntary recruiting for the British army in Ireland during the First World War' (unpublished PhD thesis, Trinity College, Dublin, 1984).

Hirst, C., 'Religious and political conflict in nineteenth-century Belfast: a case study of the Pound and Sandy Row 1820–1886' (unpublished Ph.D. thesis, Queen's University of Belfast, 1997).

McCracken, D., 'The impact of developments in South Africa on Irish politics, 1877–1902' (unpublished DPhil thesis, University of Ulster, 1980).

Index

The following abbreviations have been used in the index:

CC – Cricket Club
FA – Football Association
FC – Football Club
RFC – Rugby Football Club

Aberdeen, earl of, 150
Allen, J.A., 4
Amateur FA [England], 192
Amien Street station, Dublin, 80
Anderson, W.J., 55
Andrews, C.S., 114
Anglo-Irish Treaty, 185
Antrim, County, 3, 5, 47, 60, 95, 114, 126
Antrim, town, 124
Ardoyne, Belfast, 155
Armagh, city, 45
Armagh, County, 5, 39, 51, 88, 118, 119, 120, 164
Armour, James, 55
army, 18–20, 172, 181, 188
Arsenal FC, 87
Aston Villa FC, 94
Athlone, 18, 47, 165
Aughrim FC, 49
Avoniel FC, 16, 33

Balfour, Gerald, 133
Ballina, 44
Ballymacarrett, 50, 91
Ballymena, 50
Ballymena CC, 47
Ballymoney, 114
Ballynahinch, 113
Balmoral grounds, Belfast, 108, 115
Banbridge Academy, 5
Bandon FC, 119
Bandon, Lord, 47
Barbour, William and Sons Ltd, 48
Barnsley, 94
Barret, Fred, 90

Barron, James, 156
Bee Hotel, Liverpool, 87
Beechmount FC, 17
Beehive public house, 46
Belfast, 1–8, 10, 11, 13–17, 20, 22–5, 27, 28, 30, 32–40, 42, 44–55, 59–61, 64, 66–8, 70–7, 80–3, 85–91, 93, 94, 96–100, 103–5, 107–14, 116–33, 136–40, 142–4, 146–57, 160, 162–74, 176–80, 183–99
Belfast [Evening] Telegraph, 71, 137, 184-5
Belfast Amateurs FC, 99
Belfast and District [Wartime] League, 170–1
Belfast Bowling Club, 154
Belfast Catholic Committee, 152
Belfast Celtic FC, 33, 44, 46, 50, 53, 54, 55, 56, 59, 61, 64, 75, 76, 87, 89, 90, 91, 93, 94, 99, 104, 115–7, 121–7, 139, 147, 148, 151, 152, 157, 167, 168, 170, 176, 185, 192
Belfast Chamber of Commerce, 11
Belfast Charity Cup, 74, 112, 113
Belfast Citizen's Association, 156–7
Belfast Conservative Association, 153, 155
Belfast Harp Festival, 154
Belfast Hibernians FC, 99
Belfast Merchantile Academy, 17
Belfast Newsletter, 7, 125, 157
Belfast Protestant Association, 151
Belfast Temperance Voters Executive, 156

Belnaleck, 31
Benson, Sir Frank, 17–8
Bessbrook, 39, 46
Birmingham Daily Gazette, 34
Black Watch, 90, 119
Blackpool, 167
Blaney, Alexander, 17
Boer War, 19, 139–41
'bogus clubs affair', 43–4
Bohemian FC, 17, 25–6, 33, 35, 44, 45, 50, 68, 93, 109, 113, 114, 137, 143, 144, 148, 150, 151, 165, 168, 171, 174, 187, 191
Bolton Wanderers FC, 35, 113
Bovril, 107
Boys' Brigade, 17, 98
Bradford City FC, 93
Brantwood FC, 177
Brennan, J.L., 180
Brighton, 94
Brighton United FC, 87
British Legion, 188
Brown Street School, Belfast, 22
Bundoran, 119
Burnley FC, 87
Burns, Robert, 153

Cahoon, Mr, 48
Caledonians FC, 4
Campbell, John, 95
Cardiff City FC, 94
Carnduff, Thomas, 114
Carrick-on-Suir, 19
Carson, Sir Edward, 126
Cashel, 134
Castledawson, 5, 47
Castleknock Butterflies FC, 44
Castlerea FC, 46
Castlereagh FC, 89
Castlereagh Road, Belfast, 61
'Catch-My-Pal', 46
Catholic Bulletin, 185
Catholic Reading Room FC, 45
Catholic University, 26
Catholic University, 26
Cavan, County, 136

Central Presbyterian Association, 45, 51, 98, 170
Centre Half Bar, 94
Chichester, Major Spencer, 46, 138–9
'Children of the Unemployed', 111
Church of Ireland Young Men's Society, 52, 98
Churchill, Winston MP, 126
City of Derry Alliance, 145–7
Clarence FC, 71
Clarke, James, 148
Clarke, Neal, 148
Clegg, J.C., 182
Clifton Street Orange Hall, 155
Clifton Ward, Belfast, 155
Cliftonville FC, 5, 16, 17, 35, 39, 44, 45, 51, 52, 53, 54, 5, 57, 66, 68, 70, 73, 104, 108, 113, 120, 121, 122, 128, 148, 154–7, 188, 194
Clongowes Wood College, 25–6, 67, 94
clubs, 42–64
    numbers of, 43–4
    origins of, 44–50
    organisation of, 50–53
    financing of, 51–53
    flotations of, 53–56
    shareholders in, 55–61
    see also under club name
Clyde, River, 90
'Coal fund', 111
Coleraine, 23, 93
Commissioners of Public Works, 12
Connacht, 30, 44
Connacht FA, 31
Cookstown, 164
Cookstown Swifts FC, 26
Coote, Orlando, 47, 165
Corinthians FC, 21, 35, 71
Cork, city, 12, 17, 35, 44, 193
Cork, County, 12–3, 24, 29, 47
County Antrim FA, 16, 23, 70, 105, 118, 119, 128, 136, 141, 143, 166, 170, 175–6
Craig, James MP, 64
Creevy, William, 94
Croke, Archbishop Thomas, 134

INDEX

crowds, 101–31
  sizes of, 102–110
  composition of, 110–117
  conduct of, 117–122, 124–131, 175–6, 185
  control of, 122–4
Crusaders FC, 46
Curragh, The, 19
Cusack, Michael, 21, 135

Dail, 185
Dalymount, 150–1
Darling, John, 76, 91
Davitt, Michael, 134, 150
Derry and District Alliance [Championship], 145–7
Derry Guilds FC, 144
Derry Journal, 145
Derry, *see* 'Londonderry'
Devlin, Joe MP, 64, 125, 151, 153
Distillery FC, 16, 33, 35, 39, 47–8, 52, 53, 54, 57, 72, 74, 75, 81–3, 86, 87, 89, 91, 93, 94, 99, 110, 111, 117, 120, 124, 147
Divers, John, 93
Docherty, Isaac, 99
Donegal, County, 119, 136
Donegall Road, Belfast, 122
Donegall, Marquess of, 138
Donnelly, Joseph, 152–3
Dorrian, Joseph, 91
Dorset, 21
Down, County, 5, 12, 23, 38, 60, 88, 89, 105, 113, 136
Downpatrick, 46, 189
Drennan, David, 81
Dublin Association FC, 5, 6, 162
Dublin Castle, 126, 127, 134
Dublin, Archbishop of, 2
Dublin, city, 1, 2, 4, 5, 6, 8, 9, 10, 11, 13, 15, 16, 17, 18, 19, 20, 21, 22, 25, 26, 27, 28, 30, 31, 32, 33, 34, 35, 37, 40, 43, 44, 45, 46, 48, 49, 50, 52, 53, 66, 67, 68, 73, 74, 80, 88, 91, 100, 102, 105, 106, 107, 108, 109, 112, 113, 114, 117, 118, 119, 120, 121, 125, 129, 131, 133, 135, 136, 137, 139, 143, 144, 147, 149, 150, 151, 160, 161, 162–7, 168, 171, 173, 174, 175–81, 184, 185–97, 199
Dublin, County, 2
Dungannon, 47
Dunlop, J., 155–6
Dunton, John, 2
Dunville's Distillery, 47–8

East Lancashire Regiment, 90
Ebbw Vale FC, 93
Emerald FC, 49
Enfield RFC, 66–7
Enniskillen, 141
Entertainment Tax, 170
Entwhistle, John, 148
Everton FC, 87

FA [of England], 4, 32, 36, 128, 131, 154, 168, 178, 181–3
FA Cup, 83, 94, 113, 129, 138
FA of Wales, 32, 195
Factory Acts, 11
Falls League, Belfast, 186–8
Falls, Belfast (see also 'Pound'), 46, 94, 126, 152–3
Farrar School, 24
Farrell, Patrick, 86–7, 94
Federation International de Football Associations (FIFA), 178, 181
Fenians, 134
Fermanagh and Western FA, 6, 30, 136–7, 141, 175
Fermanagh Herald, 120
Fermanagh, County, 30, 31, 39
Fermoy, 20
Fiana Fail, 85
Fitzgerald, Dick, 80–81
Fontenoy FC, 49
Football Association of Ireland, 178, 179, 180, 181, 182, 186, 187, 188, 189, 191, 194

Football Association of the Irish Free State (FAIFS), 181–3
Football League [English], 35, 76, 105
Football League of Ireland, 178–80
Foreign Office, 181
Fountain, The, Londonderry, 145
Freebooters FC, 68, 109
Freeman's Journal, 7

Gaelic Athlete, 131
Gaelic Athletic Association (GAA), 21, 28–31, 39–40, 44, 66, 80–1, 106–7, 128–9, 131, 134–5, 137, 150–1, 161, 180, 186, 192, 195
Gaelic games, *see also* 'Gaelic Athletic Association', 12, 18, 24, 27
Gaelic League, 30, 135
Gallaher's of Belfast, 48
Gallia FC, 181
Galway, city, 2, 31
game, 1–41, 159–96
  origins of, 2–5
  early development of, 4–16, 36–8
  dissemination of, 16–27, 38–41
  opposition to, 27–32
  style of play, 33–36
  partition of, 162–96
  effects of Great War on, 167–75
Gaussen, Arthur, 67
Germany, 49
Gibson, Andrew, 153–4
Gibson, Robert, 70–1
Gibson, William Kennedy, 132, 153–7
Gilford FC, 51
Glasgow, 16, 150, 153, 199
Glasgow Celtic FC, 46, 76, 86, 130
Glasgow Rangers FC, 83, 104, 130
Glenavon FC, 53, 55–6, 57, 60, 170, 173, 175, 177, 193
Glentoran FC, 50, 53–5, 57–60, 64, 72, 75, 87, 89, 90, 91, 94, 95, 99, 101, 110, 120, 121, 144, 149, 153, 160, 176, 177
Gogarty, Oliver [St John], 26, 85
Golfing Union of Ireland, 188
Goodall, Archie, 25, 94

Goodbody, M.F., 21, 197
Gordon Highlanders, 70, 90
Great Famine, 3
Great Northern Railway, 105
Green, Alice Stopford, 125
Greenwood FC, 45
Greer, William, 22, 114
Griffith, Arthur, 135
Guinness Brewery, 48

Hackett, Thomas Kirkwood, 21
Hamilton, Marquess of, 151
Hammill, Mickey, 94
Hampshire, 18
Hannay, Rev. James, 48
Harland and Wolff, 169
Harrington, Timothy MP, 151
Harris, Valentine, 171
Harrison, J.F., 179–81
Hegan, Hugh, 156
Hertford FC, 38, 62
Heuston, Thomas, 67
Heuston, William, 67
High Pressures FC, 49
Hilden FC, 48
Hill, A.J., 75, 77
Hill, Robert, 70–71, 75, 90
Hillbrook School, Co Down, 23
hockey, 47, 188, 193
Holmes, Robert, 25
Holywood Swifts FC, 89
Home Championships, 7, 74, 160
Home Office, 11
House of Commons, 12, 139, 149

Ibrox disaster, 121
'Improvement Commission', 82, 124
Independent Order of Rechabites, 46
International Board, 32, 38, 77, 84, 167–8, 178, 180, 181–2
Ireland's Own band, 150
Ireland's Saturday Night, 1, 9, 65, 80, 81, 101, 152, 156
Irish Amateur Athletic Association, 29, 67, 192
Irish Bowling Association, 188

INDEX

Irish Champion Athletic Club, 68
Irish Cup, 5, 6, 16, 19, 23, 34, 51, 67, 68, 69, 70, 71, 74, 80, 90, 100, 102–6, 108, 109, 112, 117, 121, 122, 124, 142, 147, 148, 155, 160, 163, 168, 171, 173, 176, 177, 184, 187, 190, 191
Irish FA, 5, 6, 7, 13, 15, 16, 18, 19, 23, 27, 30, 31, 32, 34, 37, 38, 43, 44, 47, 49, 51, 54, 66, 68, 69, 70, 71, 72, 73, 74, 75, 76, 77, 79, 81, 82, 83, 84, 86, 87, 88, 89, 91, 92, 94, 102, 104, 107, 108, 112, 113, 118, 120, 122, 123, 124, 126, 131, 134, 135, 136, 137, 138, 139, 140–1, 142, 143, 144–5, 146–7, 148, 152, 154, 155, 156, 157, 160, 161, 162, 163, 164–5, 166, 167, 168, 169, 171, 173–9, 180–95
Irish Folk Song Society, 154
Irish Football League, 5, 19, 63, 76, 77, 79, 89, 100, 104, 105, 109, 120, 121, 125, 127, 128, 142, 143, 167, 168, 169, 173, 174, 176, 187, 191, 193
Irish Football Players' Union, 173–4
Irish Free State, 12, 139, 181–3, 189, 194
Irish Guards, 140
Irish Intermediate Cup, 119, 191
Irish Junior Cup, 23, 176, 191
Irish Land Conference, 151
Irish News, 7, 125, 147, 156, 177
Irish Parliamentary Party, 31, 64, 133, 134
Irish Republican Army (IRA), 85
Irish Republican Brotherhood (IRB), 133
Irish Society, the Honourable the, 52
Irish Sporting Chronicle, 9
Irish Times, 7, 28, 162
Irish Transport and General Workers Union, 112
Irish Tweed House, 16
Irish Unionist Party, 126

Irish Volunteers, 149
Irish Worker, 150
Italian FA, 178–9

Jacob's Biscuit Factory, 48
Jews, 45, 99
Johnston, Ezekiel, 87

'Kaffirs', 139
Kennedy, Robert, 66
Kent, 35
Kildare Street National School, 22
Kildare, County, 20, 25
Kilkenny, Statutes of, 2
King's Own Scottish Borderers, 19
Kirwan, John, 94
Knock FC, 5, 45
Knock Lacrosse Club, 45

Lancashire, 35, 87
Leinster FA, 6, 12, 17, 18, 19, 20, 21, 73, 81, 137, 144, 163, 165–6, 171, 175, 176, 177, 178, 185, 187, 190–1, 192, 195
Leinster Nomads FC, 6
Leinster Senior Cup, 17, 26, 108, 112, 113
Limavady, 15, 33
Limavady FC, 117
Linfield FC, 33, 34, 35, 44, 47–8, 53, 63, 64, 70–1, 72, 74, 75, 76, 77, 80, 87, 89, 90, 91, 92, 94, 95, 99, 103, 104, 111, 113, 114, 115, 119, 122, 124, 125, 126, 128, 137, 142, 143, 144, 151, 155, 156, 160, 179, 181, 188, 192, 194
Lisburn, 15, 23, 45, 48, 62, 88, 119
Lockhart, Henry, 21
Londonderry, city, 15, 17, 23, 51, 52, 66, 73, 83, 103, 110, 119, 120, 127, 144, 145–6, 151, 165, 167, 188–9
Londonderry, County, 5, 47, 67, 136, 164
Lurgan, 55, 60, 105, 170, 173, 177

MacBride, Joseph, 157
Mackie and Son, 48
MacLaughlin, Sir Henry, 194
Mallon, Tom, 55
Malone Protestant Reformatory, 140
Manchester City FC, 35
Manor School, 24
Marlborough Barracks, 150
Marshall, Matthew, 55
Maynooth, 24
Mayo, County, 134–5
McAlery, J.A., 4, 16
McAlinden, Hugh, 55, 153
McAnerney, James, 147
McCandless, Jack, 93–4
McCann, Daniel, 153, 157
McCartney, Alex, 87
McClure, George, 87
McCracken, William
    32, 65, 82–5, 91
McCrum, William, 42
McElborough, Robert, 22
McIlroy, Brice, 153
McKnight, Lizzie, 70
McLarnon, Francis, 67
Meath, County, 39
Middlesbrough, 7, 160
Mid-Ulster FC, 5, 136, 175
Milford FC, 5, 42
Millar, Jack, 150
Milltown FC, 87
Milne, Robert, 70–1, 90, 95
Moles, Thomas, 186, 188
Monaghan, County, 23, 136
Monaghan, town, 16
Montpelier FC, 17, 18
Moody-Manners Operatic Company, 18
Moore, Thomas, 153–4
Moran, D.P., 135
Mountpottinger YMCA FC, 45
Moyola Park FC, 5, 46, 67, 138
Munster FA, 6, 31–2, 44, 166, 175
Murphy, Harry, 75
Murphy, J.F., 180

national anthem, 150
National Athletic and Cycling
    Association, 192
nationalities of, 89–91
Nevin, James, 114
'New FA', 7, 143–4
New York, 89
Newbridge, 20
Newcastle United FC, 83
Newry, 49
Newton Heath FC, 34
Newtownards, 38
Nomad's Weekly, 132
Norfolk Regiment, 90
North End FC, 52
North ward, Londonderry, 188
North West FA, 15, 73, 144, 146, 175
Northern Cricket Union, 188, 193
Northern Ireland, 64, 138, 186, 189
Northern Ireland Amateur Athletic
    Association, 192
'Northern Ireland FA', 182
Northern Union [Rugby], 192
Northern Whig, 4, 7, 43, 119, 125
Nottingham Forest FC, 35

O'Leary, John, 134
Oldpark FC, 16
Orange Free State, 139
Orange Order, 50, 99, 125, 155–6
Ossory, diocese of, 2
Oxford FC, 119

Paris, 185
Park Drive FC, 48
parks, 10
Parnell, Charles Stewart, 31, 134
Partick Thistle FC, 35
Passchendaele, Battle of, 173
Peden, John, 34
Pembroke FC, 49
Phoenix Park, 12, 17, 21, 135, 149, 171
Pieter's Hill, Battle of, 140
'Plan of Campaign', 151
players, 65–100

religions of, 66, 97–100
class of, 67–8
professionalism amongst, 68–75, 86–9, 93–4, 99–100
pay and conditions of, 75–80, 95
attitudes towards, 80–6
nationalities of, 89–91
ages of, 92–3, 94–5
occupational backgrounds of, 95–7
Plunkett, Horace, 133
police, *see* 'Royal Irish Constabulary'
politics, 134–58, 184–195
Portadown, 105, 120, 156
Portadown Celtic FC, 50
Portsmouth FC, 18
Pottinger ward, Belfast, 61
Pound, The, 126
[Presbyterian Working Men's] Institute FC, 144–6, 151
Preston North End FC, 25, 33, 35, 85
priests, 45, 61
Prince of Wales's War Relief Fund, 168
professionalism, *see* 'players'
publicans, 56, 58, 61, 106

Queen's College, Belfast, 23, 67, 160, 178, 194
Queen's College, Cork, 24
Queen's College, Galway, 24, 160
Queen's Hotel, 5
Queen's Island FC, 16, 69
Queen's Park FC, 4

railways, 9, 13, 80, 105, 176
Ranfurly, Lord, 47
Rea, Robert, 93
Red Hand of Ulster, 48
Reilly, Matthew 'Ginge', 18
Renfrew, 16
Reynolds, Jack, 90, 94
Ringsend, 46, 49, 50, 80
Roberts, Field Marshall Lord, 139–40
Roosevelt, President Theodore, 156
Roscommon, County, 47
Roseville FC, 62
Ross, Nick, 33

Rossall School, 21
Royal Artillery, 18
Royal Belfast Academical Institute, 24
Royal Dublin Fusiliers, 140
Royal Engineers, 197
Royal Irish Constabulary, 123, 125–6, 127, 128, 176
Royal Irish Fusiliers, 140
Royal Scots, 19
Royal Society of Antiquaries in Ireland, 154
rugby football, 4, 5, 20, 23–5, 27–9, 32, 36, 81, 98, 108, 113, 114, 161, 188, 191–2
Ryder, J.A., 177–8, 191–2

sabbatarianism, *see* 'Sunday play'
Sandy Row, Belfast, 99, 114, 126
Sandymount, 80, 150
Saturday half-holiday, 11–3, 14, 48, 49, 75
schools, 21–6
Schools Cup, 23, 66
Scott, Elisha, 171
Scottish Cup, 130
Scottish FA, 4, 16, 32, 36, 131, 167, 168
sectarianism, 61–4, 97–100, 125–30, 135, 137–49
Sexton, Thomas MP, 138
Shankill Road, Belfast, 155
shareholders, 53–61
Sheehan brothers, 17
Sheffield, 94
Sheffield United FC, 35
Shelbourne FC, 18, 33, 44, 46, 50, 53, 54, 57, 74, 80, 88, 105, 109, 117, 143, 144, 150, 151, 168, 173, 174, 177, 184, 187, 190, 191, 192–4, 195
Sherwood Foresters, 90
Simms, 'late of Renfrew', 11
Sinn Fein, 133, 185
Skene, Leslie, 87
Sloan, Donald, 75, 76, 77
Sloan, T.H., 151

Smithfield ward, Belfast, 152
Smurthwaite, J., 179–80
soldiers, *see* 'army'
Soloheadbeg, 176
Somme, Battle of, 186
Southern Irish Loyalist Relief Fund, 194
spectators, *see* 'crowds'
Sport, 9, 162, 186, 187
Springboks, 108
St Columb's Court FC, 51, 52, 151, 165
St Columb's Hall Celtic FC, 103
St Columb's Hall FC, 34
St James's Gate FC, 48
St Malachy's School, 17, 44, 66
St Vincent de Paul Society, 50
St Vincent's College, Castleknock, 25–6
Stanfield, Olphert, 54
Stockport, 126
Stoke FC, 87
strikes, 111, 149–50
Sunday Closing Act, 106–7
Sunday play, 2, 31–2, 39–40, 106–7, 134, 148, 166–8, 192
Sunderland FC, 154
Swan, Samuel, 91

tennis, 77
Times [London], 125
Torrans, Samuel, 80, 92, 95
Tottenham Hotspur FC, 94
Trainor, Oscar, 85
Tralee, 106
trams, 9–10, 49, 105, 150, 176
Transvaal War Fund, 139
Trinity College, Dublin, 21, 25, 27, 43, 67, 16, 178, 197
'Triple crown', 7
Tritonville FC, 31, 34
Turner, William G., 155–7
Tyrone, County, 88, 136, 164
Tyrrell, John, 157

Ulster CC, 4, 53
'Ulster FA', 166
Ulster FC, 51, 52, 53, 71, 75, 87, 88, 118
Ulster Football and Cycling News, 9, 71, 75, 119, 147
Ulster Hospital, 140
Ulster provincial side, 82
Ulster Schools Cup [Rugby], 24
Ulster Spinning Company [Linfield Mill], 47
Ulster Volunteer Force 186, 188
Ulster's Saturday Night, 9
United Irish League, 152
United Irishman, 135

Victoria ward, Belfast, 61, 153

Wall, Sir Frederick, 154, 183
War Office, 167–8
Warwick, John, 156
Waterford, 2, 29, 140
Wattie, Peter, 89
Waveney, Lord, 47
Wellington Park FC, 69
West Bromwich Albion FC, 34
West Ham FC, 87
West, John, 94
Westmeath, 24, 47, 165
White, General Sir George, 139–41
Wigoder, Saul [Barney], 187
Williams, David, 169–70
Wilton, Capt. Sir James, 179–82, 186–8
Windsor Park, 142
Wrexham, 7, 160

York Road, Belfast, 46
York Street Mill, Belfast, 38
Yorkshire, 93
Young Men's Christian Association, 45, 52, 66